A STROKE OF HEAVEN

Processing a Brain Injury and the Events Thereafter through a Spiritual Lens

M A L O R I   R O G E R S

WESTBOW
PRESS®
A DIVISION OF THOMAS NELSON
& ZONDERVAN

WestBow Press books may be ordered through booksellers or by contacting:

WestBow Press
A Division of Thomas Nelson & Zondervan
1663 Liberty Drive
Bloomington, IN 47403
www.westbowpress.com
844-714-3454

ISBN: 978-1-6642-7006-0 (sc)
ISBN: 978-1-6642-7005-3 (hc)
ISBN: 978-1-6642-7007-7 (e)

Library of Congress Control Number: 2022911551

Print information available on the last page.

WestBow Press rev. date: 10/12/2022

ACKNOWLEDGMENTS

To God, who spared my life and gave me a message to share.

To my dad, whose faith can move mountains and whose encouragement never lets me quit.

To my mom, who selflessly and generously raised me, twice. You are an angel.

To my brother, whose perseverance, courage, and excellence are inspiring and whose humor keeps me afloat.

To my sister and best friend, whose joy and personality light up my life.

To Papa, who fought the good fight and finished the race and whose legacy continues to multiply.

To Nana, who lives as a selfless, fruitful, God-fearing saint and whose example is firmly imprinted in my heart.

To my aunts and uncles, who have maintained Godly traditions and established enlightening, Christlike principles within their families.

To my cousins, who have chosen to follow God and make faith their own, as part of our legacy in various forms.

To my childhood church home, Green Lawn, whose foundations and principles continue to nourish my faith.

To my friends, who have chosen to walk alongside me through thick and thin, honoring me far greater than I deserve.

To Dr. Kamath, whose perseverance and skill saved my life; God is real, and He is working in you every day.

To the hospital staff at Kell West, for never giving up the night of November 10, 2015.

To Dr. Welch, whose steady hands finished the race in my treatment and gave hope to my family.

To the hospital staff at Zale Lipshy, whose knowledge, service, and love blessed my family and nourished me back to life.

To Coach Lawrence, for believing in me, giving me a chance to play volleyball, and preparing me to be a leader.

To my LCU volleyball team, whose sacrificial faith was and is selfless, inspiring, and life giving; keep being fruitful.

To the professors, staff, and student body of LCU, whose prayerful hearts continually look to the Father.

To brain injury survivors and all those who fight invisible injuries, may you always live with hope; there is essential purpose in your pain.

To my children, McCrae and Roan, who gave me a new sense of purpose and taught me a new level of love that inspires me. You are the baton that has helped me finish the race.

To my husband, whose love and faithfulness (Proverbs 3:3) brought about the greatest version of myself. Thank you so much for believing in me. You inspired this book, and your daily sacrifices are not in vain.

To all prayer warriors, never give up.

PREFACE

I am so grateful to try to follow in the footsteps of the faith giants before me. My maternal grandpa, Papa, was a preacher, steadfast and sound in the truths of God's Word. He had a passionate desire to make sure those around him knew God and were obedient to be baptized. He inspired others to share in the privilege of having a relationship with God and often practiced a sense of urgency to know Him and His Word in the Bible. My maternal grandma, Nana, pursued this calling alongside him so faithfully, till death did they part on November 12, 2017, all the while multiplying their fruitfulness through obedience to God's Word. Nana continues to live in the fruitfulness they established together and shares it generously with others; she walks in the light every day. *Fruitful* might not be a strong enough word to describe her example and life. She gives, pours, and loves with her every living breath; she is a walking light who lives with her arms extended to all.

I wish I could ask Papa more about his preaching journey; all of his articles and notes left behind share his perspective very clearly, and he never wavered with the changing views of this fallen world. He planted a healthy fear of the Lord in all those who knew him in a way that was loving and gracious. When Papa passed away on a Sunday morning, after taking the Lord's Supper, I remember a feeling of peace and accomplishment rushing over me. It was weird and unexpected because I ought to have felt broken, I thought. Of course, I was deeply saddened to not be present for such a profound and emotional moment; Tyler and I had moved away for his school at that time. All of our family had gathered around in worship and fellowship as Papa took his last breaths. That feeling of uncertainty of not being able to be there has inspired me to make him proud in a new way and strive to honor him differently. Papa and Nana's marriage was the definition of faithfulness, and their deep Christian legacy maintained through the vessels of their roots convicts me to write this book.

I am particularly inspired by my parents' examples—their faith in action through raising children, loving people, and serving the needy. They have maintained and nurtured rich family values in their home while showing generous love to any under their roof. They deserve more honor than I know how to express.

For Christmas one year, my dad gave me a book titled *My Father's Gift*, by Sixtus Z. Atabong. Atabong writes about "purposeful charity." He emphasizes the value of giving in the short term while empowering for the long term as well; that is what his dad did for him. He tells of ways his dad's example inspired him to do great things while he strives to carry on his legacy.

In reflecting on the example and love of my parents, I can't seem to find a way to honor them adequately. I don't feel like I have the physical stamina or endurance to give, live, and love like I truly would like to. I pray this book is the small seed of faith that God can miraculously multiply to His doing. With the commandment in mind to "honor your father and mother," I yearn deeply for the most powerful way to do so (Deuteronomy 5:16). My hope is that this book is a small package that continues to share the light to others that my family has so richly given me. I pray this book shares a heavenly perspective that inspires people to seek the eternal Father with a yearning that is never quenched or satisfied.

Parents have such a great opportunity to create humans, influence their perspective and worldview, plant seeds of faith, and maintain fruitful and powerful relationships with their children. That is what my parents have done—and more. When I thought about the story I wanted to share, I kept thinking about my parents—my superheroes. They willingly gave me life and continue to maintain the most generous, caring relationships with their three children and son-in-law.

I truly believe that I have grown up in the greatest home, in the richest country, with the greatest parents, the most incredible and talented siblings, and the most supportive grandparents. My aunts, uncles, cousins, and friends are so loving and are also heroic examples to me. I even have a husband! God has been good to me since the day I was born.

When I think about the individual God created in me, I sometimes search desperately inward, putting pressure on myself to live up to His rich blessings and try to follow the legends of faith before me.

As I wondered for quite some time about what to do with my new life and how to maintain the rich legacy before me, I kept trying to knock on doors that God kept closing. There was one door that I kept ignoring, not wanting to go near to knock, and that was to write this book. *Would anyone read it? Would it encourage anyone? Would it even make a difference? What if for just one, would it be worth it?* Jesus said yes (Matthew 18:10–14).

Though a true believer in God's grace, I didn't want to get to heaven without having completed my task. I felt like I should *not* be the one to write it because I'm *not* the hero. But because I am convicted by God and my husband, parents, siblings, grandparents, and all my family to continue to maintain a rich Christian heritage, I am thankful and compelled to share this testimony.

God's presence and our problems are equally real, but we get to choose what we focus on. In my life, I want to choose to focus on His presence rather than getting blurred vision because of the latter. Having the privilege of getting to know God intimately is like having a private wellspring of joy within us and is independent of our circumstances (Young 2004). Let's share in it for a little while.

Learning to live with a brain injury is something I never envisioned happening to me. Those with invisible injuries have a voice that needs to be heard. A new sense of protection and trust is so deeply yearned for and so vital to capture. God alone is the only one who truly knows the real story behind the scars.

My mind has often wandered to meditate on Job, a richly blessed man of God who endured treacherous storms and sternly kept his faith. In the midst of a terribly great trial, he grasped boldly to his faith even when questioned by his friends. Job said, "But He knows the way that I take; when He has tested me, I will come forth as gold. My feet have closely followed His steps; I have kept to His way without turning aside. I have not departed from the commands of His lips; I have treasured the words of His mouth more than my daily bread" (Job 23:10–12). The fear of God sustained a conviction in Job to never waver from obedience to him.

"But He stands alone, and who can oppose Him? He does whatever He pleases ... That is why I am terrified before Him; when I think of all this, I fear Him. God has made my heart faint; the Almighty has terrified me. Yet I am not silenced by the darkness, by the thick darkness that covers my face" (Job 23:13, 15–17). When I start to feel discouraged and weary, my foolishness is calmed by this story in His Word. The story of Job is one of many of His tools that gives us an example of patience to endure hardship.

We all ought to remind ourselves more that we are not entitled to anything. The book of 1 Timothy says, "For we brought nothing into the world, and we can take nothing out of it" (6:7). Our lives are the Lord's, and "it is God who works in [us] to will and to act in order to fulfill His good purpose" (Philippians 2:13). While we're here on earth, as long as there is breath in our lungs and His Spirit in our hearts, we have the opportunity to praise Him and live for Him.

In searching for a life calling in my new life after a brain injury, everything seemed meaningless to me if not directly connected to the Lord. I felt as if I had been spared for just *His* purpose, not my own. Maybe it's because He's the King of the universe. Maybe it's because of the miracle He worked in me. Maybe it's because I can't do anything without Him, and I have to be *all* in.

My passions are surely influenced by the relationship I have with my earthly father; they are also influenced by the testimony of my marriage. The men in my life serve as uplifting and generous providers and leaders, which inspires my view of our heavenly Father. The book of Luke reads, "From everyone who has been given much, much will be demanded; and from the one who has been entrusted with much, much more will be asked" (12:48). God has given me a rain shower of blessings, and I was sick of feeling drowned by them, unsure of how to pour from this cup that only God could keep full.

Without a memory, things were hard. The only thing I knew was to look to God and His strength. His knowledge is supreme, and He makes anything good. Some things are hard to admit, but I am convinced that all struggles must be brought to the light so God can saturate them and take control. Praise the Lord for His tender mercies and divine power. He is forever on the throne, His ways are perfect, and His love never fails.

I was very guarded with the precious energy I could use in any given day until brought to a halt with a headache, usually a sign to get more rest. Wise advice was given to me that maybe a blog would be a good platform to love people: I could pour all my thoughts and energy into one focused source that God could work through to reach people however He seemed fit.

My dad always reminds our family that God does the extraordinary things, not us; His work is greater than ours, and we all have the privilege to ask Him to take the stick to run that anchor leg and finish the race *with* us. After a few blogs, my next post reached thirty-five pages. Then it broke one hundred ... God remained so patient with me as I tried to process His working and gradually acknowledge a new fork in the road: to write a book.

One thing my simple mind has had to pray often is, "God, please show me how to accept these blessings! I don't want to just sit on them or be spurred to action by wrong motives or anything impure. Lord, lead me by Your Spirit. Thank You." And my fingers just started typing ...

I felt compelled to tell the story revealed to me upon waking up from a miracle. As my mind continues to wander in the spiritual realm, I have found that God and His ways are beyond my understanding. But I must cling to His simple, concrete, and calming truths. I *never* thought I would write a book. I've never been accused of even liking to read. But there was an unquenched fire that continued to burn inside of me until I started putting His voice to paper. The testimony enclosed in this book is something that is scary to bring to the light, but I prayed for His Spirit to lead my steps and guide my thoughts. Although this journey has been crazy to endure, discern, and process, I knew I couldn't just sit on it. This book is an account of what I experienced and want to try to make sense of.

This new life that He spared is a blessing. This new life is a new state of frustration. This new life is different and challenging but full of faith and hope. This new life is different every day, unpredictable, and a little scary. The book of Psalms says, "Look to the Lord and His strength; seek His face always" (105:4). He gives us confidence, generously.

This book is Christ centered: an aroma of thanksgiving and praise; an encouragement to everyone in the midst of, in victory of, and especially those in preparation for the trials that come with the life we are born into; and a transparent, Spirit-filled, honest testimony to our heavenly Father and His powerful nature. This book has to be from a real and honest perspective of a less than ordinary human. Some of it (most of it) was even crazy to type, mind rattling to truly accept and live in, and convicting to share.

My hope is that this book will spark a flame in your desire for a faith journey and ignite a passion to cling to the rock. May His name and His power be forever acknowledged as we all yearn deeply to feel His presence. God is always good.

"Let this be written for a future generation, that a people not yet created may praise the Lord ... The children of your servants will live in your presence; their descendants will be established before you" (Psalm 102:18, 28 NIV).

"Your testimonies are my heritage forever, for they are the joy of my heart" (Psalm 119:111).

"How abundant are the good things that You have stored up for those who fear You, that You bestow in the sight of all, on those who take refuge in You" (Psalm 31:19).

"The name of the Lord is a fortified tower; the righteous run to it and are safe" (Proverbs 18:10).

REFLECTION

*For the Lord is good and His love endures forever; His
faithfulness continues through all generations.*

—PSALM 100:5

"Marray, hurry! I don't think she's with us anymore," my mom said frantically.

"I'm trying, Sarah, but I can only go as fast as the police escort in front of me," he answered. Maci's heart was beating out of her chest, but she kept quiet in the back seat.

* * *

As the wheels of the plane neared the edge of the runway, we slowly started to ascend. Going to Africa had always been a dream, and I was uncertain it would be anything more. But God had provided the greatest opportunity to explore the miraculous country of Rwanda with special people, twice.

After my brother, Peyton, graduated from Lubbock Christian High School in 2015, we had the opportunity to take a mission trip to Rwanda, Africa, and stay with a familiar and loving host family. It was absolutely the experience of a lifetime, as I got to join my brother, boyfriend, and two friends on a trip I had always dreamed of. Having been on the same trip the summer before, I was anxious to experience it again with these people I loved so dearly. Peyton; Tyler, my boyfriend; Mallory, my best friend; Connor, another friend who is like a brother, and I cherish several life-changing memories from this trip.

It was such sweet timing that God allowed such a rich experience in that perfect season. The hilarious effects of no sleep for my brother after a long night of Project Graduation, coupled with our long plane rides and the frantic rushing through foreign airports, created an experience to remember before we finally landed in the gorgeous country of Rwanda.

The Amos family, who generously hosts so many visitors and missionaries, is so incredibly fruitful in the selfless ways they live their unique calling to the fullest. Heath and Rebecca both grew up in the States, but they share the desire of long-term mission work overseas. They raise their three kids alongside them in their ministry, while serving as a bright light in their Rwandan community. After spending time with them doing mission work the summer before, I wanted to recruit more people to witness and experience God's working through them.

God, in His perfect timing, allowed just that. The Amos family works with several friends, American and Rwandan, in their nonprofit organization called Africa Transformation Network (ATN). Their vision is discipleship, partnership, service, and development in their African community. Witnessing their faith in action firsthand was such a life-changing experience; it was inspiring to see how God gives such a powerful sense of unity despite deep diversity within a group of people.

We quickly dove into the African culture as we shadowed the Amoses' daily duties of discipleship. A typical day consisted of eating a wonderful homemade breakfast from Rebecca before loading up to go work with Heath in various teaching and service activities. It was typically still light outside when we got back from the day, and it was fun to walk around the village and play with the sweet kids in the area before dinner.

With the help of a translator, Gilbert, we got to teach a vacation Bible school, sing, and play with the sweet children in the area. We were ready to do whatever the Amoses allowed as we followed them around with wide eyes and hearts full of joy. We got to help teach English classes, play language games, engage in conversation, and admire the hard work of the ATN organization. Everything about ATN equips Rwandans with the tools needed to live a rich life, spiritually and physically. In the midst of their jobs and service work, the Amoses were gracious tour guides, giving us a glimpse into the daily lives of Rwandans.

None of our luggage with teaching material made it until the trip was almost over, but Heath and Rebecca were gracious to share their things and help us make do with whatever we could find to put on a vacation Bible school. It's funny how God can use anything and anyone with a willing spirit to accomplish His will; what an honor just to be His puppet.

One of the most powerful and moving days of the trip was when we went to tour some of the deep monuments of Rwandan culture, such as the Genocide Museum. This country was once broken so painfully with what seemed like no hope. Once flooded with evil and hatred in the horrific genocide of 1994, Rwandans are now united as one—Rwandan—rather than using tribal discrimination. The testimony of a typical Rwandan is full of love, mercy, forgiveness, and inspiration. Praise the Lord for His gracious work and for shining through those people.

Some of our favorite times during our stay in Rwanda were simply getting to hang out with and admire the Amos family. Each of their hearts is so full and pure; their whole family radiates life and warmth. After a fun day of work, we got to enjoy a wonderfully cooked meal around the table. Rebecca is an incredible homemaker, cook, and source of deep love; the way she poured herself out to provide for her family and a large, obnoxious group of visitors was worth the trip in itself. She reminds me that the greatest beauty is that of the heart, where the Holy Spirit resides. We enjoyed games and laughter in the evenings as we reminisced on the activities and funny happenings throughout the day. We also talked about special events that had happened so we could all process together and reflect on how we'd witnessed God at work throughout the day.

God was so gracious to allow this special time of deep connection with Him and more of His people in that season; He is so good. This trip helped grow deep spiritual roots that God continues to anchor us with daily. What a blessing to have had this experience before all our next life chapters. Peyton was about to go to college and play baseball at Southwestern Oklahoma State University (SWOSU). Mallory was ready for another volleyball season as an upperclassman leader at Lubbock Christian University (LCU), Connor was ready for his senior year of high school, Tyler was ready to tackle another basketball season as a junior at LCU, and I was preparing to finish my volleyball career and graduate from LCU. Life was good. God is always good.

God's working in my life keeps me accountable; it gets me out of bed in the morning. It gives me hope. He has painted a picture for me of a lifestyle with a fullness that I never want to perish or spoil. The assurance I have in my Christian walk stems from the base of this bubbly, benevolent, loving, generous, and kind Christian family. I never want to put an end to His heritage and legacies. I often pray, "God, I love You, and may my life prove it." When I think about what I really want to do in life, all I think about is being like my momma, and Lord willing, getting to be a momma and homemaker someday, in hopes of carrying on the legend. My mind is constantly on the simple, basic needs, and I strive to learn how to keep things rich with simplicity in the home. It would be a blessing just to *try* to imitate the love that has been shown to me all my life; that love fuels and inspires me.

God has been so good to my family, and we have danced in His blessings all our lives. I have never known hurt or pain, what it's like to go without, or any kind of tragic heartbreak. The God who loves, sustains, and blesses us is forever the God of the universe.

My dad has always said, "Life is a marathon." His zeal and energy encourage everyone who has the honor of knowing him; his life is truly radiant. The way he keeps going and going and giving and giving just doesn't seem human sometimes; he could run circles backward around the Energizer Bunny. His legacy shows truth to the command "Give, and it will be given to you. A good measure, pressed down, shaken together and running over, will be poured into your lap. For with the measure you use, it will be measured to you" (Luke 6:38). Dad *always* gives his all to others; he is equipped with countless spiritual gifts and wears many different hats to serve. He constantly maintains a life of character and integrity while juggling numerous responsibilities as a leader. It seems like the man who took me to school everyday growing up, with the tradition of reading a verse or saying a prayer, hasn't changed a bit. But in reality, he's just a greater version of himself everyday.

My mom is an unbelievable light and joy to our family, and none who know her would be able to make it without her. She is an angel and continues to dance in God's will since that day, just as she has done every day of her life. She is a friend to any in her path, makes everyone feel special, and loves in very passionate, generous, and spontaneous ways. She makes life fun and is always a source of laughter, providing an opportunity to "exercise your liver," as she always says. I am humbled daily at the faith it takes to try to mimic her role in the home; I had no idea how much work it must have taken to make that job look as easy as she did all my life. Praise the Lord for that woman.

Our family has always enjoyed our big green backyard, and it has often been a place of community to share with others. Dad planted trees along the border of the fence and left a big open space for a baseball diamond, perfect for home run derby. When those trees were little, we jumped over them to celebrate rounding the bases for a home run. My brother, the baseball star, definitely had the homerun record. I never understood how he could hit the ball so naturally when we were kids. Sometimes, he would let me follow him around the diamond as I pretended I could hit too.

My dad played football and basketball and ran track in high school before graduating from Texas Tech with an exercise sports science degree. He was the first one in his family to graduate from college. His knowledge, interest, and practice of health and exercise have allowed him to lead our family to great and exciting endeavors. The perseverance he showed to reach his goals inspires and fuels me to bless others with my accomplishments awarded through hard work.

My mom has always been an athlete too; she ran cross-country and track and played basketball. She won state in high school in two track events: the 800-meter run and 1600-meter run. Her competitive spirit continues to thrive, as she has also supported my siblings and me in reaching our full athletic potentials as well.

As a kid, Peyton loved any sport with a ball and always displayed the quickest, smoothest hand-eye coordination. He played football, basketball, and baseball in high school and won a state championship in both basketball and baseball. His skill, grit, determination, perseverance, and ability to be a team player granted him the opportunity to pursue baseball in college as well. His successes as a team player and leader also paved the way for him to graduate from LCU and pursue his business degree.

After Maci spent her early childhood following Peyton and me around to all of our sporting events, she decided to establish her own athletic career, and she has thrived in a variety of ways. She set a record in every race in track in middle school, also dominating in every volleyball and basketball game that she played. She had a phenomenal basketball career, accumulating numerous high school accolades before choosing to pursue that passion and gift as a college athlete. She shows so much joy on the court, always playing with a big smile and a lot of energy. I strive to embody Maci's energy and zeal for life everyday, especially the ordinary days. She is definitely the big sister at times, though six years younger. The spark inside of her is undoubtedly a flame of Jesus.

We are innocently born into a broken world that our holy God looks down on to care for, deeply and faithfully. How do we get access to the richest spiritual blessings that are fully felt in this physical world? Jesus. Jesus made a way to this passage and right when He died on the cross for our sins. What a miracle. We will never comprehend this gift in all its fullness, but we get to accept it before we even understand it. Jesus gave His whole life for us, yet it's still hard to sacrifice parts of ours?

In March 2003, my mom went to the doctor for a mole that my dad noticed and thought looked peculiar. One of our family friends, a highly skilled dermatologist, was able to remove and examine it and then determined it to be a melanoma. She was taken care of in a timely manner, a truly powerful and fruitful blessing, as it was further removed through a more invasive procedure to get the whole thing. *Thank You, Lord, for Your healing hands that surrounded my momma.* Her life is a continual fragrant aroma to so many. God is always at work, watching and protecting His people. His ways are far beyond our understanding, and His will always prevails; sparing my mom's life marks a tally in the miracle column.

In July 2014, my mom and sister loaded a full car for church camp and headed toward the mountains of New Mexico. My family has always enjoyed being a part of this special week dedicated to spiritual growth with our church. That year, my sister had been having a nagging stomach pain that gradually grew worse. Unsure of the cause, she tried to endure it with pain medicine as my mom continued to monitor it; church camp was one of their favorite weeks of the year and would be so sad to miss! When the pain grew unbearable, my mom decided it was essential to load up and go to the nearest doctor. Tests determined that Maci had appendicitis and needed to be treated before her appendix ruptured, releasing harmful bacteria that could lead to a serious systemic problem.

My dad, brother, and I were in Lubbock, as we had our work and team workout schedules going in full swing. We immediately loaded the truck to meet my mom and sister in New Mexico when we heard that the severity of her pain led them to go to the hospital. Driving as fast as we safely could toward their direction, we then caravanned to the doctor in Lubbock for an emergency appendectomy. We all remained calm and hopeful through the situation because we just knew God had everything taken care of as we rolled her into the hands of the medical team with confidence and thankfulness.

In the waiting room while Maci was being treated, our family and several others prayed and trusted God. After about an hour, Maci was wheeled out in a timely manner, and the doctor assured us that everything went smoothly. *Thank You, Lord.* He is always working for our good and always providing for us. The nature of His power and might are so constant through seasons of trial and victory.

It amazes me to just stop and ponder God's ways that are far beyond our human understanding. We could never thank Him enough or live right enough. Truth is we could never love, serve, or thank Him adequately because of His love *first* shown us on the cross when He willingly sacrificed His Son, Jesus, to free us from sin. The most we can do is to be all in and live for Him and to "not quench the Spirit" (1 Thessalonians 5:19). We are all unworthy of the gracious nature of how God treats us, but His steadfast character never wavers despite our inadequacies. His unchanging nature ought to always keep us accountable; we *always* need Him.

I am forever in awe of the way God has worked in my family and continues to do so. My dad was brought into this world in a unique way as an adopted son, and it is obvious that He has a very special anointing on his life. It is impossible not to notice the radiance in his presence as Jesus shines through his every pore with continual acts of service through his Spirit-led life.

He is forever a hero to me, for countless reasons. He has always been different, with a childlike innocence and curiosity that continually lead him on the right paths. He worked so hard to be the first one in his family to graduate from college and has used that accomplishment as a tool to bless others. He continues to provide so richly for all those in his path, with a special passion for his family. It's amazing what God does through a willing vessel.

Dad is one of those people who can instantly make your day by seeing him or talking to him, and he is the most generous, intentional provider for a family. His gift of encouragement is so obvious as he puts it to use so generously; he has a special way of empowering people by the way he believes in them and inspires them through his example. I can't believe God chose me to be his daughter.

I am so grateful for the family values instilled in me by my parents, and I'm encouraged to be fruitful because of them. They make it look so easy to raise children and live holy lives. I try to see things with a spiritual lens, exactly how I was raised, so I can also be a pleasing aroma to God as I live in this rich legacy. My view of our heavenly Father is deeply influenced by these incredible family relationships, specifically the faith of my dad and the love of my momma. Praise the Lord for how good He is to His people and for the eternal privilege to *all* be called family. A Christian family is such a special gift that will forever carry divine responsibilities.

FIRM FOUNDATION

*The Lord is righteous is all His ways and faithful in all He does.
The Lord is near to all who call on Him, to all who call on Him in
truth. He fulfills the desires of those who fear Him; He hears their
cry and saves them. The Lord watches over all who love Him, but
all the wicked He will destroy. My mouth will speak in praise of the
Lord. Let every creature praise His holy name for ever and ever.*

—PSALM 145:17–21

Diamonds, in all their beauty, are created through a process of intense pressure and temperature. Iron, a strong metal, is sharpened by itself and can even be used to team up with carbon to make steel, a much stronger material (Steel 2019).

It is inevitable that we are going to experience a storm or some sort of experience that tests or refines us. In life, we, too, must be ready to endure and bounce back when enduring our seasons of living through such intense pressure.

I guess I knew that but never really *knew* it. I had heard of other people's stories, and it always seemed easy to encourage but never to relate, to sympathize but never empathize. Then God gave me an opportunity to understand what it's like to be broken.

After an exciting summer of 2015, with a trip to Africa, an

incredible family vacation to Gulf Shores, Alabama, disciplined workouts at the gym, and a lot of spontaneous fun with family and friends, I was ready to attack my senior year of college. I had graduated high school as salutatorian with thirty some odd dual credit college hours, so I was anticipating graduating college in three years. When applying to LCU, I had no intention of playing college sports after being a four-sport varsity athlete at Frenship High School; I thought I was ready to know what it was like to have a little bit of free time for a change. But if I had stuck to that plan, I am confident I would not be alive.

Having the opportunity to play volleyball at LCU for Coach Lawrence was such a sweet miracle from the start. She had given me an opportunity to practice with the team toward the end of the first semester of my freshman year because they needed an extra player for scrimmaging purposes. I was hesitant because I was sure I wasn't good enough to play at the college level, but she insisted I try it. God transformed that decision into a life-changing privilege for me; I forever see Coach as an angel for giving me the chance to be a part of three volleyball seasons at LCU.

Summer workouts in preparation of my senior year had been great, and our team was anxious to get another volleyball season started. As one of our team captains, I couldn't wait for everyone to finally get together and dive into the deep roots of our team culture that had been so intentionally established over the years.

Our first team meeting in August felt like Christmas, as we all bounced into the locker room together, excited to see all of our new gear and equipment from the coaches placed neatly by each locker. Everyone brought so much energy as we hugged and laughed and shared fun stories from the summer; we were all tanned up and excited to jump into our spandex and hit the floor. The team chemistry was awesome, as we all fought competitively with a unified vision. It's truly a gift to be a part of a team.

The 2015 LCU volleyball season was full of adventure. Every road trip was always a good mix of business and laughter; it was an honor to step on a nice charter bus and then put on a jersey representing something greater than ourselves. Volleyball is so fun; there's just something about throwing your body on the ground to get a dig, watching the setter meet the ball with soft hands and then push it to the hitter to pound at the floor on the other side. Of course, the main focus was screaming and running to the middle with a bunch of energy and focus after getting that hard-earned point. That year, we even went to a tournament near the beach, making the most of every second on the court and the sand. A few of the moms joined us for that trip, and I was sure thankful my momma got to come. My parents never missed an event for us kids, and I'm speechless with gratitude for their consistent, supportive, and selfless parenting.

So many fun college memories took place that year; I was living with one of my best friends, Mallory Powell, on campus at LCU. We had great accountability with each other as roommates, and it was a priority to sprinkle our studies with fun, or our fun with some studies, always striving to be disciplined college athletes. The volleyball team had consistent meetings and devotionals and enjoyed events on campus that were uplifting. We all had a firm base of foundation that was vital for everyone, individually and as a team. We were very close and completely transparent with one another, eager to share in one another's struggles and joys to remain a team. It's important to have "a band of sistas" or a group to plug into and grow with; as Christians, accountability is vital.

Every part of a sports season can turn into a life lesson, especially in retrospect. Getting up early for morning workouts, pretending like you're awake enough to lift a bar with weight on it, conditioning until you can't even take another step … those moments of grind and self-discipline are what stay with us to sharpen and refine us later on. It's so cool to be able to look back on a task or event that sounded physically impossible and know you did it.

Coach Lawrence always had a special way of tying meaning to everything we did and learned. Coach and/or one of the team captains frequently led meetings and devotionals throughout the season, continually remembering the Source we drew from. It is important to recognize the why and the how by which we all do something; it is vital to remember our purpose. One lesson that sticks with me was drawn from the word *yet*; this tied a struggle with a mindset of confidence.

"We didn't reach the team standard in _____ ... yet."

"I don't feel confident in that area of my game ... yet."

"I didn't reach my goal in _____ ... yet."

Rather than sulking inwardly with discouragement at a mistake, we would instead recognize that it was crucial to perk up with motivation to get better. This is true for any and everything in life.

On November 7, we had just celebrated senior day with the last home game. We had such a sweet team meeting before the game and were all inspired to play one last time on that home court together. For the four of us seniors, it was a particularly special memory. There were lots of tears and laughter, making for such a truly heartfelt and Spirit-led time. That group of girls is surely special.

On November 10, we loaded the bus toward Wichita Falls to play a nonconference volleyball game during the middle of conference play. It was a normal day. I had taken an anatomy test earlier that morning before loading the bus. We drove three hours east of Lubbock, and then the team got ready for the game. We went through our normal warm-up routine and did the introductions and announcing before starting the game. The lights seemed unusually bright in that gym, coming from the tall ceiling, and we all tried to adjust accordingly during warm-up so we would be ready to play.

When the game started, I remember missing some easy routine plays because of what felt like a lack of depth perception. Something felt off, but I tried to shake it off and "get the next one." Maybe it was due to the bright lights in the gym throwing me off, but my judgment was completely skewed. When I rotated off and sat on the bench, my head was throbbing. I grew concerned, thinking the pain was not a normal headache. After just a minute of sitting still, I couldn't take it anymore; I thought my head was going to split. Noticing my behavior, our trainer and my dad escorted me to the locker room so I could close my eyes and rest. I lay down and propped my feet up, but within seconds, I was gone. That was my last waking memory.

My mom and sister had followed us into the locker room. The fact that Maci was there was unusual because it would be a late school night, and both friends she had planned on staying with were sick. God was already working through every detail for our family to be together, although my brother was still in Oklahoma for school.

"Marray, carry her to the car; she's having an aneurysm," my mom said once she witnessed my condition. I was carried, unconscious, to the car from the locker room, where a man, the Midwestern State soccer coach, ran into my dad. He advised my dad to go to the small, rural hospital; he said there would be too long of a wait if he went to the big one that seemed more practical to go to for a serious case like this. He had just taken in one of his players the week prior and said the wait would be too long there.

As it turned out, there was a neurosurgeon, Dr. Kamath, at this small, rural hospital who had just finished a long day and was about to go home. But he thought it was best to wait, as he had gotten a call that a patient was about to be brought in, and it sounded like a neurological case.

After carrying me to the back seat of the car, right next to Maci, my dad followed the police escort to the hospital. Shortly after, my mom jumped to the back seat to scoop vomit out of my mouth as I postured, stiff in her arms. Dad drove steadily while my eighth-grade sister was watching wide-eyed.

Members of the Kell West medical staff were waiting for us as soon as we arrived, armed to partake in timely action. Prayer warriors were contacted, and God was sought as a tremendous outpouring of family, close friends, and community flooded the waiting areas of the hospital after hearing the news. God's angels were at work, interceding for me.

The ER staff transported my body to a table inside the hospital, too stiff to be put into the wheelchair that was originally planned. While my parents were getting things reported to the hospital staff, Maci was trying to keep up with messaging family and close friends about what had just happened. Dr. Kamath, the neurosurgeon, came out and said, "I have done a CT scan, and this is a terminal condition. She has a brain bleed. She's got an arteriovenous malformation (AVM) that has ruptured, and her condition is worsening by the second." He implied that I needed to be taken across town to do the surgery at a bigger hospital, or even to a hospital in Dallas that was more suitable for such a high-risk surgery. He said, "But we don't even have fifteen minutes because she's got many signs of brain stem herniation, and we don't have much time once you get to that point. I will have to do surgery here. I cannot guarantee she will survive this surgery. I cannot guarantee that she won't be paralyzed, have brain damage, or many other complications. Brain infections are a high risk for this type of surgery at this facility. I cannot guarantee any of these things, but it is what I have to do to attempt to save her life."

My parents listened and said, "Please do what you can to save our daughter. We will be praying for you and the whole medical team out here in the lobby and praying that God will save Malori."

My parents and Maci immediately started praying together, completely in shock and unsure if they'd ever see me again. They later found out that while their heads were bowed, a nurse sprinted behind them to run to the blood bank because, when on the table for surgery, I had no blood pressure. The ability to perform a surgery was uncertain due to the amount of blood I had lost. I was given five units of blood to get a blood pressure reading after the transfusion, and then the surgery started. Because my brain had so much swelling from the bleed, a craniotomy was performed: they removed the left portion of my skull, sawed it in half, and put it in the lower left abdomen to keep it viable to reuse down the road if they were able to save me.

Dr. Kamath, who had canceled a trip to India last minute for his mother's hip surgery, along with his amazingly talented team of professionals, persevered for hours trying to get my brain to stop bleeding. Ideally, a surgery of this severity calls for a crew of ten to fifteen people, but this procedure started with three. During surgery, a nurse kept relaying messages from the operating room to my family, updating them on the progress of the procedure.

"She is holding her own," she continued to say. My dad would then update everyone in the hospital lobby who was praying; his leadership of positivity, believing, and pleading with God in prayer was powerful. I can believe that wholeheartedly without seeing it. Dad faithfully trusted and believed that God could not only save and heal but that *He would*. He even had the courageous hope to pray for the "impossible things," like being able to walk out of the hospital holding my hand.

The volleyball team beat Midwestern in three games, and Coach Lawrence said, "No ice. Get your stuff and get on the bus. Malori had a brain bleed, and we are headed to the hospital." The team and families who traveled to watch us play that night met at Kell West.

At one point during the surgery, a nurse brought a gallon-sized Ziploc bag full of my hair to my mom. She was told this was for funeral purposes if need be.

About six hours had passed since the start of the surgery, and Dr. Kamath came out to talk to my family. After trying and trying for hours, using the same methods in precise, expertise fashion, the bleed finally stopped. He had tried a clotting device, and it just *stopped*. The Kell West staff performed a life-saving surgery that night. Praise, thanksgiving, and honor were given to God in prayer. But the fight was not over. The next few hours would be critical, and the future was not promised. The risk of infection and being paralyzed was not out of the picture; the amount of brain damage at this point was unknown. Dr. Kamath said that he kept looking at my sister, Maci, and saw similarities to his own daughter, so he kept pressing on.

Dr. Kamath's plan was to monitor me until he determined I was in a stable enough condition to be flown to Dallas, Texas, to a brain suite for continued care. This was one of two of the best locations in the country for neurological treatment. First, I had to be wheeled through the lobby to undergo a CT scan so the doctors could make sure the bleed had stopped. People in the lobby witnessed a new "Mal" being wheeled through the lobby: I was completely bald on the left side of my head, tubes were down my throat with several wires and IVs, and I had a huge question mark–shaped incision from my left temple to underneath the left side of my ear. There were bandages around my staples and incision, and my skin was as white as paper. It was a shocking scene for everyone.

After several hours at Kell West, my dad boarded a small plane with me for a scary ride through bad weather to Dallas. Several of my family members and dear friends got in cars to drive straight to the hospital in Dallas. This was possible because of a dear soul who had cleaned the vomit out of the car and bagged the items that smelled strongly of it. Several of those who were at the hospital in Wichita Falls continued onward to Dallas in a caravan, trusting God and praying the whole way. At four thirty that morning, my dad and I made it, by God's grace, to the open arms of the nurses who were ready for our arrival.

At the Zale Lipshy Hospital, my dad was met by a doctor who told him that the care I had just received and experienced was unheard of for a small, rural hospital. What Dr. Kamath had done was exactly the protocol that the neurosurgeons at Zale Lipshy would have done. Miracle.

I stayed in the intensive care unit (ICU) for fourteen days at Zale Lipshy Hospital. When I was taken off the ventilator in ICU, no one knew if I would be able to talk again or what I would remember. When asked, I confidently said that my name was Sarah and that I was born in 1972, my mom's name and birth year. The right side of my body was so weak and immovable. I didn't voluntarily move it at all unless someone coaxed me through the movement. My family pushed me and encouraged me to always use my right arm when eating, drinking, or grabbing for things. They would always stand at my right side, trying to trigger neuron connections linked to limb movement. Such patience, grace, and faith that must have took! But my family is full of those qualities. I don't even remember having this deficit; there was always someone by my side coaching me back to full strength, and I was never alone. My family celebrated every baby step of progress that I made, leaving me blissfully unaware of my deficits and always full of joy in the moment. In the book of Isaiah, God says that He strengthens us and helps us; He upholds us with His "righteous right hand" (41:10). His presence always trumps our weaknesses, and I feel that specifically by how His right hand continually gives strength to mine.

Upon adequate stabilization, I was then moved to a regular hospital room for ten days. I gradually started regaining consciousness and woke up, though completely unaware of the reality and magnitude of what had just happened. With the love of my family continually surrounding me, it just seemed like one big holiday, and I was just so happy to all be together. Quality time has always been my love language, though I'm not sure how much *quality* everyone else perceived that time to be. Because of the powerful love of the Father and my family, who was so generously available to me in every waking moment, I never focused on the needles that were poking me, the tubes that were taped on me, or the wires that entangled me; I was truly encapsulated in the greatest sense of peace during a horrific tragedy. God's presence was and is *truly* unexplainable.

Throughout the treacherous days in ICU, unsure of the quality of a not so promising future, I remember vivid moments of certain things while relying on pictures and videos for others. There is no explanation for why I do or don't remember certain moments, but I'm thankful for any light bulb that has tried to squeak its way on.

During one of the later days of the hospital stay, my neurosurgeon in Dallas, Dr. Welch, another courageous hero to me, came in and started talking to my parents about the *next* surgery. I looked at them and remember thinking, *What do you mean next surgery?* I had no idea half of my skull was missing, as Dr. Kamath had removed it to relieve pressure in that initial, life-saving surgery. He had stored it in my abdomen and planned for it to be replaced during the procedure for the AVM removal scheduled for several weeks later in January.

An AVM is an arteriovenous malformation; it is something I was born with, and people who have them may never know until an event happens that causes it to rupture or bleed. This rupture was not caused by any sort of external or physical force, and some people with an AVM may never experience a rupture.

After the news from Dr. Welch, my parents gently calmed me down as they read my confused facial expression, and I trusted their every word of reassurance. I never felt scared. It was like everything I was told, no matter how shocking, was received with such peace because of the gracious buffer of my family's presence. That peace, His peace, truly surpasses our every ounce of understanding (Philippians 4:7). I was so trusting with everything my parents told me; they surely set the tone for this journey and pointed a lot of people to God's sovereignty, so naturally. God just kept meeting every new "obstacle" with a greater measure of His *mighty* presence, allowing everyone to grow in spiritual momentum.

One moment of light I am thankful to partially remember was when the volleyball girls, my team of rock stars, came through to the hospital on their way home from the conference tournament in Arkansas. I was still in ICU, and at that point, I remembered all of the girls. I also remembered I was once one of them, but in my mind, that was in a different life. I knew those girls were very dear to me, another heart memory; I love them so much. I was so happy they had thought to come visit me, and I remember being so giggly. I was told that they had to make a courageous decision to go play in the conference tournament after such a rattling event with what had happened to me, and I am so proud of their bravery to go fight through such unique adversity as a team. They were encouraged to do so by several important leaders who had stepped up during that time to support them.

Tyler wrote the team a letter that inspired and encouraged them; he gave them confidence to play again for the right reasons. I am just speechless but believe with my whole heart the things I've heard that people endured for me. My three fellow seniors, Kacey, Maddie, and Kyleigh, had played volleyball for the majority of their lives, and they were willing to hang up their careers in an instant. Wow. All of the girls on the team will forever be the "band of sistas," as my dad called them throughout that journey.

In the hospital, I continued undergoing therapy sessions regularly. Therapy included speech, physical, and occupational activities. I sincerely enjoyed every session and was always motivated by my family or a sweet visitor who stopped by to bring some sort of love or encouragement. My parents always greeted everyone with kindness and appreciation, and it fueled me that the atmosphere was so constantly positive. I felt favored to have had received God's love in such generous measures.

Having been previously interested in becoming a physical therapist, I was genuinely excited when a therapist knocked at the door and pushed me to work. Although in retrospect every task asked of me could definitely be considered babyish, I always felt motivated and accomplished getting to do anything. My therapists soon became friends, and it was always a fun time, for me at least.

The Zale Lipshy Hospital breakfast always provided a great start to the day. Breakfast ties with lunch and dinner as my favorite meal for the day; I was always excited to wake up and eat. I felt like royalty getting to order a five-star breakfast every morning, brought in by the sweet hospital aides who also soon became dear friends. My parents always helped narrow down the options, as too many choices overwhelmed me.

Each day was continually filled with more and more hope for a promising future. That specific request prayed by my dad to all *walk* out of the hospital, while he held my hand, was graciously granted. On December 4, God allowed just that. A cart was loaded with all of our acquired belongings there, as so many generous souls sent or brought their love to us in some form. My parents led the way as we hugged doctors and nurses and thanked them deeply. I genuinely couldn't wait to see them again, even though that meant another surgery was coming up.

On the drive through Dallas, my parents asked if I was hungry, and I told them I was craving Rosa's, a family favorite restaurant. Although it was about a forty-five-minute drive to the nearest one, my parents and I headed straight there. Those two bean and cheese burritos with chips and queso never tasted so good. My dad continued to drive us to the Ronald McDonald house, where our family was able to stay during our time in Dallas. That organization is such a gracious blessing to a lot of needy families going through hard times, providing a luxurious home with delicious meals. We were so grateful to be able to live there and all be together. It was a great day.

I was enrolled to begin therapy at Pate Rehabilitation until my next surgery in January, which was the reason we lived there for two months. I had a fairly strict schedule that my parents, siblings, extended family, friends, and teammates encouraged me through. I had a therapy session from 9:00 to 12:00, a lunch break until 1:00, then another therapy session from 1:00 to 4:00. I rarely had the endurance to make it through a whole day's work without a nap break. I was exhausted by the end and typically fell asleep during the car ride back to the Ronald McDonald house. After a good nap, it was fun to wake up to a meal with my precious family and oftentimes a new visitor.

Memories of the days prior often came to me after a good rest, proving the healing power of sleep. I would often remember something new in the morning after a good night's rest or upon waking up from a nap. It was always exciting to wake up to what felt like a new treasure being gifted to my brain.

Throughout this recovery journey in Dallas, I remember several instances of just being so giggly. I had so much joy when my family helped me through therapy activities; my parents were always there, and my brother and sister were in Dallas as much as they could be in the midst of busy school schedules and sporting activities. They are truly incredible. Because of their presence, I didn't even realize anything was wrong with me. They would play games with me and bring excitement to whatever task I needed to complete; they are why I stayed so motivated as a patient.

My boyfriend also reorganized his schedule of college basketball and school to be at my side as much as possible; he was constantly flying back and forth in between games to show his love and faithfulness to me. On November 9, he had just played in an exhibition game the night before my AVM ruptured. He had twenty-two points that night, rolling off of the momentum he had built from his hard work during the off season. Although he says otherwise, the sacrifices he chose to make for me during his "business" time are beyond measurable. Tyler is a legend of a human, and I know his example of faith inspired everyone on his team to look to God during this time as well; he handled the circumstances in absolute heroic fashion. I wish everyone could be shown the kind of love he has shown me. Love empowers.

CLING TO THE ANCHOR

"For My thoughts are not your thoughts, neither are your ways My ways,"
declares the Lord. "As the Heavens are higher than the earth, so are
My ways higher than your ways and My thoughts than your thoughts.
As the rain and the snow come down from Heaven, and do not return
to it without watering the earth and making it bud and flourish, so
that it yields seed for the sower and bread for the eater, so is My Word
that goes out from My mouth: It will not return to Me empty, but will
accomplish what I desire and achieve the purpose for which I sent it."
—ISAIAH 55:8–11

My family is so special; all of them are so patient, loving, kind, and heroic. It takes a special squad to love on a baldheaded goober like me.

Christmas happened to fall in the window of time between surgeries. Just like Thanksgiving had felt so special, even in a hospital, Christmas did too. This was due to the amazing humans I get to call family. Holidays have always been special for us, as my immediate and extended family is all so close; we get to celebrate fun traditions together. I didn't even realize our traditions shifted because of me; because my family was still together, everything felt so right and normal. For me, the presence of family trumped any sort of negativity due to the sudden changes in my life. God is so good.

A special lady named Cathy Delaney let our whole family enjoy Christmas together by opening her home to us. That was such a powerful and kind deed, as her home was stocked with good food and Christmas cheer. All of my family, including grandparents, cousins, aunts, and uncles, always make for a memorable and special time when we are together. We played games like Yahtzee, Wahoo, spades, Skip-bo, and other family favorites and ate all sorts of yummy snacks that were instantly burned off by gut-wrenching laughter. I was blown away by God's provisions, then and always. We all enjoyed cruising through town to see the beautiful Christmas lights and decorations. All of us were filled with the Christmas spirit and enjoyed this special time of opening presents and fellowship. We all appreciated this refreshing time together.

After a few fun days of celebrating, all of us went our separate ways back home. Each family went to their own town, and my family went back to the Ronald McDonald house. When we were about twenty minutes down the road, we got a call regarding my papa. He had become very lethargic and started leaning over to the left as his body went stiff. My nana, who was driving the car, pulled over to a gas station because he had started throwing up. All of the family stayed close together and met at the nearest hospital in order for him to be examined. At this point, everyone was a little rattled, but we all remained calm and hopeful.

Papa stayed there for several days, until stable enough to make the drive back home to Lubbock. We have some incredible spiritual leaders in our family who are always ready to stand firm. We were continually reminded that everything that happens in life, good or bad, points us to Christ. All of our family continued to portray unshakable faith through every splash of this storm.

Later on during the Christmas holiday, Ms. Cathy Delaney offered her home a second time for us to also do a Maddox/Rogers Christmas. Kindness and generosity ran deep throughout this sweet time as Spirit-filled family traditions carried us through; time spent together consisted of games, walks, and more fun. This carried us to the next milestone, as January 5 was a day that everyone seemed to be waiting for. I say *everyone*, excluding myself, because I had no sense of date or time; every morning was literally brand-new. But because my immediate family was together and I was mentally in my childhood years, it seemed normal and felt as if we were all in vacation mode to me.

This day marked the day for an angiogram with an embolization procedure, which was the preparatory work to remove the AVM the next day. Several close friends and family came to Dallas to be with my family for this day, and the atmosphere continued to feel so positive.

In Wichita Falls, Dr. Kamath had performed a life-saving surgery to stop the bleed and stabilize the pressures and conditions of my brain so I could be flown to one of the best possible hospitals in the country for continued neurological treatment. After being released from that hospital in Dallas and then completing about a month of therapy at Pate Rehab, it was time for this second surgery.

An embolization is a procedure where all of the blood vessels surrounding the AVM are plugged or blocked. A catheter goes in through the femoral artery in the leg and travels to the area of the brain needing to be treated. This enables the doctors to distinguish which vessels feed the AVM or other important regions of the brain (AVM 2019). This procedure was covered in prayer, and everyone seemed very optimistic. Completion of the planned embolization was done in unusually rapid timing, as Dr. Welch brought great news shortly after to all those in the waiting room. He announced that the AVM did not require any sort of embolization; he was confident in its full removal during surgery the next day. We celebrated by going to eat barbeque with our faithfully supportive friends and family.

With everyone's spirits high, I continued walking with the greatest peace. I was even more encouraged during the evening as these sweet family friends joined my family's gathering for another time of fellowship and more prayer covering the next morning's surgery. I remember everyone sharing some of their heart around the room, speaking with gratitude, faith, and confidence in the Lord for what He had done and for what was to come. These faith memories have been stapled in my heart forever, triumphantly defeating memory loss.

The next morning came early, as my family, extended family, and continued faithful friends drove to the hospital with hope and what felt like excitement. Excitement? We knew God was in control. In the words of my brother, "After seeing what God has already done for Mal, I know everything is going to be OK for the rest of the journey." Amen, brother.

We got to the hospital, and everything felt so smooth. I was always smiling with the constant outpouring of reassurance felt in the presence of my dearly faithful family and friends. My mom, dad, brother, sister, and I drove together and went to get checked in at the front desk for surgery. Even more people drove in to support my family for this big day.

One specific memory I have was when our preacher, Dale Mannon, came in before going to the surgery room and asked me what I did for a pregame routine in volleyball. It's funny because while not completely remembering I was an LCU volleyball player, I knew exactly that folder of Bible verses on my phone that I would read before each game. I shared this routine with my teammate and warm-up partner, Kyleigh Leslie. I knew them each by heart but always felt more ready and confident after reading each one. Mr. Dale encouraged me to do this same pregame routine before surgery as well.

My list of verses included the following:

"But as for you, be strong and do not give up, for your work will be rewarded" (2 Chronicles 15:7).

"Jesus looked at them and said, 'With man this is impossible, but with God all things are possible'" (Matthew 19:26).

"Jesus looked at them and said, 'With man this is impossible, but not with God; all things are possible with God'" (Mark 10:27).

"What, then, shall we say in response to these things? If God is for us, who can be against us?" (Romans 8:31).

"Finally, be strong in the Lord and in His mighty power. Put on the full armor of God, so that you can take your stand against the devil's schemes" (Ephesians 6:10–11).

"I press on toward the goal to win the prize for which God has called me heavenward in Christ Jesus" (Philippians 3:14).

"I can do all this through Him who gives me strength" (Philippians 4:13).

"Whatever you do, work at it with all your heart, as working for the Lord, not for human masters, since you know that you will receive an inheritance from the Lord as a reward. It is the Lord Christ you are serving" (Colossians 3:23–24).

I am thankful for Mr. Dale's advice. Holding those verses in my heart gave me the peace and Godly confidence I needed to ensure that everything would continue smoothly, even as I was dressed in my gown and waiting for the surgery team to roll me down to Dr. Welch.

I remember being so grateful and calm while more people who drove in took turns showing me some love before surgery. At least one of my immediate family members was always there in the room with me, and each of them felt like an anchor for me; their peace was powerful. Tyler stayed until the last second before catching his flight to Lubbock for practice later that afternoon. He is incredible.

The book of Deuteronomy says, "The eternal God is your refuge, and underneath are the everlasting arms" (33:27). The amount of joy and hope I felt lying in a hospital bed didn't make sense; I didn't fear a thing. I know it was because of those everlasting arms that were so gentle and gracious in the form of the humans around me. A nurse soon came in to take me back, and I think I was laughing as the anesthesia hit, waving to my family before falling asleep. All of my prayer warriors went to God in prayer to battle for me again.

My brother and I jokingly made a deal before going into surgery: when I heard him play the song "Brainwash" by Nicole C. Mullen, I would know that I had made it out. My first conscious memory with my new brain was seeing his goofy, smiling face and hearing that song. That dude can find humor in anything.

I stayed in ICU for a couple of days with the same sweet nurses I had before; I am grateful to call them friends. I knew I was hard to handle, specifically being extra sassy about wanting water. Water intake had to be minimal because I couldn't hold anything down after all of the anesthesia from surgery. When given a sponge, I would suck it dry and demand more. Gratefully, I was shown a lot of grace, and we can laugh about my sassiness now. Those tiny, wet sponges were the best things ever, but I typically prefer a water bottle now.

My nurses and parents continued to nurture my every need. In physical therapy, it was a joy to be able to take any amount of steps; just walking felt amazing to my whole body. I was so joyful to God for that ability.

When a resident doctor came in to take out my drain, he asked for all of the visitors to leave the room. It made me kind of nervous to hear a rather stern command, but he assured me I was going to be OK. I tried not to imagine what it looked like inside my noggin as he started pulling something out that seemed to go on for eternity. He had really steady hands, and I told him he was really good at his job.

When moved to a regular room, we had high hopes that the hospital journey was coming close to an end. I needed to clear a couple more checkpoints to be able to go home, one of which was a bowel movement. When I heard what might need to happen if I couldn't, I tried the best I could, not that that is necessarily a controllable. But this particular detail had a good ending.

I enjoyed each of my last sessions with my therapists, as we had also become good friends. My sweet nurses also shared joyful goodbyes with my family, as they, too, were very dear to us all. A final angiogram was scheduled for April as one last checkup to officially be AVM-free, but that monster already felt out of sight and out of mind. January 10 was a truly victorious and joyful day, as it marked the official ending of a long, tiresome, and beautiful hospital journey. God is so good; praise the Lord.

ONWARD TO DEEP
HOME ROOTS

Because of the Lord's great love we are not consumed, for His compassions
never fail. They are new every morning; great is Your faithfulness.
—**LAMENTATIONS 3:22–23**

The drive back home to Lubbock seemed very long. I knew we were going home, but I always felt at home wherever my family was. Home had been Dallas, Texas, for two months, but we all looked forward to being officially home. It was such a miracle to have such a relatively close location for all of the treatment and care of my catastrophic injury. So many gracious visitors came to show love to my family and me during this time. Although I don't remember everyone, I wanted to be confident in knowing they felt honored, recognized, and special for their noble and humble deeds for me. Even without a memory of some, the love I feel through deep relationships continues to bring me confidence and purpose. Loving people is the second most important commandment that God gives us; His presence is so evident when that love is active among us.

During the drive back to Lubbock, being the spoiled little thing I was, I would crave something and stop the whole caravan at the next gas station. I always tried to make light of silly little things, but it was weird how intense those cravings were. When my body wanted something, I couldn't think or function until I ate or drank that thing. I was a diva with a capital D. During this car ride home, I asked for pickle slices, then dill pickle–flavored sunflower seeds, then Sprite. That got us about one hundred miles. God bless my precious family.

My parents said we were en route to go through Wichita Falls. It would be a great opportunity to stop at Kell West Hospital and was also on the way for my brother to get back to Oklahoma. We drove into what seemed like a homecoming parade in the hospital lobby. It was a Sunday, and several people were dressed in scrubs, while some were in everyday clothes. Everyone there immediately embraced our family in love and the warmest kindness.

My mom had been in contact with a few of the ladies from the hospital for this gathering; everyone already knew and loved one another. I was led to a man who seemed to know me. I looked at my parents as I grabbed his hand and gave him a hug; he embodied such a strong sense of boldness and grace. I was told this was Dr. Kamath, the man who had saved my life. The hospital staff gathered there had all been instruments of this miracle in some way. All of those humans were and are angels to me, and I praise God for His tools of such mighty power.

Dr. Kamath took me by the hand, while I held my heated owl pillow in the other. I was anemic for a couple months during recovery and always felt cold; my heated owl always made me feel better. Dr. Kamath led me through the hallways of the hospital and showed me the room where I had been taken care of. I had no idea of the significance of that place at that time. God had looked down from heaven to perform a miracle in that very place. Now, anytime we drive through Wichita Falls, I see Kell West and know that must be holy ground.

We enjoyed visiting with all of the hospital staff, and they even offered us a meal so we could all stay and eat together. We enjoyed a good laugh when Dr. Kamath went and bought me a Powerball ticket, joking that I probably had a good shot at the lottery with the odds he had just experienced with me in surgery.

They learned of surprising details, like how Dr. Kamath tried every trick he knew to stop the bleed, then finally tried something one last time and got it stopped. How the nurse kept giving my family and Tyler updates and saying, "She's holding her own," just to be so very kind and reassuring during a grim situation. How there were several moments with no blood pressure reading at all, and the nurses kept running to get more blood for transfusions without any family seeing and worrying. How they started a major brain surgery with three total people, one being an emergency room nurse. How the lady who had given my mom a Bible that night was at Kell West to visit someone in the hospital there and really existed in human form instead of angelic form, coupled with the gift of the hospital staff later contacting her to let my mom thank her. And finally, how a true miracle was witnessed that night at Kell West, and how much love and gratitude my family felt for every angel involved and prayer that was said. Everyone involved in this miracle experienced his or her own journey of faith too. In the words of my father-in-law, "God is so kind to us." I am grateful to forever stay connected to this precious Kell West family. They give me encouragement, fuel, hope, accountability, and inspiration to keep moving forward.

After our time together in Wichita Falls, Peyton headed north to Oklahoma while my family and the Rogers continued west toward Lubbock. My sister and I were in the back seat of the Tahoe, and we heard our parents say something about meeting at the church with a few people. We were just excited to be going home. I remember my arms feeling numb and tingly, and I kept trying to shake them out the whole ride home. It was a restless ride, but I always had a full heart around my family.

As we neared Lubbock, we were en route for Green Lawn Church of Christ, my family's home church for more than ten years. It looked like there were a million cars in the parking lot, and I thought, *Oh goodness, what's going on?*

The Lubbock community is a special place. Though a rapidly growing city, there is such a passionate connection shared within what has always felt like an intimate circle, and love runs generously deep. A few of the elders of the church had met us at our car in the parking lot and led my family inside. My family was escorted into the most indescribable scene. There must have been a thousand people, with signs and warm smiles, so graciously there to welcome us home. God's love filled the whole atmosphere as everyone sang the most beautiful worship songs. My dad spoke, thanking all of the prayer warriors on our behalf so sincerely. It is crazy what a body of believers can provide: encouragement, love, kindness, reassurance, and hope. Prayer was the greatest gift of all.

I was led to where the volleyball girls were sitting, and a sweet boy, Case Driskill, came and sat on my lap. I had babysat him and his brother for several summers and became very close to their sweet family. It felt so good being around all of these people that I love; the power of God's love felt in that church building seemed to ooze out of the walls. I was in awe of what was going on around me. Although I didn't remember much about volleyball at this point, it felt so right to be with the girls from the team again too.

I had heard of things people were doing back home: advertising for prayer, making T-shirts, and hosting fundraisers for our family. In that moment, we got to see a new form of love that was crazy deep, and I will never understand it. I have struggled with trying to thank people adequately and never feel fulfilled in that category; I never will. But that fuels my spirit to strive to be "a living sacrifice, holy and pleasing to God," or to at least try (Romans 12:1). I believe that the best thing you can do for someone is to pray, and I received the most powerful answers to those prayers firsthand. I was in awe, truly emotional and speechless, but so encouraged in spirit. I also said a few words, through happy tears, just hoping to show as much gratitude as possible to the people who had gathered there to worship

God for His miracles. Stopping at the church was a milestone of a memory, saturated by feelings of joyful gratitude and thankful praise. Thinking of this moment reminds me that we ought to always live in a spiritually unquenched state (1 Thessalonians 5:19).

Our black Tahoe finally made it to my family's driveway in Lubbock, Texas, and we got to enjoy the luxury of a sparkling home. Carpet Tech, a company in Lubbock, had done some deep cleaning for us, making it extra sweet to walk in the door. Others had stocked our pantry and refrigerator and had left our home filled with the richest blessings. God is so gracious, and His vessels so real.

PERSPECTIVE

I will exalt You, Lord, for You lifted me out of the depths
and did not let my enemies gloat over me.
Lord my God, I called to You for help, and You healed me.
You, Lord, brought me up from the realm of the dead;
You spared me from going down to the pit.
Sing the praises of the Lord, you His faithful people; praise His holy Name.
For His anger lasts only a moment, but His favor lasts a lifetime;
weeping may stay for the night, but rejoicing comes in the morning.
When I felt secure, I said,
"I will never be shaken."
Lord, when You favored me, You made my royal mountain
stand firm; but when You hid Your face, I was dismayed.
To You, Lord, I called;
to the Lord I cried for mercy:
"What is gained if I am silenced, if I go down to the pit?
Will the dust praise You?
Will it proclaim Your faithfulness?
Hear, Lord, and be merciful to me;
Lord, be my help."
You turned my wailing into dancing; You removed my sackcloth
and clothed me with joy, that my heart may sing Your praises
and not be silent. Lord my God, I will praise You forever.

—PSALM 30

Charles Swindoll said, "We cannot change our past ... we cannot change the fact that people will act in a certain way. We cannot change the inevitable. The only thing we can do is play on the one string we have, and that is our attitude. I am convinced that life is 10% what happens to me and 90% how I react to it. And so it is with you ... we are in charge of our attitudes." Our attitudes can sustain and empower us, but we have to choose to believe in that power and mental toughness.

My family has always looked up to the way Aunt Lola sees the world through "rose-colored glasses," as we say. She has a special and unique way of making any situation good, as she always sees the best in any and everything. She can turn darkness to light and sadness to joy, and she never holds back the love and zeal in her heart. Her example has been a tremendous contribution to the legacy of our family as we all try to mimic her positive, simple, and hopeful outlook on everything.

Practicing an intentional perspective is crucial. It's crazy how the same situation can be perceived so differently because of our own little ways of processing. God saturates life into everything when we open our hearts to Him and strive to see with His vision; He loves us enough to invite us into a lifestyle of fullness together.

When God's love fills us, it expresses itself in wonderful and powerful ways. I truly felt God's light on me, as my heart and spirit were always full from the love I was shown; it felt so good to be home, saturated with the sweet culture of my family.

At the time of my injury, I was in college at LCU and living in the apartments on campus with my roommate and best friend, Mallory Powell. However, day one at home with my parents and sister was the start of a new life, a second childhood, as I now see it. My outward appearance was visibly tattered with scars, staples, and a lot less hair. It's funny how I didn't even realize how different I looked or felt from the Mal before November 10. Being at home with my sweet family felt so normal and right because our family legacy was powerful. I guess what people didn't realize, and couldn't realize, was my loss of self on the inside. I didn't realize it either.

My sister, Maci, and I were getting excited about some sister sleepovers. However, my mom would not let anything or anyone get near my head or stomach, as the staples there were still fresh. So, I slept with her in a barricade of pillows where my head stayed elevated. We often got so tickled and laughed so much at silly little things that it was hard to differentiate between our home and Disney World. As everything was perceived as new and exciting from my eyes, I just soaked it all in like a sponge.

There was someone who brought us a meal every night for about two months, and it was so encouraging to have this fellowship in our home. I am proud and thankful of the reputation and relationships that my parents have nurtured for our family. I love people so much and am always ready for a good conversation; the loss of self from not being able to drive was muffled by the fullness I felt from these sweet visitors in my parents' home.

I stayed pretty guarded in this new state of headaches and minimal energy, so being at home was perfect; I felt so protected and complete. Tyler came by almost every day, which was always something to look forward to. I loved to hear about his day: his workouts, practices, and classes. He always brought some form of good news and was always exciting to see.

After about a week of being home, a man came over to talk about starting therapy at a place called Transitional Learning Center (TLC) in Lubbock. He asked a bunch of questions to ensure that their program would be the best for my needs. My mom answered all the important stuff, while I just listened. At the end of the meeting, he gave me a little memory quiz; I don't remember how much I was able to retain and recall from the information he had presented to me, but I know it wasn't much. Needless to say, I was set up to start therapy at TLC shortly after this meeting, feeling ambitious to get on a productive schedule.

My dad is part owner of Physical Therapy Today (PTT), an outpatient physical therapy clinic in Lubbock, and I had always aspired to become a physical therapist someday. TLC was next on my list of settings to try and shadow for observation hours, but little did I know I would get all of my observation hours from an inside perspective as a patient myself.

I had worked at PTT as a physical therapy tech for a few summers prior, while also observing at two different pediatric physical therapy clinics in Lubbock. I loved studying the human body, engaging in the gift of exercise, fueling my body with nutritious foods, and learning how to more specifically encourage people in the realm of physical health. This interest was influenced heavily by my upbringing.

As a family, we have always enjoyed physical activities together and love being outside. We have been on so many camping trips and joke about the advantages of being small and agile. Our family of five has always fit comfortably in a camper, and one summer we were even able to all squeeze on one seat of a Ferris wheel during one of our family vacations in Colorado. Growing up, we were always outside in the yard being active and sometimes moved the craziness inside. I remember watching Peyton and Dad play pillow football in the living room a lot. Dad and I have always enjoyed running together, and all of us like walking the dogs around the neighborhood. My mom is the queen of the backyard volleyball court, and my sister's athleticism always glosses her bottomless energy in incredible ways. She will wrestle anything. All of us even like mowing the yard, with the riding lawn mower of course, and we enjoy evenings on the porch swing or patio.

Just having childhood memories seemed more than enough because my family is the greatest. My mom is forever the world's most fun and tender-loving momma bear. Her extravagant deeds have always kept our family afloat. During my recovery, she gave me all of my medicine, food, drinks, comfort, and care. She drove me to every appointment and led my every step. She could tell when I was weak, and she guarded me extra carefully then. I felt like I was doing her a favor if I could breathe and go to the bathroom by myself.

My mom was the one who had told everyone in the locker room I was having an aneurysm and needed to go to a hospital the night of November 10. She was the one who had scooped vomit out of my mouth as I was stiff in her arms on the way to the hospital. She was the one who had told my dad to go faster on the way to the emergency room because she didn't know if I was going to make it. She was the one who caught me when I fainted from getting up too fast to go to the bathroom in the middle of the night in Dallas. She was the one who helped me shower, get dressed, and feel like a pretty girl again, dolling me up. She was my angel, and she is forever an angel to everyone. I could never express my gratitude to her for raising me, twice.

My dad handled the responsibilities of his job from a distance in an incredibly honorable way, as the employees of PTT were able to graciously share duties through tremendous teamwork. Dad is a hardworking, successful businessman, but no one would even know what he does for a living. He never uses the word *I*, as he doesn't ever have time to think about himself in the midst of all of his service for others. I think his humility, encouragement, and wisdom are the most powerful combination in a human, and I've never even heard of anyone like him. My dad is such a leader, and it's obvious that his example inspires others to reach their best too.

I feel closer to knowing God's heart as I try to greater understand the command to "honor your father and mother" (Ephesians 6:2). It's like my parents' whole purpose was to raise their kids with the most extravagant life and righteous view of our heavenly Father. Their examples led everyone to embody a perspective of hope during my recovery. I love them so dearly; they are role models to all who know them.

Everyone experienced a unique spiritual and physical journey, and it seems crazy that people so willingly volunteered to walk this road with me. Together, our family acknowledged what a blessing and privilege it was to enjoy physical, mental, and spiritual health.

Upon plunging into the full swing of life again, all of us continued to process and try to find our own way again, catching our breath from what had just happened. After an event like this, it seems fitting to feel awkward or different, or to take the label of an outcast, but that was not the case for us. Divine intervention from our heavenly Father glossed our every chapter; He always does when we look to Him, but I never realized it until becoming so desperate for it.

While I have always looked up to my family for their incredible examples, many talents, and strong faith, my post-stroke life has made me even more of a sponge to my family's influence on me. Childhood memories have been my main source of things I confidently remember and trust. Although I am the oldest of the siblings, I, for a time, felt like the youngest, hungrily searching for the meaning of life through my family again and treasuring the roots of how I was raised. I am grateful for my sweet family upbringing that has helped me tie all of life's newness together as a stroke survivor trying to navigate through adulthood. God's love is radical.

TRUSTING HIS ROOTS

For though the righteous fall seven times, they rise again, but the wicked stumble when calamity strikes.

—PROVERBS 24:16

Even when we try to do right, we can mess up. It's hard to be obedient and persistent in our faith when doors start closing that were once so wide open. The book of Proverbs says, "Trust in the Lord with all your heart and lean not on your own understanding; in all your ways submit to Him, and He will make your paths straight" (3:5–6). So, we don't have to *understand,* thank goodness. God is always in control. How does it get any better than the black and white truth of a promise like that?

My dad, mom, brother, sister, and Tyler seemed to jump right back into life with complete ease and normalcy. Dad was always excited to go to work, doing the marketing for PTT. He enjoyed conversations with everyone and let the extra attention from our family event fuel him, as he used it as a segue to give glory directly to God.

My mom had put her life on pause as the librarian of an elementary school so she could stay home with me and tend to my needs. She drove me to all of my therapy sessions and even participated in several of the activities with me. The way she carried herself made me believe everything was normal and right, a way of living that only my momma could do. Her energy always lifts people's spirits and makes everything fun. There is not a stroke patient in history who laughed as much as she made me through that time.

My brother continued with his classes and baseball with admirable focus and determination. His team showed such tremendous love and support to our family and even shaved their heads in my honor. I'm glad they made that style look good because I surely did *not*. Maci jumped right back in to eighth grade, also juggling school and basketball; her team was full of energy, love, and support for our family. I admire so greatly the mental toughness displayed by my siblings to be able to do and handle what they did for me.

Tyler also showed great courage by the way he handled his classes and role as a leader on the basketball team; his faith was courageous and contagious, just like it has always been. True grit has a chance to emerge when looking to God is the only way to take another step forward. These heroes made that look easy.

At this point in time, I was in what's called a mental state of euphoria. I had no memory of life before my AVM, but I knew my family and always felt safe with them. Everything seemed like a big celebration, as every moment was full of life and love. With such a positive environment, I didn't realize that a big portion of my brain and memory were still pending. I didn't notice any missing pieces of what once was my life.

I kept living in what felt like an absolute parade of love and kindness, which was such a great and truly empowering blessing, through the sweetest family and friends. I felt normal being around these people I loved; it was always so fun. I knew that there were so many familiar faces throughout this journey who had showed support to me, but I wasn't exactly sure how all of the dots connected. There was always so much going on, all good things, that I never took time to let myself really think or process it all.

Because I was so severely one-track minded, whenever someone was with me or talking to me, all of the focus had to be on that person so I could be fully engaged. It took literally every neuron for me to direct my attention so strongly for even short conversations. Nothing else in the world existed to me except for what was going on right in front of me. My empathy was on full force because all of my focus had to be very direct and intentional; I didn't know how to just talk to someone without trying to *be* that person.

I never took the time to process and realize that I was still Mal, but a lot of my memory was missing. We were always able to laugh off the short-term memory issues, small things I forgot that didn't really matter. But the long-term memory and identity loss was a whole new category. It is a bizarre thing to research the person you used to be and try to attain the good qualities of that person.

Everything seemed to be focused on the physical things that were plain to the eye, while a lot of screws were still loose on the inside. No one could see how broken I actually was, including me. In just trying to keep up with everyone and everything going on around me, my sense of self gradually slipped away as I poured and poured from my shallow cup. I was just happy for whatever drops were left, but I didn't seem to care to guard them because I was so eager to give back to others.

Through the beginning phases of getting on my feet again in therapy, it felt good to belong to something again, although I didn't realize my new label belonged with an injured population. A brain injury is a double-edged sword. The more you get better on the outside, the more you realize on the inside, and it's scary. But I stayed highly motivated and encouraged to get better.

After the draining mental task of picking out a comfortable outfit for the day, I would eat the breakfast that my dad had made me and then get in the car. Then my mom would drive me and walk me into therapy; she would always stay there with me all day to observe, and she even participated in activities with us when appropriate. I am so thankful for her loving presence all of my life, and her character never wavered even through this season.

The first full day of therapy started with a meeting with my case manager, Tia. While she and my mom reviewed paperwork, I was instructed to jump into a group activity going on with several other patients. Within our group, there was a strong sense of unity and drive to work. Everyone in therapy seemed normal to me, even with visible deficits noticed by wheelchairs, canes, or other equipment. Obviously, being a patient in the neurological setting was not necessarily in anyone's plans, but the atmosphere always stayed positive and motivating.

Starting with a group was comfortable and inviting, and I tried to catch on as best I could to the game going on. All of the patients and therapists seemed to be having a lot of fun, and we all smiled at one another through our activities. Any silly mistakes were always glossed with positivity through gentle correction from the therapists. The atmosphere was full of grace.

A typical day at TLC consisted of physical, occupational, and speech therapy sessions, just like the therapy program in Dallas. It was nice to have one-hour sessions at a time and then switch to a new task. Getting to work toward a goal for an allotted amount of time evoked a deep drive for whatever I was doing; small increments of work were very attainable.

I enjoyed physical therapy the most, feeling so blessed to be able to move my arms and legs with no limitations. Running has always been an outlet to me, but now I find great joy in walking too. Any type of movement, in moderation, feels so good. Walking is relaxing, simple, and therapeutic. When I walk, I love to imagine all of the nutrients being delivered to thirsty cells in my body as my circulatory system pumps steadily. It is such a rich blessing to move.

Shortly after being home from Dallas, I remember getting to walk with my dad around the track at his work; he packed us a lunch and drove us to the clinic. After walking a few laps, he gave me permission to try to jog a few steps. I was hesitant at first, thinking the things in my head might bounce around or maybe even fall out my ears. But then my motivation and curiosity emerged enough to try it. I held my head with both of my hands, just to keep everything secure, or at least it made me think so.

I took about ten slow jog steps and started laughing; it felt so good even though I knew I looked awkward. I walked a few strides and then started the jog back up again, this time for a little longer of a distance. The more I jogged, the more I wanted to keep going. It's like I had never run before but somehow knew that was a part of me that was wanting to come back again. It is a blessing to move a healthy and able body freely, and I don't ever want to take that for granted.

It continued to fuel and intrigue me that physical activity gave me energy; I often became more tired from a single worksheet in therapy as compared to any form of physical activity. Although the cognitive aspects of recovery tired me the most, I continued to stay motivated. I felt best when I was able to balance my workload by alternating between physical and mental functions of my body.

In therapy, group activities were always interesting, though I was less motivated for these sessions. I have always been highly driven and disciplined in anything I do, and I felt anxious "wasting recovery time" doing things that I didn't feel contributed specifically to my improvement. I just wanted to get back to my own schedule with independency in my pace. In retrospect, I realize that being so one-track minded with a brain injury made me very selfish. But working with others, like a team, sharpens us. Maybe that was the whole point.

I tried to recognize when I felt selfish and then switch gears to love others. Mentally, it was hard to completely turn off the pathway of action I was doing at the time in order to respect someone else's attention and respond to their command or comment. To me, accepting interruptions meant throwing my current action or thought process in the trash can because I wouldn't remember it in the next few seconds after responding to something else. But, after learning about the repercussions of my condition, I couldn't expect others to actually relate to what I dealt with. Learning how to act around others in this new state was an unspoken aspect of therapy that also helped me in transitioning to the real world. I realized I had to maintain a fine balance within myself to operate with energy, personality, and respect to those around me.

Certain situations during therapy that come into mind upon being "more conscious" are quite humiliating. For instance, I remember working so hard in occupational therapy on this certain worksheet; it worked logic and had to do with labeling and organizing certain groups together. When I proudly turned it in, my therapist so cheerfully said, "Good job, Malori! That was a third-grade level." I tried not to let my smile fade too noticeably as those words sunk in to my wounded confidence and made my blood boil. Those types of moments led me straight to the treadmill, where I tried to remind myself of the blessing it was to walk and move.

Most of the time, silly errors were easy to joke about. One evening when my family was all at home, I was feeling giggly and rattled off a joke. I asked everyone, "Is your doorbell ringing?" I wasn't sure what came after that but was referring to the joke, "Is your refrigerator running?" We still laugh about that. Several times, when I'm going full speed somewhere, I will absolutely ram into something on the right side. I know I don't have right peripheral vision, but I still don't seem to want to acknowledge it. Oftentimes, things that are important to me that I ought to never forget slip my mind so fast that it's like they never existed. Memory loss was often a scary battle for me.

When in public or in a social setting, I was very sensitive with how others poked at me for my attention or time, but I tried to hide it because I loved them and knew they meant well. A lot of times, the way people would present information to me made me feel anxious; my head and heart would immediately start to pound when given an overload of information. I often felt trapped inside my body because no one else seemed to feel that way about the situation. But it was easy to shake it off and be joyful because I had so much support through the greatest family and home life.

MOMENTUM: P = MV

Being an encourager requires humility; it's not encouragement when you look down to speak to others from a pedestal. An encourager speaks from their knees.

I have always had compassion in my heart for the "least of these"; God seems to be more clearly present in those situations, with such an obvious platform to perform (Matthew 25:40). Although it had always seemed so natural for me to try to encourage, serve, or volunteer with this population as an outsider, after my stroke, I grew to see myself as *part* of that population. In doing so, I learned that trying to lift up the spirits of those around me by relating with them really just lifted up my own and built unity.

In the early days of therapy, I was gaining confidence and staying highly motivated. After getting a rhythm amid working through new learning strategies to live with my new body and mind, I was ready to start my schoolwork. As a senior and having left off during the end of my fall semester, I lacked a handful of assignments and finals to complete the 2015 school year. I am so very grateful that God had led me to plan to graduate early so that the majority of my college career was under my belt before my stroke. *Thank You, Lord.* My therapists had helped me get organized and ready to attack the course load that remained for me to graduate with a bachelor's degree from LCU. The first class on the list was Physics I.

I knew physics was hard, even for my healthy brain, so I was very nervous to attempt to conquer this class. But I started the journey with a stack of blank paper, a handful of colored markers and pens, my old notes, and a bunch of stubborn determination. My therapists had advised me to rewrite all of my notes in different colors, part of a new learning strategy for me that helped me to remember details. I had always been a strictly kinesthetic learner, but now I needed additional aids for my memory; different colors seemed to help information stick.

Rewriting old material that I had learned prior to my stroke seemed to rekindle old flames quite quickly and was very encouraging to me. It was like I was relearning who I used to be and slowly gaining confidence that girl was still in there. It took a lot of self-motivation to keep going, but I didn't even realize it at the time; I just knew I was supposed to keep working as hard as I could and strive to move forward. I didn't know where forward led to, but I wasn't worried about it. My work ethic, drive, and encouragement from others distracted me from acknowledging the fact that I was in the bottom of a deep well; sometimes, being so stubborn can work in your favor if that drive is used for good.

I continued gaining momentum when I was able to perceive therapy sessions as productive. My desire to hurry up and heal always pushed me. I didn't know what the definition of *healed* meant, but I was always striving for something greater. I think I'll always feel like a work in progress; it seems scarier *not* to be.

As therapy progressed, I started to get frustrated when I felt like I wasn't. I tried to stay positive and told myself that getting annoyed and impatient was a good sign. That ought to be normal in this case because, obviously, being a patient in the neurological setting wasn't necessarily on anyone's list of goals.

With a new and shortened attention span, I enjoyed activities that required focus for a limited amount of time with a specific, attainable goal. It didn't matter to me how small the goal was; I just liked the feeling of accomplishment that gave me momentum and confidence. Then I wanted to conquer something else in a different area. For instance, in each of the fifty-five-minute therapy sessions, I tried to complete a workout, solve a logic puzzle, or copy as much of my physics notes as possible. The silent frustrations at myself seemed to rob my personality for a time; I was so strictly driven that I didn't even want to waste time for small talk.

One particularly frustrating activity was when I was told to do a connect-the-dot activity while standing on a rocker board. This worked my mental focus, challenged me to scan to the right for open dots, and silently sharpened my balance. I knew it was so simple, which made me even more irritated that I was taking *so long* to complete the activity. After about fifteen minutes, I saw a treadmill in the corner and dismissed myself to go walk. I hoped no one noticed the steam coming from my ears as I walked away. I apologized for what probably seemed like disrespectful behavior to my sweet therapist.

Other days, I felt more lackadaisical and free. I got giggly at some things that just reminded me that it's OK to laugh and be silly. Sometimes I messed up so badly or felt so dumb that the only choice was to laugh it off. Things like ping-pong or activities that required fast reaction or thinking time were not exactly my forte. How in the world did I play college volleyball? At this point, I didn't remember I had.

I truly enjoyed therapy when I knew it was sharpening weaknesses. I felt thankful to call my therapists friends; it takes a special heart to have active compassion for a wounded population and a deep drive to put that love into creative practice. The positive culture amid the therapists and patients meant everything; it was also crucial to have friends visit and observe different activities there. My friend Mallory Powell always made me laugh when she was around. She had a unique way of treating me with dignity when she encouraged me; it was always like old times with her sweet friendship. Her ability to laugh at some things while respecting other things made me feel normal and thankful.

"A cheerful heart is good medicine," and that was always Mal Pal's gift she shared (Proverbs 17:22).

People who talked with a baby voice to encourage obvious things were so humiliating that it pushed me to grit my teeth and work hard to get out of therapy. I appreciated their intentions of trying to show love and support, but I remember my blood boiling at the ignorant comments of some. After about three months of dedicated therapy, I started to get impatient and frustrated. I knew overall this was a good thing and made me feel normal in a way. As positive as I wanted to be, I would be fake not to acknowledge these silent feelings creeping through.

I was ready to have the reins on my life again. Not being able to drive because of my vision deficit and slower processing and reaction time made me feel like a mouse trapped in a tiny box. I just went with the flow of my people, which was amazing, but over time, this started to strip away my identity. I loved people, but the ways I enjoyed doing so were no longer available to me without keys, so I had to get creative. All I could do was follow what everyone else did; that seemed like the full extent of my social life. My mom and dad were so graciously willing to care for and drive me wherever I needed, which was such a blessing. The way they live with such generous love and kindness is truly amazing. But my true self was sneakily starting to vanish along with freedoms I had always taken for granted.

Usually after therapy, I was excited to satisfy my need of rest. After I would wake up, my family would have dinner together, truly soaking up this quality time. Oftentimes, a visitor or two would join us. I have always been a homebody with my dearly close family, so time at home was always a treat to me. But the concept of losing my keys gradually nipped at my pride by erasing my freedom.

In April 2016, about three months after the last surgery to remove my AVM, I had a final checkup in Dallas with a vision doctor and Dr. Welch. My parents had said they were so confident and optimistic to hear a final doctor's approval of healing and a good prognosis after what had just happened in November. So, Mom, Dad, and I got in the car and headed to Dallas, while Maci stayed in Lubbock with Nana for her school, track, and other activities. My family's willingness to maintain such confident hope throughout this whole journey continued to contribute to such a positive tone for us.

My first appointment in Dallas was with the vision doctor. I didn't really know what to expect; I knew I could see, and my peripheral deficit was not really noticeable for me in daily life. Everyone seemed to talk about it with a great concern, which made me wonder if it was a bigger deal than I thought, but it never bothered me. I was hopeful that I was going to be released to drive, but I also knew the big picture was great even if I could not.

The ophthalmologist instructed me to put glasses on and sit in what felt like a bubble of machinery. I was told to click a button to signal when I could see certain dots appear on the screen, while keeping my gaze straight ahead. This tested the depth of my periphery.

After a couple more visual field tests, the doctor then came in to go over the results with my parents and me. As he spoke, I was happily in a daze when I thought I heard the words "never going to improve and therefore never be able to drive again." I just looked at my parents for reassurance and then looked back at the ground.

Surely not, I thought. The doctor was very blunt and knowledgeable, and I didn't have a care to fight back. Yet. After he left the room, my parents clarified what had just happened.

"So, did he say that I'd *never* be able to drive again?" I asked my parents to make sure.

They said, "Yes," and smiled without a hint of disappointment on their faces. Their looks implied that it was not a big deal and I shouldn't worry. So, I didn't.

We piddled around Dallas and looked forward to seeing Dr. Welch the next morning. My mom was working on a picture frame gift for him in order to show respect and gratitude for his team's noble work. She is so good at that kind of stuff. We couldn't wait to see this heroic medical team again; they were *family*.

Our alarm went off at four thirty that next morning in order to allow for traffic or any unexpected events along the way to the hospital. At about five thirty, my parents and I were waiting in the holding room at Zale Lipshy while I lay there in my fancy hospital gown, expecting Dr. Welch to walk in any minute. I remember being ecstatic to see him. After all, he is a hero. He answered our bubbly excitement with a shy smile, continuing in his constant, calm nature.

After an eager moment of catching up, I was rolled back for what seemed like the fastest procedure ever. This angiogram was expected to be the final step, medically, of this journey, and our hopes were high to receive the all clear. During the procedure, I was highly medicated while remaining able to talk with the doctors as they worked on me, but I don't remember any part of it.

Upon completion, I was placed in a recovery room for a couple hours and was instructed to lie flat. There was a sweet nurse who kept checking on me; he kept reminding me to be still and told me how much longer I had in that quiet room. I needed to go to the bathroom so badly but was not able to move my body upright yet. Although he had brought me a bedpan, I physically could not go to the bathroom while lying down flat.

Finally, I got rolled back to the room where my parents were, and I felt more comfortable and awake. The doctors who performed the angiogram came in with such positivity and energy as they continued to monitor how I was doing. I just remember being excited to tell them how good they were at their jobs and that I was so thankful to be in their care. It just felt like I was hanging out with the coolest squad.

One of our sweet friends through this journey, Valerie Gregory, brought cupcakes to the hospital to share in celebration with us. She had an AVM two years prior to mine and was able to reconnect with the same doctors I had. She is such a constant encouragement to me still, and I deeply appreciate her example and willingness to reach out to me and others. She has taught me what to expect with new normals and how to best handle them with intentional strategies. It is important for me to have a sense of community living in such a new body, and I am so thankful for how God has orchestrated that for me.

Upon the final visitation with Dr. Welch, reviewing all of the procedure and expectations from that point forward, his official words of "See you in ten years!" didn't seem real to my parents. That was what we had hoped and prayed for, but it seemed like a surreal blessing. We offered our gratitude and goodbyes in a celebratory fashion with such good friends. All of us were exhausted from the early-morning procedure, with all it had entailed, so we headed to the hotel to rest.

After a few hours of sleep, our three growling tummies were ready for some nourishment. I wasn't able to eat before the procedure, and my parents chose to fast along with me until we could all eat together. Our hungry bellies led us to eat at a delicious taco place. After enjoying some chips and salsa along with a full plate of tacos, we walked next door to a Kendra Scott jewelry store.

While I was in the hospital, Kendra Scott (herself!) wrote a sweet letter of encouragement to my mom and sister and sent them each a special piece of jewelry; it meant so much to us! That had to be one of the most memorable deeds anyone did for me—to honor my mom and sister like that. We wanted to go into the store and express gratitude to the whole Kendra Scott organization. After several minutes of conversation, we smiled for a picture with all of the girls who worked there. Then they told me to pick out two pieces of jewelry, whatever I wanted! This kind deed was overwhelming and precious, and we felt so honored that such a noble company would do such a thing for us. We then went back to the hotel for the remainder of the evening to take it easy before driving back home the next day.

STEPPING BACK
TO REALITY

The human spirit is the lamp of the Lord that
sheds light on one's inmost being.
—PROVERBS 20:27

Ignorance is bliss, as they say. No matter the situation, everything was always good with family; that was just our culture. My parents have intentionally established an enlightened mindset of unity and comfort within our family. I know to live *in* the world and not *of* the world as long as I'm alive on earth, as implied in the book of 1 John (2:15–17). Our Maddox family standards and values have engrained this truth in us deeply, which has kept us optimistic through so much.

My parents and I were en route for Plainview, Texas, where an auction event was going on that evening, put on by some sweet family friends. I was working on some physics homework in the back seat, trying not to get too nauseated on the way back. It seems comical to think of the things I attempted in this wounded state. What might have once seemed to be brave might be better labeled as naïve. Nonetheless, the Tahoe was filled with good vibes as my mom updated everyone on the great news from the doctor visit.

The Goldens, who are talented auctioneers, had invited the Rogers family to the auction that evening, and I was honored to tag along. The Golden family has more talent than I would know what to do with, and they are always ready to share with others in unique ways. I happily tagged along as my parents dropped me off, while they continued on their drive back home to Lubbock. It was an exciting evening!

I was able to make it through dinner and about half of the auction before Tyler took me to rest at the Rogers' house. I was still a little weak from the procedure and in constant need of rest. The next morning, we slept in and had a gourmet breakfast by Tyler's dad, Tye. Later that afternoon, Tyler's mom asked me to go get my nails done with her at a salon down the street from their house. I jumped up from a nap and said, "Sure!" We met the boys later to just hang out for the evening.

After a weekend in Plainview, Tyler and I headed back to Lubbock. He had school starting back up Monday, and I had therapy, pretty romantic. But in reality, that dude is romantic as ever, even through the most dreadful circumstances. His faithfulness and love continually prove as steadfast as humanly possible to little ole me, even when bald and a little stilly. Now a cowboy in shining armor, he continues to ride his way through my bubble of crazy like he has since my junior year of high school.

Although it was not evident to anyone but me, a lot of my past had been erased. My memory loss was obvious in the short term, but what people couldn't see was that my whole life, twenty years' worth of growth, struggle, victory, and experience, was gone. It's inevitable that a person's past shapes personality, character, preference, and purpose, but that block of life with all of its connections was gone for me. The victory of healing on the outside was also coupled with a deep sense of emptiness and realization on the inside. No one else could see that or even remotely understand, and it was hard to be joyful when others were celebrating what they perceived as victory. Faith and patience were tested to the maximum.

In trying to couple the present with the retrospect memories of our relationship, faith was the glue to connect these two worlds together because of the void caused by my brain injury. "Christ's love compels us" to live with courage and confidence, just like Tyler's love compelled me to adjust my life plans to follow his (2 Corinthians 5:14). God is the first and strongest strand in our relationship and forever will be. My courage grows when I reflect on Tyler's embodiment of the verse, "Jesus Christ is the same yesterday and today and forever" (Hebrews 13:8). Tyler's love never wavered through the storm.

But during our car ride to Lubbock, I muttered out a memory that I had tried so hard to sweep under the rug.

"So I guess we can't get married this summer," I said, looking out the window. I brought up the fact that I knew he had a wedding ring for me, but since it was already mid-April, I had decided we couldn't get married that summer. It took me a long time to process and prepare for things, especially such a big adjustment as marriage, so I had given up on the thought of getting married that summer. I knew I wasn't fit to anyway. We couldn't get married during the middle of his basketball season, so I guessed we would have to wait another year. I was looking down and embarrassed to even bring it up because I knew I was a fool to even think that anyone would want to marry me, much less Tyler.

I shouldn't even be alive, I always thought. Tyler told me later that he was trying not to laugh when I brought that up; I had no idea of the plan.

He had told me about having a ring while on a date to Waffle House when I was in Dallas for therapy. He had asked my parents and called Waffle House to have a special table set up for us ahead of time. I dressed up in my tennis shoes, yoga pants, jacket, and toboggan, with my half head of hair in a side braid. I rode in the back seat while Tyler drove us in my mom's Tahoe. I always sat with the missing bone flap side of my head toward the inside.

We had walked in to the sweetest waitresses showing us to our table, decorated with flowers and a tablecloth. It was the sweetest thing ever and one of my favorite memories of our time in Dallas. Tyler wanted to give me something to be excited about and knew I would forget about the ring. After all, I could barely remember my name or what I ate ten seconds ago. So telling me about having a wedding ring on this date didn't seem like a big deal in his mind. My memory loss was *very* severe, but this little detail didn't seem to vanish in the void of my injury. I was so giggly the whole time we indulged our chocolate chip waffles, our favorite part of the all-star special meal at Waffle House. We thanked the sweet ladies who had made that special night possible and had catered to us so well. They were precious waitresses to treat us to such a planned-out evening. Then we headed back to the Ronald McDonald house to go for a little walk outside.

That memory of the wedding ring continued to mess with my mind as we neared Lubbock, and I was kind of in a bad mood because of the lack thereof in the proposal aspect. (What a goober, I know.) I just knew if he hadn't asked me by then, there was no way I would be able to handle things in a rushed manner. It was only about a fifty-minute drive to my parents' house from Plainview, and upon arrival, we were welcomed warmly by my parents and then continued inside.

9

THE DOOR

Trust in the Lord with all your heart and lean not on your own understanding;
in all your ways submit to Him, and He will make your paths straight.

—PROVERBS 3:5–6

April is always a fun season with a change in weather, new plants growing, more sunshine peeking through, and competition on the horizon with spring sports. My sister was in the midst of her track season, and I loved watching her compete. She had the district meet coming up and had been training hard for her races. She ran the 800-meter dash, 300-meter hurdles, and the mile relay, arguably the three toughest races in track. But she has always attacked everything she sets her mind to and never holds anything back. Difficult tasks have always been her forte.

My brother was in the peak of conference play for baseball at Southwestern Oklahoma State University. His team was having a great year and was ranked in the top of their conference. They had so much talent and were moving with momentum at just the right time. In the classroom, his business classes sparked a new interest that allowed him to grow, learn, and envision a motivating future. Being a college athlete is not easy, but the challenges and struggles that accompanied his growth were matched with blessings from all angles.

My family was looking forward to summer activities; we never missed an opportunity to take a vacation and enjoy special family time. We always had a camper growing up and enjoyed traveling to new places, exploring new land, meeting new people, and engaging in outdoor activities. Blessings were always on the horizon because our parents nurtured our family unit so tenderly with intentional planning and generous love.

I can't help but praise the Lord for the amazing and sweet family He has given me. I always felt safe around them; our family is established in a way so that our mind's buffer is to always cling to spiritual truths when things get rough. The verses that have so intentionally decorated our home, coupled with daily spiritual nourishment, have kept all of us afloat. His Spirit is alive and active through the Christian morals and discipline that fuel our family.

My mom always reminds me of God's goodness through her daily life full of selfless deeds, and we share several Bible verses that fuel our deep bond. When I was younger, we went to a mother-daughter devotional group together called Caterpillars and Butterflies. We met once a month for crafts, snacks, and a Bible study. This planted seeds for spiritual growth along every stage of our life journeys, always working toward the end goal of maturation like a butterfly. The theme verse of our group was found in Psalms: "I praise You because I am fearfully and wonderfully made; Your works are wonderful, I know that full well" (139:14). My mom and I continue to read this verse together, as it encourages and unifies us through sweet childhood memories. We have since learned that a butterfly is a symbol for AVM survivors. What a sweet touch of His presence.

As things started to look up in my recovery journey from the outside, a little bit of anxiety had started creeping into my mind very sneakily. The gift of healing and blessings ought to be balanced with wisdom and preparation, but I was lacking in this step of direction in trying to plan ahead with vision for my life. It was as if my physical body started climbing a ladder, but my mind couldn't reach the next step.

I lived only in the moment, as it was all I could do to try to focus on the task right in front of me. Every activity required 110 percent of my attention, whether it was trying to match my clothes in the morning, putting my name on a paper, or carrying on a conversation with someone right in front of me. I knew my personality might have seemed short fused because of the amount of intense concentration needed for anything I did, so it was important for me to continue to grow in being flexible and patient. I had to learn to give myself a new level of grace that would probably seem silly to everyone else.

The monotonous routine of therapy and sleep didn't quite excite me anymore. The day was gone after the completion of those two things. I started looking down, getting weary and impatient with fear of the unknown. I began losing purpose, motivation, and trust; I didn't want to claim my person anymore.

What was even left to take hold of from the past before November 10? I wondered. At this point, that chunk of twenty years' worth of living had vanished. The severity of the loss of self that accompanied this memory issue was a sharper knife than anyone realized, including me. After cruising ignorantly using the training wheels of those around me for so long, I slowly started waking up and getting anxious. Looking more normal from the outside was hard because people expected more of me. The deficits that were unseen by the naked eye from my brain injury now made me a greater target for people. I had to learn to not be such a victim but to be transparent and honest with people who lovingly prodded me for things.

Being what almost felt like a celebrity in my hometown of Lubbock, Texas, was awkwardly dangerous. It took everything I had to focus with people for even the simplest conversations, but I loved them enough to invest the little I felt that I had. I loved people so much and treasured good conversation, but I didn't realize the sense of self that was secretly vanishing away as I tried giving everyone my all. This led to a little bit of bitterness and confusion, which, I learned, can dangerously cloud even the purest, greatest gifts if not addressed. Satan had a plan, but God's is always greater.

As I continued working hard in therapy, I was motivated and inspired by my family and boyfriend every day. I even felt accountable to our whole community, church, and school to never give up. I wanted to defeat that physics monster that wasn't getting any less scary. Trying to finish the tidbit of my 2015 fall semester felt like trying to move Mount Everest one teaspoon of dirt at a time.

In my mind, a productive day in therapy was getting to exercise and work on schoolwork. I typically copied about two pages of notes per day out of a spiral that held almost a semester's worth of material. Getting to work on school gave me a lot of motivation even though it was challenging. Relearning something that was difficult to me before my injury made me feel connected to my old self in a way. The ignorance of the weight I was trying to pull with all of my mental wounds continued to be a good thing.

The goal I had of finishing physics and graduating therapy gave me such tunnel vision that I seemed to lose connection with the rest of the world. In my mind, until I was able to shake this monster off by defeating certain things in my way that I felt were unfinished business, I was not capable of truly living to the fullest. This was selfish in a way, but I tried to be patient with myself. I felt a fire in me that reminded me I had to keep moving, to accomplish, and to conquer.

During the grind of therapy, there appeared a surprise door on my path, one I was not even remotely prepared for. It was a gorgeous door, a beautiful door, a kind door, a dreamy door, but it was a door that would take a lot of faith and courage to walk through in a state like this.

On April 14, 2016, there was a team scavenger hunt set to take place with the volleyball girls. I was so excited to finally get to hang out with those girls again, without the focus being on me or my condition. We met in the locker room to go over some ground rules and instructions for the scavenger hunt. It felt so good to be in there, while old memories of pre- and postgame talks brought about a sense of normalcy and comfort. We all sat at our lockers while the coaches gave us instructions for the evening. We were so bubbly and giggly to all be together; those girls are sure special.

I was so full of joy to *finally* get to do something with the team that wasn't about me, after all the girls had been through on my behalf. After being assigned to different teams of four, we piled in cars and went out to start the hunt in a mad rush, chasing different clues around Lubbock to try to finish our list of tasks first. But really, it was a creative twist that the coaches had planned to go along with what Mr. Rogers had in mind to do for the evening.

I was on Kyleigh, Mallory, and Channing's team, and our intensity was through the roof. We raced through Walmart to take pictures with random items, grabbed food in the Chick-fil-A drive-through, bounced around campus taking pictures with the Chap mascot, and completed several other goofy to-dos from the list. Every activity had to be documented, so there were all kinds of silly videos and pictures sent to the coaches for approval.

Upon completion, the plan was to meet at my parents' house to get ready for a team picture. Our 2015 season had had an abrupt ending and was so eventful, so it seemed totally normal for a fun gathering full of silliness and a good picture. It was like a party, getting all dolled up and sharing stories and laughter from the scavenger hunt as we bounced through my parents' house, all anxious to hear what team was the winner. I am so thankful my momma was there, always ready to help me dress up and do my hair, so graciously. She did so much to make me feel beautiful and believe it, even in my wounded state with such short hair that I didn't know how to fix; she is truly an angel. We were all trying to organize a picture idea as we finished up and carpooled to the RIP. We were all smiles.

We piled out of the cars like circus clowns and walked into the gym through a side door. All of the lights were off, but we heard some soft music playing. We all just bopped in like crazy people with a lot of energy, and I was oblivious to the whole scene. Coach had her phone out and said, "Mal, come here." My heart sank because she sounded really serious, like something intense was going on. I followed with curiosity but was still clueless.

My brother, Peyton, was dressed up and met me right when I stepped onto the concrete floor leading to the stairs of the gym. I couldn't believe he had come home from college in Oklahoma, so I started asking him a bunch of questions about what he was doing in Lubbock. Peyton wasn't saying much but just smiled as he led me down the stairs to the court.

He handed me off to Tyler, who was looking real handsome down there on our home court. My heart was just beating really fast as I tried to understand what was going on. I could see several faces looking through windows around the gym, but I just kept my focus on Tyler as I grabbed his arm and followed his lead. We danced to Aaron Watson's new song "Unbelievably Beautiful," which he had kept a secret from me because he had wanted it to be new and special for this night. After a good ole two-steppin', he got down on one knee and popped the question.

"Malori, will you marry me?"

I honestly have no idea what I did or said, but I knew deep down this was a beautiful and sweet act, despite the anxiety that was beginning to overwhelm me from all of the stimulation. There was a handsome, tall, strong man kneeling in front of me, looking up at me with a big smile and a beautiful ring. Maybe that was why I had three offers to go get a manicure the week before. I smiled and clung to Tyler's arm as tightly as I could.

Afterward, the lights were turned on, and people came out from the stairs, the tunnels, and the athletic offices, and we took all kinds of pictures. It was absolutely perfect and wonderful, it seemed, as I got to talk to people who had made special trips for this event.

But during that whole time, my brain was just on overload, and everything was cloudy. I couldn't take hold of the excitement and joy that everyone else showed; it was too slippery for me to hold on to as my brain kept swirling and tripping. When Tyler and I were down there dancing on the court, I had noticed people hiding and looking down at us. When we finished, everyone came pouring out to the floor to join us. Through the excitement and joy, my wounded mind felt as if there were ants crawling around it with all of the surprise and stimulation. I didn't realize I was so mentally handicapped.

We enjoyed cake and conversation and, of course, the team picture that we had all dressed up for. Once again, this sweet volleyball family was joined with love and grace as we shared this time together. Several other friends drove in to celebrate with us, some even driving hours. Tyler's basketball team, coaches, several sweet LCU friends, and dear extended families even chose to join us for this special moment. It was such an honor to feel Christ's love and encouragement through all of these sweet vessels.

A local TV station was also there. They captured the moment and asked for an interview. I just clung to Tyler as he answered the questions, and I followed his lead of love and gratitude for those around us. We felt overwhelmingly blessed. Everyone scattered after saying grateful goodbyes as the evening came to a close.

"So the 'pray for Malori era' must be over," I ignorantly concluded. I was feeling overwhelmingly blessed. I joined my family in their car to make the short drive to my parents' house for the night. I always felt safe and secure with my family and was thankful to be living with them in this season. I didn't realize the *power* of what they were doing for me or the *magnitude* of how God was providing for us. I shared in the exciting atmosphere of what was going on around me, but deep inside I was starting to spin with confusion as a fog clouded my perception of reality.

10

NEW LIFE

We know that suffering produces perseverance; perseverance, character; and character, hope. And hope does not put us to shame, because God's love has been poured out into our hearts through the Holy Spirit, Who has been given to us. You see, at just the right time, when we were still powerless, Christ died for the ungodly.

—ROMANS 5:3–6

The concept of "flooding" after a brain injury refers to how to process information. There is not a discernment factor, or filter, to distinguish or categorize oncoming stimuli. So, when a lot of things, even good things, are introduced as a stimulus to the brain, the brain often floods to the point of shutting down. Within this state, there is an inability to get excited, recognize, or discern the good because the brain is just too overwhelmed.

In therapy, I started to learn about what had actually happened to me, scientifically, with my brain bleed. I understood there was an AVM that had ruptured and caused a lot of damage, but I didn't really know all of the details. It was probably best that I didn't know them, but I needed to be aware of the repercussions so I could know how to defeat them.

The brain is divided into two hemispheres; the right hemisphere is the abstract, insightful, and creative side of the brain, while the left is responsible for the more logical, analytical, and reasoning functions. Before my injury, I was a strong-willed and stubborn left-brained child. I was smart, routine oriented, confident, and determined. I have always loved people, and I usually expressed that in rather simple ways so naturally. But once I actually realized the deficits of my injury, I had to get creative in how I could bless others. I had to believe that I should, in fact, be alive and that my being alive was not a mistake. I had to believe in myself and gain confidence that I was worthy of something, though my new calling might seem radically different from what I would've ever imagined.

Once I realized the hard truth of new normals, I had to explore what it was I might be able to do to make a difference in the world. I became motivated to discover how I might be able to use the deficits of my injury to my left brain to highlight the strengths of my right brain. Learning this about myself carved me into an extrovert that wanted to strengthen other people by pouring love into them. Able to connect loving others to a spiritual and intellectual purpose motivated me to explore this new right-brained self, seeking to grasp the new strengths that it brought. It gave me so much confidence and purpose to defeat the AVM monster by utilizing the strengths I was left with from the event that had tried to take me down, right as I was ready to enter the chapter of adulthood that my whole life had led up to.

The brain is pretty intricate, fragile, powerful, and interesting, and every neuron connection needed to be reestablished one at a time. This felt like counting from one to one hundred infinity million very slowly, one decimal at a time. But each link was precious and needed to be highly valued. When people helped me, I often felt so small and that I was such a charity case; I wasn't confident that I could do anything helpful for others anymore. I often became impatient, losing sight of the bigger picture during this process. Lack of patience is common in people with a brain injury, and learning this made me feel connected to a population that gave unity. It helped me want to give myself grace; I became softhearted to myself when I realized that I was impatient because I knew my memory couldn't last longer than my attention span.

In therapy, I remember Mrs. Cindy, our program director, being interviewed by a local TV station in Lubbock about brain injuries. She asked if I would join her in the interview, and I happily agreed to. It caught me off guard to hear her say that a brain injury was a disease, but I thought maybe that part didn't apply to me. I was too stubborn to believe that.

I don't have a disease, I thought, planning how to prove it.

While reality is often alarming, I have tried to own my weaknesses the best I can. Continuing to grow through this new state took a lot of character, patience, and grace, not just with myself but also with others who didn't understand. I tried not to crumble when people gave ignorant compliments to me without understanding the mental fragility of my new reality. I often felt uncomfortable when people made comments to me in a baby voice, as if I was a toddler doing something for the first time. Now *I* humbly needed the encouragement that I had so easily dished to others all my life.

Because I wasn't around the same people or doing the same activities anymore, my old life was not even remotely familiar. I didn't even give myself time to daydream because I was either working in therapy or focusing on trying to look normal for whatever it was I was doing.

When teammates or old friends came to visit in therapy, I just got happy to talk to them; it felt so natural when my emotional right brain worked in my favor through relationships. Every now and then, I would hear a voice in my head that sounded like me, like the girl who *once was* me. I got excited and wanted to be like her again—to walk with confidence, boldness, and the toughest strength. But it was like trying to hold on to a bar of slippery soap trying to claim her again.

Am I even supposed to? I often thought. So many voices of questions in my head seemed to constantly torment me with confusion. I often played Jesus music or clung to scripture to try to fight these battles.

At therapy the next morning after the proposal, I got to share the news and proudly show off my beautiful ring. I almost felt guilty and silly to be excited because I knew I was lacking in so many areas of how I thought I ought to be. I wondered what my therapists thought about me and if they thought I was foolish and naïve about the state I was in.

The thought of continuing therapy and planning a wedding could not coexist in my mind. I am not sure if it was because of my pride or my lack of ability to multitask with a brain injury. In a completely overwhelmed and frustrated state, I cried to quit therapy.

After the proposal, I started clinging to scripture harder than ever. I was so overwhelmed and confused that I wanted truth and simplicity. That was found only in God's Word. My spinning whirlwind of thoughts walked into therapy with embarrassment and awkwardness, and I just wanted to quit and be normal already.

But as I began to find my new population, I started to learn of other people who had AVMs; I was always encouraged to hear their stories of coping and triumph. Valerie Gregory, a courageous AVM survivor, has been such a role model to me in motherly ways, offering advice and gracious wisdom, and I am thankful to call her a dear friend. She is a beautifully strong woman who makes a daily choice to walk with her head up high. Carmen Smith, another victorious AVM survivor, continues to spread the umbrella of God's love and grace by boldly sharing her testimony. She even leads a ministry that speaks life and truth to countless women. Lillian Hyde was planning to go to LCU but had a brain bleed during her senior year of high school. She still walked the stage to graduate and continues to work toward her dream of becoming a teacher someday.

I feel so graciously blessed and fueled by these friends who share common ground with me and know what it's like to live with similar new normals. My parents have connected with countless other families as well, offering advice, prayer accountability, and priceless encouragement in such intentional ways. Because of the fuel through relationships, I felt a whisper of purpose to get married and seek God with my teammate forever. God is always working through people who are bold enough to share their testimony, and, though uncomfortable, I wanted to let Him keep the pen in His hands.

GOD IS SO GOOD

When anxiety was great within me, Your consolation brought me joy.
—PSALM 94:19

Sleepovers with my sister are the best. At this point, we were both getting to sleep in her room, as my mom gave permission because my scars were healing. At first, my mom didn't want me sleeping beside anyone but her, because my scars were still vulnerable, tender, and bandaged; she wanted to protect me from any danger of an accidental movement that could be harmful to my wounds. Maci and I have always shared a special and close sister relationship, and I love her so much. During this time of living at home, we got to have some special time of just us again. We have always enjoyed a quick little snow cone outing or a Starbucks run, anything we could do to sneak away together. But I couldn't drive at this time with my vision deficit and slower reaction time, so we enjoyed a bunch of time at home together instead. She keeps me smiling so big.

It is so fun to be a big sister to two of the world's greatest humans, Peyton and Maci. Our family stays so busy and close because there is always something to celebrate with them. Our parents are the most supportive and encouraging humans in the world, raising and equipping us to be able to do anything. Family support and closeness has always been a backbone for us, and I thank God for that blessing. I have always wanted to carry on the Maddox family dynamics the best I can in a fruitful way.

It felt so natural to live in my parents' home again and reestablish what a pure gift my family unit is, truly a rare and special gift from the Lord. It seems like God was allowing me to study the dynamics of my sweet family while soaking up every waking moment so that I might be able to implement those statutes in a household of my own someday. Our family plays a lot of games. Skip-bo, Yahtzee, spades, and hearts are some of our favorites, and we were all able to get a lot of quality time in that way. I am grateful for this opportunity to rekindle the childhood backbone of who I was created to be before I was called to the real world again.

Discernment is hard. God tells us to ask Him for wisdom, and He will give it to us (James 1:5). At this point, I struggled with the decision to leave my family with the new blessing of a wedding proposal. Everyone said I was doing so well, but my memory and identity were lacking in several areas, so I was scared to leave the only thing I remembered confidently, which was the house that built me. When I started growing outwardly silent and reclusive, my dad's voice echoed in my mind, saying, "When faith is all you have, you have all you need." All of my thoughts were scripture, as spiritual nourishment was continuing to digest in my soul. I didn't have anything going on of my own to take hold of; I relished His Word that rang clearly in my heart.

I read Bible verses about marriage, explaining how God must always be the head of every relationship, especially marriage. I also learned from other verses that encouraged the act of submission for women. Ultimately, marriage ought to model the relationship that God has with each of His children, the church: a husband's love for his wife, a willingness to patiently and faithfully fight for her, a husband's role of leadership, a willingness for the wife to obey the husband's lead and trust him fully, and so on. I feel that marriage is a *huge* act of trust that mirrors how a follower of Christ must leave his or her old life, by faith, to engage on a new journey with Him. Though gracefully broken, I felt motivated to fulfill a spiritual prophecy.

In a way, Satan had twisted Bible verses in my mind, making me think I must literally lose myself in the act of submission, and I started to feel humiliated and lost through such blind obedience because of my memory loss. At first, I thought I would just finish therapy, completing my Physics I class while wrapping things up with my therapists. To me, this route meant I could be enrolled in a class at LCU in the fall semester to slowly chip away at the small work load I lacked to graduate and be on the road to normalcy, so I thought. I would split one semester's load into two so it would be less overwhelming and then graduate in the spring of 2017. Then, we could get married. But everyone else seemed to know things I didn't and strongly insisted I go on with the wedding. So many voices swirled around in my mind, and I felt overwhelmed with so much going on.

Deep inside, I wanted to get married fast. I loved Tyler. But marrying him at this point meant that I would need to quit therapy, pause school, and trust that something good would happen if I put a stop to everything I had planned for my life: college graduation, then marriage, then PT school.

I sought as much counsel as possible but knew we were in a hurry to make a decision if a wedding was to take place in three months. I wish I had been prepared. Or trusted. Or communicated. Or believed that I was worthy. There just appeared a black cloud on my mind that I couldn't seem to shake to think straight. Everyone else had a free-spirited and lighthearted mindset, ready to celebrate. I was just trying to understand.

I have always been very thoughtful in my decisions, taking ample time to do *anything*. The spotlight during this season started to blind me, as the microscope was now zoomed in further, and I began to shrivel. I questioned every thought I had, wondering what all was missing from my memory that everyone else seemed to know about me.

How does a news station know more about my introvert life than I do? I thought. I tried doing research on myself, but it was just weird and awkward. I didn't want to look at that really.

I knew God had the lead role for this journey, and may He always be the Captain. Faith is the only way, but it had never seemed like the scary way to me before. I've always walked with confidence, assurance, hope, trust, and motivation to follow God. But this time, His way was the painful way. I felt stretched, uncomfortable, and anxious. It was like the more I sought to obey God, the harder my life was. Was I under a curse? I didn't understand. But even without an ounce of human understanding, God's Word remains true forever. "When God is all you have, you have all you need."

Tyler is such an incredible man and is loved, trusted, and admired by everyone. During this time, I was just struggling so hard to get married because of the surprise factor, which led to lack of preparation on my part. This forced me to desperately cling to the Father for His guidance. *Isn't that the point of everything in life?* In this instance, I couldn't rely on what I could remember but rather on what I knew, and that was my faith. It was awesome and scary.

I literally couldn't think on my own. Any thought I did have couldn't be trusted once I realized I was missing something that everyone else had: a working memory and the real understanding of what had just happened to me.

"He says, 'Be still, and know that I am God; I will be exalted among the nations, I will be exalted in the earth'" (Psalm 46:10). I thought it should be easy to be still and submissive, but I would toss and turn all night long as so many things ran through my mind. I didn't know that a racing heart and inability to sleep were called anxiety.

Surely I don't have that, I thought. But in reality, I just couldn't handle the pressure of the constant attention and big decision-making, and I didn't know how to get everything to the surface. I didn't want to cause another big scene for everyone, so I kept the truth bottled in as I tried to just keep up. I always felt so mentally behind.

Exciting things began to happen quickly. A short engagement sounded great; of course I wanted to marry Tyler! Several others I had asked also promoted a short engagement with a summer wedding. But without processing *anything* of what had just happened with my brain bleed, it took a lot of courage to trust people's stories and direction to follow this unfolding plan. Tyler is a special man whose trust in the Lord and confident leadership convicted me to live for something greater than myself.

A wedding date was set for July 29, 2016. In Mark chapter 8, Jesus was teaching a crowd about "the way of the cross." He said, "Whoever wants to be my disciple must deny themselves and take up their cross and follow me. For whoever wants to save their life will lose it, but whoever loses their life for me and for the gospel will save it" (34–35). It wasn't that I was "losing my life" to get married, but it did mean that I must trust God's Word when obedience called for the closing of certain doors without full confidence in my abilities to walk through this new open one.

Extended family showed up excitedly to help my mom and me with the planning and deciding of wedding details. They encouraged a short engagement, promising to take care of anything they could to help. Their spirits were so sweet and brought me a lot of hope that good things could happen quickly. Family is so precious.

There were several categories of things to tackle for the wedding: choosing a venue, colors, wedding party, guest list, and so on. Our wedding planners were incredible, and there seemed to be a new and precious angel volunteer who always appeared to help with whatever was lacking throughout the process. I was especially thankful to have my momma's encouragement as I tried to follow in her steps.

On Mother's Day, my sweet mom and sister, along with my nana, aunts, and girl cousins, went together to David's Bridal to find a wedding dress. I appreciated them so much for taking part in that with me and for making excitement out of it on a day that *should* have just been focused on the incredible mothers in the family. Their selfless examples spoke volumes to me through this season.

As I tried different dresses on, I just felt so humiliated without hair that nothing seemed to look good to me. Anytime I looked in a mirror, I just wanted to cry. I bottled that in as they all made me feel so beautiful while trying on every dress with their sweet opinions and comments. As always, we shared a lot of laughter with good stories. Upon finding *the one*, I rang a bell and nervously made the announcement, "I said yes to the dress!"

It meant so much to me that my momma, sister, nana, aunts, and cousins chose to spend that day together by continuing to show love and joy to me. I have an incredibly special family, and we are constantly reminded we are a rare bunch by the crazy, goofy things we do. Our hearts are always full when we're together; God is so good.

12

GOTTA BE READY WHEN HE CALLS MY NAME

He has shown you, O mortal, what is good. And what does the Lord require of you? To act justly and to love mercy and to walk humbly with your God.

—MICAH 6:8

Each new day neared one day closer to the wedding day. Through all of the positive excitement, anxiety continued to grow underneath the surface for me. The physical and mental exhaustion from stimulation, decision-making, and attention was pulsating its way through my joy, violently. With the goal of trying to finish school looming on the horizon, it was so hard to switch gears from wedding planning to physics. I had no discernment of what was more important and felt ignorantly burdened by the weight of such exciting tasks. But it's a miraculous thing when God uses our weaknesses as His stage.

I had several coffee dates and meetings with gracious souls who were willing to share their wisdom and encouragement in order to try to prepare me for this change of marriage, and I tried to let everything soak into my thirsty desire to do right. Tyler and I also met with a premarital counselor, the dean of students at LCU, who we also call a mentor and friend. Josh Stephens walked us through several evenings of lesson and study, and I tried to be as alert as possible, striving to absorb every ounce of wisdom. Even though I couldn't take in much information efficiently, I knew God saw my trying heart.

I remember being particularly dumbfounded one moment when asked of our life plans and goals for one year, five years, and ten years. The miracle of marriage was already beginning to unfold as Tyler led us through these meetings with confidence and authority by contributing his vision. But I, on the other hand, replied, "I just don't know anymore," trying to cover my discouragement with faith. I trusted God to lead and sustain me and us, but I still felt silly being so exposed through this new journey of marriage. I felt so discouraged and lost in just trying to keep up. But all of our meetings were very helpful and encouraging, and I'm grateful to have had the opportunity to meet with Josh for his teachings to us. Spiritual guidance was, is, and must always be our foundation.

I continued waking up in my parents' home next to my sweet sister. Things were comfortable and joy filled; the Maddox squad is a special bunch. My family never made me feel wounded, slow, or sorry but rather hopeful, joyful, and thankful by dwelling on the miracle as opposed to the tragedy. Praise the Lord for His creation of angels in my family.

I was working so hard to finish that load of schoolwork that I lacked; I wanted to catch up and be normal so badly. It was hard for me to feel excitement about what was going on with the wedding because I knew I had unfinished business in my head. The weight of my injury was clouding my joy because I knew it still needed to be conquered.

Through the encouragement from my family, professors, and dear friend and tutor Shanae Ammons, I was finally able to tackle the physics monster. Shanae had walked me through every old lesson of notes from the fall semester; she also taught me the new material from the remaining last unit that I needed to know for the final. My mom drove me to school for these tutoring sessions and always encouraged me that I could do it. She carried so much of my heavy burden through her acts of service for me.

While tutoring, Shanae was so gracious and patient; she believed in me and always spoke physics in a way I could understand. She is another angel to me. Her patience, willingness, and grace spoke volumes in this season. My adviser, Toby Rogers, administered that physics final to me, which was probably a good test for his patience because I took full advantage of my extended time accommodations, allowing four hours for the test. Turning that thing in was one of the greatest feelings, but I just celebrated with a nap for my crying brain. Sleep with a grateful mind felt like one of the most powerful tools for healing and sanity.

As July started creeping up, things were getting more and more real. The heat of the summer sunrays in Lubbock was equally comparable to the hot speed of my world spinning in motion. The twenty-eighth came around, where a rehearsal took place followed by a wonderful dinner at the Rogers' home. Tyler's parents shared a blessing of encouragement and love to us, followed by my parents' reading of a letter full of wisdom and deep support. Tears were flowing as their sweet words touched our hearts. We took lots of pictures at the photo booth that Kelli had prepared and gradually drifted through the evening conversing with everyone. It was wonderful and sweet.

I rode home with my sister to pack a suitcase for the honeymoon. Tyler's grandparents had given us the treat of a five-day cruise to the Bahamas! My sister and I then drifted to sleep for one more sleepover, as we were exhausted from the full day.

The sunrays crept through the shutters in my sister's room, declaring the arrival of July 29. My mom, sister, and I prepared to head to the first event of the day, where Mrs. Jana, Tyler's aunt, had prepared an incredible breakfast for all of the women in the wedding party and any extended family who wanted to join. We enjoyed delicious food, coffee, and conversation and soaked our souls with prayer and spiritual encouragement; it was such a sweet time. I felt so special and celebrated while also in awe of the blessings that flooded my heart. With the wedding set for seven o'clock that evening, we all headed to the venue to get ready directly after. Kaitlyn Stephenson, Tyler's cousin, was waiting there for us, ready to put her glamorous beautifying skills to action.

We all had so much fun getting ready together. We were dancing and eating Chick-fil-A as we watched one another's beauty unfold. The boys of the wedding party went to shoot guns, of course, and gave themselves all of a few minutes to get ready before taking pictures.

As the clock neared seven, prayers were ascending from different directions. I knew that whatever happened that night would be incredibly meant to be, as everyone had poured out their hearts with the most tremendous efforts for this to take place. While the wedding party was lining up, nerves sat in as the familiar songs rang through the air. As I found my dad, I was thankful to grab hold of my hero's arm; his steadfast character felt as solid as a rock and gave me a blanket of peace, just like he always did. He always knows exactly how to handle every moment with the perfect balance of excitement and transparency. When we heard the musicians beautifully begin the hymn "Come Thou Fount," we knew there were just seconds left before walking down the aisle.

I clung tightly to my dad's arm for comfort, balance, strength, and encouragement; he is such a vessel of the Rock. He reminded me to look around and soak in all of the people there to support us. I wish everyone could feel the type of love shown to me on that day, with all of the work, sacrifice, and generosity put into practice to make another miracle happen for me to walk down the aisle to my husband. That amount of love penetrated my heart powerfully, but I was also completely overwhelmed.

My heart was racing from typical wedding day nerves, but also due to complete overstimulation. The venue was overflowing with people, but I could only see the left half as I walked down the aisle because of my vision deficit; that was a God wink.

As I looked ahead down the aisle at Tyler, his reaction touched my heart unlike anything else in my whole life. The most handsome and strong man spoke volumes to me without saying a single word as such sweet tears glossed his bold face. In that moment, I finally felt enough.

I held tightly to my dad before he handed me off to Tyler, and then our families prayed. Andy Laughlin, a professor and dear friend to Tyler and me, then proceeded with the wedding.

My aunt Rachel sang, along with a sweet friend, Cailey Lawrence, to start the ceremony. Everything was absolutely beautiful: the colors, the people, the ceremony, the music ... everything. I was thankful that my sister was standing by my side and my brother was standing with the groomsmen. Tyler's cousin, Kara, made magic on the piano, while Abbey Langford played her fiddle to "Come Thou Fount" as we walked down the aisle. My cousins were the flower girls and ring bearer. The power of family was a staple that allowed this season to unfold, blessing by blessing. Tyler and I have the greatest parents, siblings, aunts, uncles, cousins, and grandparents, whose examples speak volumes of the legacy we seek to pursue.

Everything seemed to be happening so fast, but our sweet wedding planners made everything run smoothly. I was speechless that Dr. Kamath brought his family to attend, who willingly sat up front beside mine. Kaitlynn Curtner, a fellow AVM survivor, made a surprise appearance to perform the song "When You Say Nothing at All" by Alison Krauss after the ceremony. It was absolutely gorgeous, and I was so thankful she and my mom had coordinated that surprise.

Tyler and I sneakily enjoyed a plate of food in a room by ourselves, away from all of the ceremony. We shared a quiet joy in the midst of such a big scene; our simpleton minds were very grateful, but the whole atmosphere made us chuckle.

One of my favorite moments was getting to dance with my sister; it seemed extra sweet for both of us to have that always needed sister time. I tried to talk to everyone before being told to hurry and change so I could get in the car and leave with Tyler. As God saturated this event with an overwhelming sense of His presence and significance, I tried to soak up joy in surrender to the unknown by smiling at all of the millions of blessings.

Gilbert, Heath, Tyler, Pete, Malori, Peyton,
Mallory, Rebecca, & Connor in Rwanda

Peyton, Malori, Sarah, Marray, & Maci on vacation in Destin, Florida

The 2015 Lubbock Christian University volleyball team

Maci, Marray, Sarah, Peyton, & Malori in Zale Lipshy Hospital in Dallas

Malori, Peyton, Maci, Sarah, & Marray at Pate Rehab center in Dallas

*Nana and Papa with Hanks, Martin, & Maddox
families celebrating Christmas in Dallas*

Tyler after a hunt with Hondo during Christmas break

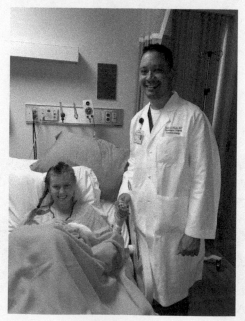

Dr. Welch with Malori at Zale Lipshy Hospital

Tyler putting a ring on Malori at the proposal

Tyler shaking hands with Dr. Kamath at the wedding

13

Included here is a chapter from Kathy Crockett's
"Courageous Women of Faith" series

A MOTHER'S
FAITHFUL HEART

SARAH MADDOX

My husband, Marray and I have three wonderful children: Malori, Peyton, and Maci. In 2015, Malori was a senior on the volleyball team at Lubbock Christian University, Peyton was playing college baseball with Southwestern Oklahoma State University, and Maci was in the 8th grade. I am sure it comes as no surprise to you—we spend a lot of our time running around in opposite directions, making it to every event we possibly can for our three children. Tuesday, November 10, 2015 is the day that changed everything for our family.

Malori's Senior Night with the volleyball team had been less than a week before, and on November 10th, we were headed out of town on a week night to watch one of her games. Peyton was working out with his baseball team, so he was not coming with us. That morning, I called Marray and arranged for him to pick up Maci from school so we could leave town in time to get to the game in Wichita Falls. Our family loves all the girls on the volleyball team so much; they became like Malori's sisters, which made them family to us. So, we liked to get there to watch them warm up and say hi to everyone. Everything seemed normal watching Malori warm up before the game. We had no idea the road we were about to go down.

The game started out a little rocky. The lighting in the gym was dim and several girls had shanked some serves, so we were a couple points behind. Malori started the game and played her back row spots, and when she came back in to serve, she served just fine, so we had no idea anything was wrong. Then, after she served, she stared missing some plays she routinely makes. However, with the poor lighting and her teammates having missed a few things, we did not think anything of it. Yet, when she missed a simple overhead pass and completely missed the ball, we began to think something might be off. Malori went to stand by her teammate, Kyleigh, and told her, "I am starting to lose vision in my right eye." Malori was so focused on losing her vision that she was not paying attention to the throbbing pain on the left side of her head. Kyleigh walked her to sideline where the trainer and Coach Lawrence checked on her. Coach motioned me over to the bench, asking if Malori ever had migraines, and I said, "No, never." So she motioned for us to meet Malori and the athletic trainer in the locker room. Marray went right away, and Maci and I started gathering our things from the stands. I just had a bad feeling; I knew something was not right because of the way she was holding the left side of her head and how she walked out of the gym. From the look on her face, I could tell how excruciating her pain was.

We got into the locker room to find Marray saying, "We don't know if we should put her in a dark room with her feet propped up and see if it is just a bad migraine or get her to a doctor." I just saw Malori rocking back and forth on the couch just holding the left side of her head. Her face looked like she was in the worst pain she had ever experienced. I know God was moving in my heart because I said, "Marray I have never seen her in this much pain. She doesn't get migraines." I asked Rachel, the trainer, "Do you think we should take her to the ER? I have never seen her like this." Rachel had never seen anything like this either, and she agreed with me, saying, "Maybe so."

Malori had had several headaches over the past three years that would randomly come and go. We thought maybe her vision was changing with all studying she did. A few months earlier, she had told me "It just feels like something is growing in the front of my head," and I told her we might want to get her eyes checked. She was trying to see her optometrist, but with our busy lives, we had not worked in an appointment yet.

Standing in that locker room, watching my daughter rocking in pain, God just put that mommy instinct in me to say, "Marray, I think she is having an aneurysm. If you will run and get the car, we will bring her out." Maci's eyes were huge as she watched all of this take place. Carrying all our things, she and I ran back to get all of Mal's stuff from the bench. Rachel and I carried Malori out because she was already to the point where she was immobile from pain and loss of vision. She was starting to go unconscious. The assistant athletic director saw us struggling to carry Malori out as she was becoming deadweight. He stepped in and said, "Let me help y'all get her to the car." Then another one of Midwestern State University's coaches stepped in and said, "Don't go to the big hospital—United Regional—because an athlete had to wait over two hours there last week. Take her to Kell West Regional Hospital, the smaller hospital." Already, at the very beginning of this trial, God was intervening.

We got Malori in the car, and were told we would have a Midwestern policeman who was going to give us an escort to the hospital since we did not know where we were going. We got in our car (Marray was driving with Malori in the seat behind him, and Maci was sitting behind me) and followed our police escort. Keeping Malori in my sight the whole time, I sent brief texts to my family and Malori's boyfriend of four years, Tyler Rogers, to let them know what was happening. All I had time to say was, "Please get on your knees and say a quick prayer for Malori. She has had to leave the game about 20 minutes into it. We think it is something going on with her brain, we are just not sure yet. We are taking her to the ER right now."

As soon as I hit send, I saw Malori start vomiting in the back seat. I jumped back there and got underneath her where she was in my lap. I was supporting her head with my left hand, and I was scooping vomit out of her mouth with my right hand. Her eyes were rolling back into her head; she was unconscious. I was scooping out the vomit, knowing I could not let her aspirate. Vomit was everywhere—all over me and her. I started kicking the back of my husband's seat. I leaned up and said in his ear, "We have to go faster. The cop is not going fast enough." I could tell that Malori's condition was getting worse by the second. Marray could not really see what was going on in the back seat, and he was hesitant to leave our escort because it was dark and he was unsure how to get to the hospital, so we just continued to follow.

Maci was beside me the whole time with fear in her face. She said, "Mom, what is happening?" I said, "Honey, I am pretty sure it is something very serious going on with her brain. Just say a prayer." Malori's eyes were rolling and her head wobbled over onto Maci's shoulder. Maci lifted it back up to help me hold up her head. I remember having Malori's head and neck in my right hand and caressing her arm, saying, "Hold on baby, God's got you. We are almost there." Then, all of a sudden, her hands just stiffened and curled up around my hands. Her legs went straight out and became stiff. Her whole body was rigid. I just leaned up and told Marray, "You have got to go." I whispered because I had heard that people with brain trauma may be able to hear things. Even if they are unconscious, they can be aware of what you are saying. I leaned up in his ear and said, "I'm not sure she is still with us. Please go faster."

Unbeknownst to us, our police escort had a dear friend who worked in the ER, so he called ahead and asked her to meet us at the ER door with a wheelchair. This was yet another example of God's intervention. When we pulled up to the ER, they were there waiting for us, but Malori's body was so stiff we could not bend her body to get her into a wheelchair. Marray and the ER workers carried her in and laid her on the table. All I thought I heard was, "Bag her." I knew I had to leave that room. They started cutting off her jersey as I walked out. I did not want to leave, yet it was getting crowded and Malori needed immediate medical attention. I knew Maci was outside crying alone, so I went to find her and give our insurance information. Marray stayed with Malori. A sweet little lady who worked there pulled me aside, said the insurance could wait, and prayed with me and Maci.

Maci took over mine and Marray's phones. She called our son Peyton, who was shopping for groceries. He stopped everything, got in his truck, and headed to Wichita Falls. What is normally a three-hour drive, he made in a little over two hours. Then, Maci called Tyler so he would not just see my text after he got out of practice (Tyler played basketball at LCU) and not know what was going on. Tyler had planned to go to the game with us, but something had come up with basketball. Maci told him we had Malori at the ER, they were working on her, and we would keep him posted.

I started giving insurance information and Malori's medical background including her symptoms of the evening. It was not long before Dr. Kamath came out and said, "I have done a CT scan, and this is a terminal condition. She has a brain bleed. She's got an AVM (Arteriovenous Malformation) that has ruptured and her condition is worsening by the second." He told us, "I need to take her across town to United Regional, or my preference would be to fly her to Dallas to Zale Lipshy to have this type of high risk surgery done. But we don't even have fifteen minutes because she's got many signs of brain stem herniation, and we don't have much time once you are to that point. I will have to do surgery here. I cannot guarantee she will survive this surgery. I cannot guarantee that she won't be paralyzed, have brain damage, or many other complications. Brain infections are a high risk for this type of surgery at this facility. I cannot guarantee any of these things—but it is what I have to do to attempt to save her life." We consented and signed. I looked at him and remember saying, "Please do what you can to save our daughter. We will be praying for you and the whole medical team out here in the lobby and praying that God will save Malori."

The little, sweet lady who prayed for me earlier came up to me after our conversation with Dr. Kamath. She told me she cuts out the scripture from the newspaper every day, and she handed me the scripture she had for November 10th. The Bible verse of the day said, "Be still, and know that I am God; I will be exalted among the nations, I will be exalted in the earth" Psalm 46:10 NIV. I still have that newspaper clipping in my wallet; it is precious to me. I held that verse in my hand for a long time that night. Throughout the night, she continually came up to us checking on us, saying, "Don't you worry, don't you fear. God has got your baby. God knows what you are going through."

After they took Malori into surgery, the three of us huddled up in complete shock, not knowing if we would talk to Malori or see her alive again. We started praying. Later, we were told that as we were praying, a nurse sprinted behind us to run to the blood bank because, when they got Malori on the table for surgery, she had no blood pressure. They were not even sure if they would be able to do surgery because Malori had lost so much blood. They gave her 5 units of blood, got a blood pressure reading after transfusion, and started surgery. Malori's brain was swelling so much from the bleed that they had to do a craniotomy: they removed the left portion of her skull, sawed it in half, and put it in her lower left abdomen to keep it viable to reuse down the road if they were able to save her. It was an old military strategy I had never heard of until that point.

The medical team worked and worked on Malori. A nurse came out about every forty-five minutes to update us on Malori's condition. She would tell us, "She is holding her own." There were probably 200-300 little things God took care of to get Malori into and through that surgery. We arrived at the hospital around 6:45 in the evening, and by 7:00, they were talking to us about the results of the CT scan and what needed to be done. Malori did not actually go into surgery until 8:00 because she needed multiple units of blood first. Tina, the nurse who met us at the door of the ER, had called over to neuro to ask if there was any chance Dr. Kamath was still there. She told them there was an athlete coming in who might need neuro care. Now, Dr. Kamath was not normally at the hospital that time of night. He had actually made travel arrangements to be in India for his mother's hip surgery, but he had cancelled those plans at the last minute. We have no doubt that God intended him to be there for Malori.

During the hours we spent in the surgery waiting room, I remember weeping out loud for the first time in my life. I have cried during sermons or certain beautiful worship songs that move me; I have had silent tears roll down my face. Yet this was a different kind of crying; I had never just wept out loud as I did during the surgery and at times over the next week. I can still vividly hear that sound— the distinct sound of my cry being different than it had ever been before. I could not even control the volume of my weeping. I am not one to ever want any type of attention. In fact, my personality is to find a corner room or table at a restaurant, and this loud weeping was like an out-of-body experience. I cried and could not control it; my heart just had to let it come out. All I could think about was if God was making that same weeping sound when he watched his son die on the cross.

While Malori was in surgery, we got word to the volleyball team about the severity of her condition. They had won the first two sets and were in the third set out of five, and Coach Lawrence told me later that she remembered thinking "If we don't win this third set, we are going to forfeit and load up to go to the hospital anyway." They won the set, and she told the team, "No ice. Get your stuff and get on the bus. Malori had a brain bleed, and we are headed to the hospital." I am told it was a long bus ride across town; the girls were in shock and in silent prayer. Around 7:45, before the team arrived, the families of the LCU players started arriving. These were all people we are close to and had bonded with over the years. We saw countless people over those hours, days, and weeks, but those first people who showed up would not leave my side at the hospital. They were rubbing my back and praying with me every few minutes throughout the surgery. It was like we were surrounded by our large, extended family.

The outpouring was incredible. People in Lubbock spread the word. Friends of friends of friends all came to support us—people we did not even know. Many came from churches there in Wichita Falls who had heard from friends who went to church with us in Lubbock. Countless people asked if they could pray for us and with us. There seemed to always be groups of people huddled up in prayer. One man who worked as a nurse anesthesiologist heard about Malori through a church email and came to the hospital to offer his services through the surgery. Normally the doctor wants 10-15 people on his crew for this type of surgery, but Dr. Kamath had to start with only three people because time was so crucial in Malori's case.

Watching Malori's teammates walk into the hospital was heart wrenching. Seeing their tears, the fear on their faces, I could tell that they were scared for their teammate, who was more like a sister to them. These girls have a special bond. Not only do they spend all their time practicing and traveling together, they also have regular devotionals and pray together. The hurt in their eyes was not just for Malori, it was for us, her family, as well. They loved on us and prayed with us. As people continued to pour into the hospital for us, the volleyball coach from Midwestern and her entire team came in. They brought us gifts: coffee, toothbrushes, water, and snacks, but more than that, they also came to pray with us.

At one point, not too long into the surgery, the nurse brought me a gallon zip lock bag full of Malori's waist-long, blonde hair. She always wore it braided in a high ponytail for her games to keep it out of the way. I just—I don't know—I had a meltdown when I saw her hair. I knew in my mind that they were bringing me this hair in case we needed it for the funeral. Thankfully, Marray and others were with me.

About an hour later, a sweet little elderly woman came up to us in the lobby. Marray and Maci were with me and the other moms were around me, loving on me and rubbing my back. Coach Lawrence had not left my side since she got to the hospital; she had lost a child of her own and could understand the anguish my heart was feeling. In front of us all, this sweet lady walked up and said, "Where is the mom of the daughter who is fighting for her life in brain surgery right now?" I said, "I'm her mom." She came and put her arm around me, saying, "Honey, I've got a brand new super-giant print, beautiful, turquoise NIV version of the Bible in the back seat of my car. I am here with a friend, I've been here for a while, and God has just laid it on my heart that when I found somebody that needed this big print, beautiful Bible that I would give it to them and bless them with it. I'm gonna run to my car because I can see that you need it right now." I thought to myself, "How in the world could she happen to know about us from a regular room down the hall, and how could she know that I don't have my Bible with me?" But the answer was simple: God knew. I have the Bible on my phone, but it is just not the same as looking at it, turning the pages, and holding God's word in my lap. He just knew I would need an actual Bible. The amount of sleep I was going to lose over the next two weeks would end up making my eyes tired and strained. God knew I needed what was called "super-giant print" to be able to keep reading his promises.

I took my new Bible to the restroom to have a little time by myself in God's word. The verse that carried me through the surgery and has carried me in the weeks and months since then is Psalm 62:1-2 NIV: "Truly my soul finds rest in God; my salvation comes from him. Truly he is my rock and my salvation; he is my fortress, I will never be shaken." These verses brought me deep comfort even in the middle of having no idea of what was happening in the operating room, and they strengthened me to go back out and be back with all of my loved ones.

Shortly after reading that verse, I remember Peyton, walking in to the waiting room. I just jumped up out of my chair and ran to hug him. We held each other and cried for what seemed like ages. I knew that the drive for him to come to us was horrible. Peyton and Malori are only 21 months apart in age, and all three of our children have always been close to each other. My sister and brother had been calling Peyton along the way to check on him, but part of me had been subconsciously watching the doors just waiting for him to get there. Having Peyton arrive was such a comfort to me because all four of us were finally together. We would receive whatever news we were going to have to endure together as a family. At this point, we knew at least that Malori was still alive, but things were still so critical. My heart not only found comfort in my family being together, but also in being able to comfort Peyton and Maci. My mommy heart was just so broken and being with them just brought some kind of peace and comfort.

About an hour after Peyton arrived, I had to just sneak off away from the crowd in the waiting room. I walked out the front doors and sat on the curb in front of the hospital. I had only been there for about five minutes when I looked up to heaven and I asked God to please spare Malori's life. I told Him I knew he was capable of miracles; I just had never personally witnessed one with a family member. I begged God for the experience of witnessing His power. "God, I just want to be able to proclaim that I have seen the power of your miracles firsthand. I know I laid my twenty-year-old daughter onto the table stiff, unconscious, with no verbal response, and no movement response—basically dead. God, I just want to witness this, and I want to be able to proclaim your power and your glory forever. If it be your will, please let her make it through this surgery. I know the odds are against her, yet I know it doesn't matter what the odds are because you are able and you can do anything—all things are possible with you. I can survive this, God, because you said I can do all things through the help and strength of Jesus. So, if it is your time to take her, I know I can do it and I will survive it—but I don't want to, and I am begging you to do a miracle."

Right as I was finishing my prayer, my mom pulled up. She had driven alone because my dad is in a nursing home with the progression of his disease. She pulled up and came over to embrace me; it was just the two of us for a few minutes. I said, "Mom, they don't know if she is going to make it. They are not sure she will survive it." She said, "Sarah, it doesn't matter what they are saying. God can do anything." I said, "Yes, I know He can," and she told me, "You just blot it out of your mind that she is not going to make it. You just hold onto the knowledge that you have—that we all know God is capable of doing anything he wants to do." Right after that, Tyler (Malori's boyfriend) and his parents drove up. I just hugged him and his parents, and God gave me the strength to try to be a comfort to him in that moment. I told him, "Tyler, we just gotta pray. We just gotta pray for God to do a miracle." After that, Tyler and his parents went inside and started engaging in prayers with everyone else in the lobby. Then, my brother and sister pulled up, and I was able to fall in their arms. We were all in tears because we are a very close family. We love each other's children as our own. With the rest of my family finally with me, I went back into the lobby and stayed close to my husband, son, and daughter. Together, we continued to wait and pray. At one point, we received a report that they had made it through what they thought was one of the toughest parts of the surgery, but there were still no promises. "She is holding her own" was all we ever heard. After each shred of news, we would gather up and pray, and then Marray would give a report to everyone else in the lobby.

After 6 hours, Dr. Kamath came out at the end of Malori's surgery, he pulled our family aside to a room. He told us, "It took me a while. I worked for hours to stop the bleed in her brain. Finally, I tried one last technique to stop the bleed with a clotting device, and somehow this time it just worked. We closed her up. I've placed two pieces of her skull in her abdomen to preserve it in the hopes that she will be able to survive these next critical 72 hours. I hope she will be able to get flown to Dallas, survive these days in ICU, and go through rehab to the point where she will be able to have the AVM removed and her skull put back together." He explained to us that the next 72 hours were very critical as to whether she would survive or not. He reminded us again of the risk of brain infection. She could end up paralyzed and we had no idea what kind of brain damage she might have.

We told him we understood and were so grateful. We hugged him, thanked him, and let him know we would thank God for him daily for staying to help us after a long day of surgery and not giving up. He told us later that he looked at Maci and saw the fear in her face and eyes, and all he could see was his fourteen-year-old daughter who was Maci's age. He said Malori also reminded him of his daughter because her physique is small and she looks so young in the face, and he hoped someday that a medical team would do for his daughter what he was trying to do for Malori in not giving up to stop the bleeding. He said, "I am going to have to wheel her through the lobby for a final CT scan to make sure the bleed has stopped. There seems to be about 150 people in the lobby with you as your support group; I may have to maneuver some of them to make a little path as we wheel her through. After we do that, I am going to let her family come back here to the holding room and see her." I responded that it would be amazing if we could just see her. He told us the plan was to get her in a stable enough condition that we could put her on a medivac helicopter and fly her to Zale Lipshy University Hospital in Dallas. Dr. Kamath had already spoken to a neurosurgeon who is considered the best of the best and who had agreed to take her on as a patient.

When we went back to see Malori, it was difficult. One minute we were watching our twenty-year-old daughter serving a volleyball, jumping up and down, and encouraging her teammates; then, we were handing her over in the ER in her stiff, lifeless body; and now, we were seeing her unconscious in a hospital bed after surgery. She was completely bald on the left half of her head, she had tubes down her throat with wires and IVs everywhere, and there was a big, U-shaped incision that went from the top of the left side of her head, all the way to the back and up under her ear like a question mark. There were bandages over the staples and the incision, and she looked as white as liquid paper from all the blood loss and trauma. I just remember thinking, "This is just not happening. This is a horrible nightmare." I could not even believe it was real; I was in shock. All I could do was clean my hand with sanitizer and rub her arm just to feel that there was still warmth and life in her. And I could pray over her. We had a prayer of thanksgiving around her bed—Marray, Peyton, Maci, my mom, my brother, my sister, Tyler, and Tyler's parents. (We knew Tyler and Malori meant to be married in the summer of 2016, so Tyler's family was pretty much already our family.) We all stood around Malori and said a prayer. We asked God to continue to take care of her, to carry her through the upcoming flight, and to help her survive the transport and the next 72 hours which would be so critical.

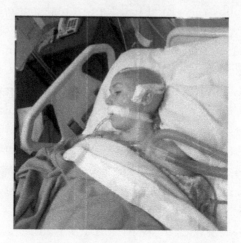

At that point, the respiratory therapist and nurse came in and said they had gotten it approved for one of us to fly with her to Dallas. I know how motion-sick I get on small planes and rides at amusement parks; I even get sick sitting in the back seat of a car. I did not want them to be tending to me throwing up on the plane. I wanted all the focus to be on my daughter. I asked Marray if he would fly with her and he said, "Absolutely, I will." We thanked everyone who was caring for her. Dr. Kamath never left after the surgery; he stayed in her room in case any complications came up. He knew that the chances of him having to take her right back into the OR during the couple of hours after surgery were pretty probable, so he stayed close. Thank God for Dr. Kamath and his selflessness throughout that whole night, not thinking of his need to rest, eat, sleep, or shower for his next full day. What a blessing! Truly, the whole medical team that stayed late and came back in and helped with the surgery was a miracle and a blessing.

At this point, it was around 2:30 in the morning, and we were blessed with the presence of my sister-in-law and dear friends, who had all arrived just before we had to start our drive. They had juggled so much with work and childcare arrangements just to come love on us and pray with us. We thanked all of our dear friends at the hospital and left to make the drive to Zale Lipshy. Yet again, God provided for us in the most unexpected of ways. A precious friend of ours had taken the time to clean up all the vomit in our car. There was no way we could have ridden in there with our empty, torn up stomachs, but this sweet angel had bagged up anything with vomit on it and had cleaned the floor mats, carpets, and seats to where we could not smell a thing. Different people volunteered to drive our various cars so we could be together without having to worry about driving. My sister is used to working nights as an RN, so she drove our Yukon with me, my mom, Maci, and Peyton. It was the most long, dreary, rainy drive I have ever experienced in my life. It was almost like a fog or a dream. We said chain prayers out loud, we cried, and we talked about all the wonderful things and wonderful miracles that had already happened and been put in place: all the wonderful people that he sent out—just vessels of comfort for us; all the prayer warriors that were with us praying—we learned of a gathering back home around the fountain at LCU; and the precious videos of prayers and singing from countless locations.

Malori arrived in her ICU bed in Zale Lipshy around 4:30 in the morning. Marray texted us that they had arrived and that Malori's vital signs were looking a little better. I could not believe it. I had been so frightened about her being transported, and to me it was a miracle that she had arrived safely and even a little stronger than before. We arrived in Dallas about an hour after Malori and Marray. Zale Lipshy has required valet parking, so we handed off our car and did not see it for many days, because we never left Malori's side. By mid-morning, our friends and family had once more taken over the hospital waiting room. The scene in that ICU lobby was unbelievable. We were camped out on mattresses, couches, and reclining chairs. There were food baskets, drinks, gift cards, and money everywhere from friends in Lubbock and people we did not even know in the Dallas area, who had heard about us. I have never witnessed such an outpouring of love.

For the first 72 hours, we all had to put on gowns and gloves before we went into Malori's room to protect her. The hospital staff conducted neuro checks every hour, and all of our family was in there every time, watching desperately for any sign of progress. We hardly slept; by the time each check was over, there was only about half an hour to briefly close our eyes before it was time for the next one. In these hourly neuro checks, they would pull Malori off her sedation and begin talking to her, asking her to open her eyes, squeeze their hands, or wiggle her toes. The first day there was no response during the neuro checks. The doctors were watching her intracranial pressure closely. They carefully monitored and controlled her blood pressure with medication and sedation. They also did a procedure where they drilled into the top of her head and placed a drain in to keep track of how much blood was coming off of her brain. We constantly watched her vital signs on the monitor. Malori started running a fever that lasted for several days. This was critical, because the fever could be a result of the trauma of brain surgery, but it could also be a sign of infection. We kept fans on her and put ice bags around her to try and get her fever down. Minute by minute, each hour slowly passed.

Early in the afternoon of the first day, we were meeting with our new neurosurgeon, Dr. Welch, when there was a knock on the door. Two nurses had come to tell me that Maci had passed out after walking into Malori's room and seeing her incision without the bandages for the first time. I walked out of the meeting room and saw Maci white as a ghost, sitting on the floor next to the door looking up at me. The nurses asked if I wanted them to take her to the ER so they could test her and treat her, but my mommy heart broke once more at the thought of having my other daughter in the ER while my twenty-year-old was fighting for her life. I reached down to hug and kiss Maci and check to see if she was okay. Her head did not feel warm, she just looked pale. I knew she had not had any food or sleep, so we decided to try having her eat a little something first before running any tests. I made sure Maci had people to be with her before returning to our consult with Dr. Welch. Dr. Welch explained to us what Malori's recovery journey would look like. We would be in the hospital for 4-6 weeks, and then 2-4 months down the road, we would have another surgery to remove the AVM. That was the first time we really realized this was going to be months and months of recovery and rehab.

On day two or three, Malori began responding to the neuro checks, but only with the left side of her body. We had no idea if she would have any use of the right side of her body, and it was not until day seven of the neuro checks that the right side of Malori's body began responding. When she would not wake up well in the neuro checks, they would give her a strong little pinch on her left side and she would lift her left arm up high. They would say, "Good, Malori. That is what we want. Let's see what you can do." The first time she opened her eyes during a neuro check, she just kind of looked around. We began to notice that she really did not acknowledge us with her eyes if we were on the right side of the bed. We did not notice at first because we were not on that side of her bed very much, because it was where the drain for her brain, the IV tower, and other machines were. We typically stood on the left side because there was more room. After several days of that we realized when one of the doctors shone the light into her eyes to check her vision that she had no peripheral vision on her right side. They asked us to start sitting by her right side to force her to turn that direction and to get her to start using her right side more often.

The hospital had rules regarding visitation in ICU, yet after a while, they gave up on the rules with us. We had the end room right by the doors entering the ICU unit, and there were usually about twelve of us at a time in Malori's room. The nurses said they had never seen anything like the number of people wanting to see Malori, and they finally said if Marray and I were okay with the visitors, they would allow it. We were never really private about any of this journey. First of all, we wanted anyone who was willing to pray for Malori. Also, as we saw the little bits of progress every day, we wanted all the glory to be given to God. We wanted any and all to see the power of His miraculous, healing hands. Anyone who wanted to go back to see and pray with Malori, we let them. We were so grateful that people would travel that far to comfort us and pray for us. People's visits were such a blessing, and the support was unbelievable.

After about four days of not leaving Malori's side, I decided I had to get a shower. I did not want to leave her, but I needed to clean up, and I thought it might make me feel better. One of Malori's nurses told me I could go up to the eighth floor of the hospital where there were rooms that family members sometimes used to shower. The eighth floor seemed so far away from Malori on the second floor, but it was better than leaving the hospital altogether, so I agreed. On my way up, I ran into a man from Cameroon, Africa who was helping me find my way. He had the most beautiful accent, and all of a sudden he said, "Stop. I feel the

Spirit of God leading me. Are you the mother of the volleyball player who is fighting for her life?" It was a surreal moment for me. It seemed like he knew everything about me, but I had no idea how he would know. He looked at me and said, "Your shower can wait. We're all going to go back down to Malori's room in ICU and I'm going to pray over every cell, tissue, artery, vein, muscle fiber, organ, and every ounce of her body for God's healing and God's protection." It was amazing. At this point, we still had not talked to Malori or gotten any real responses from the right side of her body. He laid his hands on her and we all gathered around her bed to pray. It was one of the most powerful and moving prayers I have ever been a part of. I vividly remember seeing Malori's eyes flutter just a little in response to his accent. Malori has taken two mission trips to Africa, and a big part of her heart remains there. It was almost as if she knew he was from the place she has come to love so dearly. It was an incredible moment.

Several days into the ICU stay they decided that it was time to put in a feeding tube to give Malori some nourishment. This was one of my first glimmers of hope. I thought, "Thank you, God. If they are going to the trouble to give her a feeding tube, she might survive this." Things continued to progress slowly. On day seven, she moved the right side of her body for the first time. They would start pinching her right collarbone and her arm, and her right hand would come up to stop the hand that was pinching her. It was encouraging to see her moving her right side. Our main concern was obviously her survival, but as her condition became more stable, we began to think about the long-term implications for her if she never regained the use of the right side of her body. Around the same time the nurse came and got us. She told us, "I just walked in to see Malori's little hiney in the air. She was leaned over to her left side on the rail of her hospital bed, and she had already managed to pull out her feeding tube. She had her hand on the ventilator tube, and was working on taking that out next!" That moment was when I realized things were looking better. We had one feisty, little fighter on our hands. I know the nurses said it could have really agitated her airways if she had pulled out the ventilator tube, yet it was also such a happy moment for me thinking that Malori could tell that something was agitating her and she did not like it. They put the tube back in and we had to start putting big white gloves that looked like boxing gloves or mittens on her hands. Malori would wiggle and try to get them off. We eventually had to go to restraints to keep her hands tied down because she was still trying to pull the tube out. As serious as it was to keep her tubes in, it was a ray of sunshine that we still had Mal's fighting spirit on our hands.

They pulled out the ventilator tube around day six or seven. They explained that a patient gets to the point where it is a little risky to leave ventilator in because you can develop ventilator-induced pneumonia. They had decided that Malori's levels were remaining stable, so they thought it was a good time to take it out and continue breathing treatments without the tubes. We were all around her bed watching her. It was like sitting in the most suspenseful movie of our life, only even more so because we were looking at our daughter. They said, "Hi, Malori!" She slowly opened her eyes and looked at us sporadically. They asked her, "What is your name?" She said in a small whisper, "Sarah." My heart jumped at her voice, and I thought, "Okay. She can see me standing at the foot of her bed." A little time went by and they asked her, "What year is it right now?" She paused for a while and blinked her eyes. In her soft voice, she answered, "1972." That is the year I was born. We were all really fascinated by all that and thought it was interesting. At the time, I did not feel anxiety because I was so excited to hear her voice after not hearing it for a week. However, I did realize that we had a long road ahead of us. I realized there were things deep in the long-term part of her brain that she just remembers like my first name and the year I was born. I remember thinking, "We have a long way to go. There are so many things we will have to teach her again." We were happy to accept the challenge to help her get to where she wanted to be.

A little later that day, Peyton stood beside her and said to her, "Okay, surely you have forgotten my middle name." She just looked at him smiling a little, closed her eyes, and shook her head no. Then she opened her eyes, smiled again, and said, "Glen." He said, "No way! How did you remember that?" Peyton has always laughed about having Glen as his middle name, since it seems like an old timey name to him. Malori had not even said her own name yet, but she remembered Peyton's middle name. After that, we would get on her left side and all take turns asking, "Who am I?" She slowly responded with, "Mom, Dad, Maci, Peyton, and Tyler." She called Tyler's dad by his nickname, Harvard, and called my mom Nana. As the days passed, she started recognizing aunts, uncles, and cousins.

By the time her volleyball team came back to visit her after their conference tournament (around days 11-12) Malori knew her coaches and teammates. About three players would come in at a time with the coaches, and she would call them by name and say, "What's up? How are you?" Before they all left, they all came in the room together with our family. Coach Lawrence said, "Let's have a prayer." It was an emotional time for the team; they had gone to play in the conference tournament without one of their sisters and they had lost their game. Coach Lawrence asked who wanted to say the prayer, and Malori piped up and said, "Let me say it!" Malori prayed for their safety and their health. It was almost like she did not even realize her own condition. The Holy Spirit just took over. Malori prayed for God to help the team show His love to others, and she prayed for all of them including herself to share God with everyone they met. We were all amazed. This was a pivotal point because we got to hear Malori pouring out her heart, the same Malori who had led team devotionals and ministered to her teammates.

It was a concern for all of us, especially for Tyler, if she would remember us. Tyler and Malori had hoped and planned to be married. Tyler was so relieved when Malori remembered him and would squeeze his hand before she would even open her eyes. Then, after she started talking, she would say things to him like "Don't leave, stay here by me." Early on, we were all so careful touching her because we did not want to give her any germs. Sometimes, Tyler would give her a small kiss on her forehead before he would leave, but after a while, she began to pucker her lips wanting a real kiss from him. Tyler had to come and go frequently because he was going back and forth for school, basketball practices, tournaments, and games.

Over Malori's time in ICU, the neuro checks moved from every hour to every two hours, and then to every four hours. The medical team determined that uninterrupted rest was very crucial to Malori's continued recovery. Malori slowly grew stronger. As soon as they took her catheter out (about a week into her time in ICU) Malori began wanting to get up. She needed help with every step, and posture changes made her a little dizzy, but at the beginning of her second week in ICU, she walked 100 feet. We were so excited that she was walking even while she was still in ICU. Her physical therapist and her speech therapist visited every day.

Malori loved her physical therapy. She would say things like, "Let's get up, let's sit in the chair today, let's get up and walk." If they asked her to walk 100 feet, she would walk 200. If they asked her to walk 300, she would do 450. She always said, "Little bit longer, little bit longer." She would get her tennis shoes on and walk around the big circle in the ICU. She went slowly, and her IV poles and machines had to come along with her, but it was great to see her moving.

Speech therapy was harder for Malori. She could not recognize colors, letters, or numbers at first, and it frustrated her. I remember at one point just grabbing on to Marray's arm, leaning into him, and saying, "This is so scary." The brain is so complex and controls everything in your body. This was our driven, hard-working Malori. She had maintained a 4.0 for her whole life, acing even her hardest college classes, yet now she could not even recognize colors. As scary as it was, it also confirmed for me how amazing God is to create such complex, detailed human beings. I just thought to myself, "How could anyone question that there is a God?"

After two weeks in ICU (and a week of therapy) we got the news that they were going to move Malori to a regular room. As good as that was to hear, it was also a little bit frightening to know we were going to be leaving the incredible, nonstop care of the ICU nurses. Marray and I began watching the nurses carefully so we would know how to help Malori when the nurses were not there. Our family had gotten a room at the local Ronald McDonald house, but either Marray or I was with Malori at all times. Usually, either Peyton or Maci was there with Malori as well, and the other would be back at the Ronald McDonald house with whichever parent was there.

Just past the two-week mark, our family celebrated Thanksgiving together in the hospital. A sweet lady we had met while in ICU brought us a huge, homemade, Thanksgiving dinner. On top of that, our class from church back home had arranged for a meal at the hospital as well. Marray's family and my family all came and we all went down to a room in the cafeteria to eat together. Malori got to come down and eat with us, which was unbelievably special. We were all in awe and experienced overwhelming gratitude that we were having our first holiday since everything had happened, and Malori was there to share it with us.

In the regular room, Malori wanted to walk two to three times a day, always pushing herself further and further. After being in bed so long, she loved being able to get up and move. The night of December 10th, she just kept going and going until we thought to ourselves that she must have gone over a mile. The neurosurgeon cautioned us not to push it, and to make sure she was getting enough nourishment and perhaps not exerting quite so much. But Malori had gotten a taste and she wanted more. It became fairly normal for her to walk anywhere from half a mile to a mile at a time. We could tell how much she loved it and how thankful she was to be moving.

During this time, our family had to find a way to keep functioning with all of our other responsibilities. I took a leave of absence from work. My principal got a long-term substitute for me so my job would be waiting for me when I got back. Peyton drove back and forth a lot to finish up his first semester of college. As he was taking finals, I suddenly had the realization that I had always sent goody bags to Malori while she took finals, but I did not have anything prepared for Peyton. I ran to Walmart and got lots of treats and snacks to send to him. Despite the crisis our family was enduring, he ended up pulling through just fine for his finals. I am so thankful he was able to focus enough to finish the semester. Even after Peyton got out for Christmas, Maci still had a few weeks of school left. Tyler's parents, my family, and our friends transported her back and forth between Lubbock and Dallas as much as was needed. Often times, Maci and Tyler wanted to stay in Dallas as long as they could, so we would put them on a 6:00 am flight back to Lubbock so they would arrive just in time to get to school. My mom moved into our house in Lubbock to be there for Maci and help take care of our house and animals. Tyler also stayed there often to help my mom keep things going. My mom would get Maci to school and to her practices, and Maci had a whole cheering section of Malori's friends from LCU who would come to watch her play. Maci's teachers and coaches stepped in and took care of her in countless ways. The way the community of God surrounded our family and carried us through that time was simply incredible.

Marray was so optimistic through the whole process. Of course, he had his moments where he would break down and the tears would flow, but he was such a rock and an encourager for all of us through this process. He would tell Malori all the time, "I can't wait until the day I hold your hand and we walk out of this hospital." On December 4, 2015, Marray's words came true: Malori was released from the hospital. We loaded up a huge cart with all the gifts and things people had brought to us. As we got to the door, I said, "Okay, let's stop. I want to get this picture." Marray said, "Yes, get this picture. I can't wait to share this picture with everyone that we are experiencing this miracle of Malori walking out of the hospital." I vividly remember that moment, and I cherish the picture and what it means to us.

From the hospital, we all went to stay in the Ronald McDonald House. Malori had therapy five days a week: occupational therapy, physical therapy, and speech therapy. She loved all her therapists, but she got the most frustrated in speech therapy—reading passages and trying to remember what she had just read. She really needed her physical therapy as an outlet between her more difficult speech and occupational therapy sessions. She would go through her therapy routines every day, and they would reverse the order every other day. We had frequent visitors at the Ronald McDonald House, so much so that we had to coordinate all the awesome people who came to see us to be sure Malori got her rest. We would get home from therapy at 4:00 in the afternoon, and then she needed to sleep. We would schedule people to visit between 6:30-7:00, and then Malori would need to get to bed to sleep. This routine went on for almost a month: from December 4th all the way to her second surgery.

We did enjoy a refreshing break from the routine to spend quality time with family over the holidays in a beautiful, spacious home. One of our many sweet, generous friends, Cathy Delaney, took time off of work from her job as an RN, went on trips, left us delicious baked sweets and Christmas gifts, and full use of her house. It was so cozy with numerous books and movies to choose from in her big den. We had Christmas with Tyler and his parents over the week of Christmas, when he had a break from basketball. Then, we spent several days over the New Year holiday with my parents, brother, sister, and their families. It was so special and having her big kitchen where we could cook holiday dishes was incredible. God really blessed us with a beautiful holiday season, in spite of all we were going through at the time.

Tyler's parents had some dear friends who let them use their condo in Plano. It gave us a place to go hang out and escape the medical scene for a few hours, somewhere that felt like home. On January 5th, the night before Malori's surgery to remove the AVM, our community gathered there: team members, coaches, friends, and family. We were surrounded by people who we knew loved us. Malori spoke a little to thank everyone. Malori said, "I hope you will all feel as much peace as I do about this surgery. I just feel God's peace surrounding me, wrapping me up in his love and mercy. I am going to be praying for y'all tonight and in the morning that y'all will be at peace about this." In the end, Malori knew that she would either wake up and see all those who love her so much or she would wake up and see God. She knew and understood that. I just remember sobbing as she talked to us in that living room. I was crying tears of nerves over the thought of another brain surgery, knowing they were fixing to cut into my child's brain again. At the same time, I was weeping tears of joy; it made my heart feel so happy that Malori was more at peace than she was scared. It was such a defining moment.

That night, after every one left, Tyler and Malori sat and talked, prayed, and cried together. The last surgery had been an emergency, so there had been no time to prepare. This time, however, they wanted to pray and be together. Aside from the serious moments they had together, there was one especially sweet moment that we now cherish. As I mentioned earlier, Malori's short term memory was not very good for quite a while. She would forget things just minutes after you would tell her. She joked and referred to herself as Dory from *Finding Nemo*. One night in early December after we had just moved into the Ronald McDonald house, Tyler and Malori sat and talked. He told her that he had bought her an engagement ring: "Mal, I got the ring. I bought you a ring." He knew he was safe to tell her because her short term memory was so bad. The night before her AVM removal in January, Malori said, "Tyler, I remember you told me you bought me a ring." He was shocked, and said, "Mal, how did you remember that? I thought I was surely safe to tell you at that point—you couldn't remember things minute to minute!" Malori's response was, "Tyler, how could I not remember that? That is a big deal for a girl!"

The next morning, we checked in for Malori's surgery and they gave us her case number. We could watch the screen in the waiting room for Malori's number to see the status of her surgery. We were only supposed to have two to four people in the waiting room with us, but we ended up having about fifty. Our church family, friends, schools, and family surrounded us every step of the way with this journey. We waited and watched her number for five hours of surgery. Then, Dr. Welch came out, and we instantly looked for his body language to see how he felt about the surgery. And there it was—he was smiling! As he came toward us, our whole clan walked toward him. I remember my mom just wrapping her arm around him saying, "Thank you so much, Dr. Welch. We have been out here praying for you and for Malori." I remember hugging him and telling him we were forever grateful for what he just did for our daughter; words would never convey our gratitude and we would never be able to repay him. He explained to us that he was able to remove the AVM without any complications of bleeding. "I feel confident I got it all, but I always do a post-op angiogram to verify that." We immediately huddled up after Dr. Welch talked to us and had a prayer of thanksgiving. It was just another miracle. Malori had survived another brain surgery.

The angiogram confirmed all of the AVM had been removed successfully. Praise God! When we finally got to see our courageous girl, she was back in a room in the ICU unit. She looked very pale and had the vomit bucket beside her in bed. The nurses said she had been using it because she was nauseated from the amount of anesthesia she had to have during surgery. It was so good to see our little warrior and just kiss her forehead, blood, bruises, and all. It was so comforting to see that the left side of her head was not sunken in any longer. We were so relieved that the AVM, the monster that caused so much damage and heartache, was successfully removed that we almost forgot about the great blessing of her bone flap being back in its original home, protecting her brain! For two months, she carried the two stacked pieces of her skull in the lower left part of her abdomen. Once she started walking well, she was very cautious not to let anything bump the left side of her body, head or abdomen. Thankfully, God made us in such a perfect way that her vision loss and side she hit the most was the opposite side, her right side. She would only have two more weeks of guarding the left, stitched-up areas of her head and abdomen, until we would see Dr. Harold Smith in Lubbock to get the stitches removed from both areas. All of this was amazing!

Yet it was also hard for us to see her back in Neuro ICU. Peyton and Maci had been telling her for several days that she would know when the surgery was over when she could hear the song, Brainwash, by Nicole C. Mullen. They all three laughed for who knows how long, just anticipating this moment! Sure enough, as soon as we saw Malori's eyes beginning to open, Maci blasted the song on her phone while Peyton danced to the beat in his comical, celebration fashion. We had all been hoping and praying for this moment for two months!

Malori spent two nights in ICU, two nights in a regular room, and then we were released to go home. We left the hospital on a Sunday, and our whole family got to go back through Wichita Falls. We made a stop at Kell West Regional Hospital to say thank you to all the nurses and all the staff who took care of Malori that first night. When we got there, Marray pulled up to the entrance of the ER, but I said, "No, we need to go in the front door." I did not want to relive going into the ER. Sure enough, someone motioned us to drive to the front entrance of the hospital. I was grateful for that; I did not want to get out of that same car and go through the same doors where I had handed off my lifeless daughter. I wanted to stay on our current path of wellness and joy.

It was beautiful to watch Malori meet Dr. Kamath and the other people who saved her life that night. They were so familiar to us, but Malori had never seen any of them. Dr. Kamath hugged her and touched her face. He took her by the hand and walked her through the hospital. He showed her his office where he had the silhouette cut-out of her in her VB jersey that said, "Pray for Malori," hanging on the wall. He took her into the room she waited in for surgery, and he even took her to the pad where the helicopter was going to pick her up (even though it ended up being an airplane.) The staff had one of the preachers who works closely with them come in and say an amazing prayer of thanksgiving for continued complete healing over Malori. They fed us lunch and fellowshipped with us. It was so amazing; they told us story after story of how critical she really was—how they were running behind us to get blood as Maci, Marray, and I were praying and how she needed all those transfusions to get her stable enough to have surgery.

We spent three or four hours with our wonderful friends at Kell West before heading home to Lubbock. We kept getting texts from our friends and family saying, "Hey, when are you going to get here? Do you mind swinging by Greenlawn (our church) for a few minutes? There are a few people here who have been praying for Malori that just want to see her briefly." We had no idea what was waiting for us. Friends were waiting for us outside the church when we pulled up. As we walked in, we saw precious children and beautiful faces from home holding signs saying "We have been praying for you. Welcome home!" The auditorium was full of hundreds and hundreds of people there to welcome us home. (I had only been back to Lubbock one night since November.) Malori's volleyball teammates grabbed her and took her to the front, Tyler's basketball teammates grabbed him, and our friends escorted us to the front. All I could do was cry at the overwhelming love I felt. I had heard so many stories about the things happening back home: people praying, making t-shirts, and hosting fundraisers for our family. But walking in to our church and seeing that crowd of people love us face-to-face was a whole new level of amazing. Malori was able to get up and speak to the room full of people we loved so much. She was emotional and tearful as the thanked everyone for their prayers and everything they had done for our family. Then Marray got up and thanked everyone. He talked about the miracles we had experienced over the past few months. There was singing and prayer, tears and laughter, worship and thanksgiving. It was one of the most wonderful hours I have ever experienced in my life.

Let me tell you about a few of the things I learned about myself and about God through this journey. I have heard throughout my whole life that God is always with us, and He will never leave us or forsake us. I have read these words in scripture countless times. However, when you go through a storm, that promise becomes incredibly real and powerful in your life. The neat thing is, all these months later with this terrible crisis behind us, I still think about that promise daily. I often find myself talking out loud, reminding myself that God is with me and He had his hand on every small detail of our journey. He provided what we needed every moment of the way, whether that was my first sense that Malori needed to go to the hospital, keeping us calm and clear-minded to make decisions, Dr. Kamath staying to help us when he should have been leaving work, or something as simple as a giant print Bible to nourish, encourage and sustain me.

Looking back, God's provision is unmistakably evident. In March 2016, I read Dr. Kamath's notes about Malori's surgery for the first time: "I have explained to the family that her condition is grave and prognosis is very poor. Yet, they have consented to let me attempt the surgery anyway in efforts to preserve her life. We will be in contact with UT Southwestern Zale Lipshy neuro surgery team to take over care as soon as surgery is over and she is stable enough to fly." When I read these words, I had an emotional meltdown. We experienced this traumatic journey, but our hearts were in shock for a good deal of it. To look back, remember how close she was to death, and see what a true miracle it is that we have Malori with us today, I can do nothing but pour out my wonder and thanks to God.

Through Malori's weeks of recovery in ICU, Satan worked his hardest to throw his fiery darts of despair, fear, and anxieties at us, and it was only through the Holy Spirit, hours of prayer, and the word of God that we were able to combat those attacks. I wrestled with fear every hour of every day. I would wake up terrified in the middle of the night and just have to see her to believe that she was still breathing. I would watch her walking around in the hospital, and I would worry that she would fall and hit her head. For about six months, my sleep patterns were very sporadic, and I would wake up every morning and ask myself if all of this really happened or if it has just all been a terrible nightmare. I am slowly getting back into a more restful, peaceful sleep routine. My time in scripture and my quiet time with God were my only source of protection against this hurricane of a storm that hit our family. My life was changed in the best way possible by this tragedy. I crave that closeness with God now. My prayer life has also been deeply changed. I will never discount a single prayer that went up on Malori's behalf. James 5:16

NIV tells us, "The prayer of a righteous person is powerful and effective." When I say I will pray for someone, I mean those words to my very core. I keep a prayer journal to remember who I am praying for and to see God's work through my prayers.

I cannot tell you how much I have wrestled with the question, "Why?" I find it hard to understand why this had to happen to Malori. She always works so hard to be kind and considerate to others, she never let a day go by without quiet time with God, she was a blessing to everyone she encountered, and she had her whole life ahead of her: graduation, PT school, marriage, and more. I am not the only one to wrestle with this; Peyton even told me he just kept asking "Why Malori and not me?" the whole time he was driving to meet us at the hospital. After being home in Lubbock for a few months and settling into a routine of taking Malori to her rehab appointments, I brought it up one day. I asked Malori, "Do you ever wonder why this didn't happen to someone who never really tried to do the right thing and might have needed more of a wake-up call than you did? Malori thought about it for a while and said, "Mom, perhaps it may not have had the same effect if it had happened to someone like that. God let this happen to me for a reason and we just have to trust that." I was blown away by her answer.

The biggest blessing in this journey has been watching Malori's heart for God stay as strong and constant as it was before this happened to her. She could not believe how many people were praying and turning to God for "little ole Mal." The way her tragedy brought others to God in prayer, others closer to God, and families stronger and closer, just made her so happy, that it was almost unreal to her daddy, brother, sister, and me. How could she be so joyful while struggling to recognize numbers, letters, colors, and learning to walk steadily again? How could this make her so happy when she had to fight to remember words she wanted to say and get them to come out of her mouth properly? For many days, she could not even recall her own name. The truth is, she always had an inner peace from God dwelling within her and never felt alone or afraid. She found great joy in being constantly surrounded by her family and friends who loved her the most. She was able to relax and let God be at work in what was happening. This blessed our family, Tyler, and his family beyond measure, and we are forever changed by this journey. Naturally, Malori still has her moments of frustration, like her loss of independence by not being able to drive because of her loss of peripheral vision from the AVM rupture. But even through the frustration, she remains grateful for the blessing of life and the gift of being able to walk, exercise, talk, get married, have a chance at graduating from LCU, and just have the opportunity to live a normal life outside of driving. On April 14, 2016, Tyler proposed to Malori at the Rip Griffin Center at LCU where both of them had spent their college athletic careers. That was such a special, joyful night. Malori's volleyball team and Tyler's basketball team were there to celebrate with them, along with both their big families.

Malori and Tyler got married on July 29th, in the presence of 500 wonderful friends and family at Autumn Oaks Event Center. They both love the outdoors! It was so special and emotional because we were so amazed that this day could even happen. We thought it was so neat that they asked one of their mutual favorite professors, Andy Laughlin, to marry them. Malori now jokes with Andy that his A&P exam she took the morning of November 10th is what caused the AVM to rupture. He and his wife are beautiful mentors to them, and every prayer he said before the wedding and every word he said during the wedding was so perfect and so meaningful.

Malori continues to see her sweet OT, Dawn, at Vision Center of West Texas weekly. She is making great strides there, and Dr. Riley explained that active therapy is always better than passive therapy. We will never give up hope for full vision return, and we won't stop praying for complete healing. Malori has now completed Physics, Physics lab, and Exercise Testing and Prescription from her Fall 2015 courses. She has four more to go, and is currently working on Anatomy and Physiology. She is also teaching a PE class at LCHS, where her amazing father-in-law is the President, for part of her internship. She will attain three hours of internship and just work on completing last Fall's classes during this Fall 2016 semester. Then, she will only need 13 more hours and a medical mission trip to Peru to graduate. God is good!

I have always felt pain in my heart for people who lose a child or have very sick children, like a different level of heartache. I have said multiple times, "I just don't know how people live through the loss of a child," and have said "I don't know how parents have the energy to keep on keeping on while caring for sick children day in and day out." But I never imagined that I would find myself in this position, and I would never have dreamed that I would have the strength to endure it. I think back to those vivid, nightmare moments, Malori stiff in my arms in our car, Maci looking at me with such fear in her eyes, and I honestly wonder how my mommy heart survived them. How could weak-stomached, soft-hearted me endure that without screaming or passing out? How could our family survive that night and the many critical days that followed? How did we go through the many months of caregiving and watching Malori struggle through the mentally challenging parts of rehab, while having great joy in watching her sail through the physical therapy side? How did we have the strength to send her back into surgery for the second time? How could we deal with the sadness of her losing her right side peripheral vision and not being able to drive again? There is only one answer to these questions: God! God sustained us through countless hours of prayer and time in His word, and He surrounded us with family and friends to love us, support us, pray for us, and hug us through this storm. God spared Malori's life that night. He turned our fears, doubts, and anxieties into incredible joy and gratitude. All the time now, Malori says, "God is so good. He is always working for our good."

"You turned my wailing into dancing; you removed my sackcloth and clothed me with joy that my heart may sing your praises and not be silent. LORD my God, I will praise you forever." Psalm 30:11-12 NIV

Sarah and Malori at the wedding

Malori   *Senior Night*

Sarah, Malori, and Marray at Mal's Wedding

**Photos of wedding courtesy of Courtney Hill Photography in Lubbock, Texas.

TRANSITIONS ARE TOUGH

For who is God besides the Lord? And who is the Rock except our God?"
—PSALM 18:31

The description of God being our Rock is forever true. When our feet don't know where to stand, finding His presence leads us to the solid ground our souls are seeking. As I blindly cannonballed into a new chapter resembling my old life, I yearned for this Rock because it seemed like I had forgotten all of my luggage.

Upon arrival to Lubbock, Texas, from our Bahamas vacation, Tyler and I jumped right into this new stage of life with a sense of wonder. It was late summer, and the school year was close to starting back up. Tyler was ready to begin his senior basketball season, while I continued trying to pick up slack from my remaining fall semester with high hopes of graduating by spring. We had the privilege of getting to live on campus through his basketball scholarship. This was such a tremendous blessing financially and also helped me get around campus without being able to drive.

I didn't have to go anywhere special to feel a sense of community; it was right there at LCU. The support from LCU during my accident is truly impossible to put into words. The encouragement, grace, sense of belonging, and accountability from the Christian body there is unlike anything I've ever heard or seen. However, feeling like an outcast in a place that once was so comfortable to me took a lot of courage; I had to conquer that timidity every day just to go anywhere on campus. I loved seeing people but also felt awkward to show my face after being "that girl that happened to" and causing such a scene.

I didn't remember who I was or used to be, or even who I was supposed to be. I was starting again from less than scratch. I didn't have the wisdom to know that there was freedom in humility, so I tried endlessly to keep up with where I felt I should be. I was trying to prove that I was normal, strenuously contending to act the part when I didn't even believe it myself.

At this point, all I remembered was the sense of safety and peace in my family's home, and I missed it. I didn't ever worry about what month, day, or time it was; I just went with the flow, not knowing my lack of awareness. It was easier to fit in with my family, who held the heaviest category in my brain of the things I remembered.

While the sense of identity I thought I had by being a Maddox, LCU volleyball player, and excelling student was gone, I struggled to find what it was I was actually living for. Nothing was familiar anymore, especially the girl in the mirror. I was definitely still in a severely wounded state, which was confusing because it started to get less obvious from the outside as my hair started to grow. I didn't realize how "I was doing so well" purely because my family was so incredibly and faithfully present; it was *they* who had been lifting me up every day while I lived at home, being graciously driven to places I needed to be. The constant joy, activity, and positive atmosphere in our home kept me smiling. My own misunderstanding of the severity of my condition shocked me as I strove to recognize I was at rock bottom in the real world. But I am forever grateful for how the childhood roots of who I was created to be, paired with Tyler's faithful love, kept me accountable while God continued to work on me from the inside out.

When the 2016 school year started, Tyler's morning alarm

would sound way earlier than mine for his team's morning workouts. He was a captain whose leadership continually gained credibility by his work ethic and character. His dedication to his team and coaches fueled him to be early for practices, carry the weight of team conflicts, be available for meetings, and so on. I could tell he had a hunger to finish his basketball career excelling at the peak of his performance, striding in greatness every day.

I sought to balance the act of supporting him while also staying focused on my goals for the semester. I planned to chip away at five remaining classes: Physics Lab, Exercise Testing and Prescription, Biomechanics, Anatomy and Physiology, and Senior Research. I wasn't enrolled that semester, so everything I did had to be on my own doing, which helped me practice a lot of self-discipline. But being married to Tyler and living on campus gave me the accountability to get out of bed in the morning; LCU is such a special place.

I needed to set an alarm every morning so I could trust myself to wake up on my own. I would look around, trying to familiarize myself with the new surroundings as I tried to gain consciousness in the morning. I had to tell myself basic things: my name was Malori, I was a student at LCU, and I needed to get going. I would see a wedding ring on my finger and remind myself that I was married. I knew Tyler, which was good, but *what all had just happened?* I still wasn't sure. Our relationship seemed to be starting over despite the past five years of our dating.

Since I had woken up in the hospital, I had always been around family or someone to take care of me. That atmosphere was how I had started this new life, but now I had to remember how to live again on my own. I hadn't done that yet, so there were no files to draw from, as my long-term memory and identity were gone. I walked through valleys where confusion led to anxiety. My new normal was feeling scared but trying to act OK. I had never felt lonely before, but now I missed a caregiver. I missed my momma. With every ounce of what I thought was my foundation falling through the cracks, my Bible was my best friend. I am so thankful that God is willing to walk with us in every circumstance.

Although I was not involved in anything anymore, I still felt a sense of connection at LCU. I always looked forward to chapel, a time when the whole campus meets for a short time of worship, with a lesson from a designated speaker. It was always refreshing to see familiar faces, engage in short conversations, and fuel sweet relationships. After chapel, I would usually go to the library or tutoring lab, where I could work in a quiet place. I remember several instances when I was working on schoolwork and someone came behind me with a word of encouragement at just the right time. Deans, professors, coaches, presidents, students ... it was all one big family on campus. Although I wasn't feeling accomplished or worthy in my own eyes, I often looked to those around me and tried to follow them to this higher ground.

I didn't remember what I used to do with downtime on campus before my injury. My last days at LCU consisted of being on the volleyball team. If we weren't practicing, we were all hanging out or studying together; we always had a tight squad and stayed busy with something. Without that old niche, I would often rack my brain on what I ought to be doing, but I was scared that if I wasted any energy on things other than schoolwork and catching up, I would keep falling more and more behind.

I felt as if I had lost my personality, becoming rigid until I encountered triggers that would remind me of my sense of self. Without knowing what to contribute to my brain injury, I struggled with inner frustration while trying to grow. I didn't know that I needed to physically tell myself what was going on or where I was in order to feel conscious. I needed to look at the date and time multiple times a day, and I was continually making lists to hide my lack of awareness and to avoid the terror of a surprise. This mental wheelchair wasn't visible to anyone but me, but I tried to keep it rolling.

In the midst of trying to process and remember things, I always had a nervous sense of needing to stay busy. I felt so behind while trying my hardest to understand how to move forward. There always seemed to be a huge piece of slack missing from my understanding, like a black hole of mysterious void, but it fueled me to keep trying to learn how this new life was supposed to work.

For me, routine provides a comfort that always makes me feel safe, and I sought to establish a new one. I don't have to think as much when I'm coasting on autopilot. I find it comfortable to have an idea of what the day will look like, be prepared for the regular engagement of activities, and be confident everything is all right. But routine may be boring for some who are intrigued more by surprise, always seeking a thrill. I am a weird one who clings to routine like no other, and I eagerly sought to establish a comfortable sense of who I was in the world.

Striving to walk through all of these things in the midst of the transition of marriage in such a wounded state was extremely difficult for me with a brain injury. I felt silently humiliated through my new battles in front of the one I wanted to impress and love. I wanted to try my best to keep up with what looked like a normal pace for a college student so that I could support Tyler rather than hold him back. But simply getting out of bed required more effort than ever before, as I woke up to an empty apartment with unfamiliar white walls and alone, except for the big headache that was always following me around. The voice saying, "I'm not fit to be married yet. I am not worthy or deserving. I am messed up," continued to roll around my head loudly.

An encounter with the evil one can make us feel completely helpless when we don't use our armor, and I feel foolish knowing that I had been flirting to believe Satan's lies. But seeking to recognize the presence of God and remembering the source of life itself grants the most abundant victory. As Psalm 18 reads, "With [God's] help I can advance against a troop; with my God I can scale a wall" (29). He is so good and always gives us strength; victory stands with Him forever. God always knows what He is doing, and we can trust that

He will always work for our good, as promised in Romans (8:28). We can hold firmly to that promise with full confidence. While God may seem less visible at rock bottom, with debris flying violently everywhere, He is truly there waiting for our hearts and minds to grow to trust and seek Him even harder. He never changes; it's our perspective that needs working on.

ALL OF SELF, NONE OF THEE ... LESS OF SELF, MORE OF THEE ... NONE OF SELF, ALL OF THEE!

Then I heard the voice of the Lord saying, "Whom shall I send?
And who will go for us?" And I said, "Here am I. Send me!"

—ISAIAH 6:8

As I reflected on the hard work and discipline I had to maintain to try to conquer the mountains in front of me, it seemed like the battle was always meaningless when searching for *my* purpose through it. I couldn't find that answer anywhere. As a selfish being, it's often hard to find purpose when the Bible says we must lose our lives to find them (Matthew 16:25). But you're not really living until you're living for something greater than yourself. Having been a part of a team all my life, I have tasted the joy of this principle often, where sacrifice is often outweighed by reward.

The song "None of Self and All of Thee" by Theodore Monod displays an example of the gradual attitude change after giving your life to Christ. From a selfish being living for "all of self and none of Thee," to "less of self and more of Thee," to finally "none of self and all of Thee," this journey sings of the truth preached in the gospel. As I searched under every rock in my life of how I was supposed to give back to God and others, God shared a unique perspective to me through our marriage.

"Then I heard the voice of the Lord saying, 'Whom shall I send? And who will go for us?' And I said, 'Here am I. Send me!'" (Isaiah 6.8). I needed to start running with purpose and passion.

The gift of marriage posed as an answer for me on how to "lose my life" in a fulfilling way, where God is the head and ultimate sustainer. He is so good, and His nature is so gracious. Getting married is a huge life transition for anyone, but paired with the moving targets of every other category in my life, I struggled with discernment on how to handle things. The weight of Tyler's willingness to faithfully love and pursue me through what was the greatest storm in our relationship thus far completely outweighed the battles in my mind, but it still wasn't perfect.

As Tyler and I continued to grow in our marriage, God provided a sense of spiritual glue that connected us in the most transparent ways. The opportunity to sharpen each other was fueled by being real and honest. It felt so nice to be able to be a recluse for a while, together, after living in what felt like the spotlight. We were just normal humans (well, less than normal in my case), yearning for that sense of normalcy again. But just like God's love compels us to new and radical things, I felt Tyler's love doing the same.

As I spent a lot of time by myself, needing to rest while trying to keep up with what was going on around me, I tried to establish a peaceful environment that gave Tyler an opportunity to recharge at home as well. He was working so hard in all of his involvements in school, basketball, and church. In order to try to merge our worlds the best I could to spend time together, I loved to have people over for meals and feel that sense of community again. Seeking to be a homemaker and establish a family culture for us became top on my priority list.

In my mind, I wanted to be that refreshing presence that encouraged anyone who walked into our home; I wanted the space under our roof to be full of love, encouragement, and peace. I believe that a strong family culture is one tool that God provides as a powerful blessing to hold people together, especially when accountability is felt through your last name. In our tiny apartment, I wanted to sow the roots of generosity and hospitality, although I didn't feel I had much to give.

Tyler had a meal plan in the cafeteria at LCU, so I didn't cook much for both of us. Occasionally, if the cafeteria closed before Tyler could eat, I would prepare a meal that we could eat together. My vision was always to whip up a delicious meal that fueled my big, strong man, but that was often not the case. We still laugh about several experiments I tried; Tyler's nervous smile kindly let me know to take that off the menu. *Who knew ginger root was the strongest-tasting ingredient in the universe?* Thankfully, cookies and milk were always able to save the day. No matter what was for dinner, I still laugh at Tyler's consistent making of sausage and eggs every night. That aroma always made its way to my nostrils around midnight when I was already in bed.

As desperate as I was for alone time after the circus of kindness and attention displayed by everyone, loneliness sneakily crept in and clouded my thoughts. The things I once dwelled on did not exist anymore, things I knew were not my foundation, though they sneakily acted as one in my mind. God was testing me to recognize Him in new ways as He removed all of the blessings that could have been labeled as distractions. I felt that He had "called me out upon the waters" to put my faith to the test (Hillsong 2013).

My walk in the forest of new normals included a lot of closed doors. I slowly learned that it had to be an intentional choice to view life changes as God knocking down every obstruction that might have been seen as a distraction from Him. While prior plans seemed to gradually disappear, God patiently and graciously chose to take my hand while walking with me through the new. But when God is guiding you, the new is *always* better. He says, "I am with you," and that promise still stands in this moment because God spoke it (Isaiah 41:10). There was so much to mourn all at once that I became ignorantly numb. As my memory continued to be nonexistent in the short term and recent past, it was as if I wasn't even alive inside of my skin. It was so obvious then and now that His Spirit was the only thing sustaining me. "When God is all you have, you have all you need."

I sought to find purpose and meaning in the housework business I filled my time with. It fueled me to try to do these things for Tyler, as that seemed to be all I was able to do without driving. But I wanted to grasp the greater purpose within it. I would often type novels on my phone during downtime or in the middle of the night, pouring out raw emotions and transparent thoughts. The storm was over for everyone else, but for me, the battle was just beginning. Little did I know that downtime would actually be my story.

Through my silent spiritual battle in trying to wait for all of the waves to be stilled, I wanted to rejoice in the Lord because of His presence in perseverance and reflect on His grace fruitfully. I was too stubborn to not be positive; I was too stubborn to not have hope. I wanted to tell of this testimony that He chose to inspire in me and speak to me because He is *so good*. Finally, I realized my purpose was not to find my purpose but to help others find theirs.

> But thanks be to God, who always leads us as captives in Christ's triumphal procession and uses us to spread the aroma of the knowledge of Him everywhere. For we are to God the pleasing aroma of Christ among those who are being saved and those who are perishing. To the one we are an aroma that brings death; to the other, an aroma that brings life.

And who is equal to such a task? Unlike so many, we do not peddle the word of God for profit. On the contrary, in Christ we speak before God with sincerity, as those sent from God. (2 Corinthians 2:14–17)

PERSEVERANCE

With Him at my right hand, I will not be shaken.
—PSALM 16:8

A lot of things are uncontrollable in life; I've never heard of one success story that didn't have adversity. I truly believe there are diamonds at rock bottom, gathered only by those who have the courage to open their eyes there. I have seen the purest joy in the poorest circumstances, and I have seen the most miserable souls in what looks like the richest state. Adversity strengthens us, develops perseverance, and reminds us to live for something far greater than ourselves.

With that in mind, we have to train our minds to think in the long term with *expectant* faith, the faith of a child (Matthew 18:3). Following my parents' examples, I have always enjoyed running, typically three to five miles. Running teaches an "eyes on the prize" mindset, no matter the cost of getting to the finish line (1 Corinthians 9:24). Through running cross-country and track in high school, I knew my favorite part of competing was crossing the finish line. It was a relief! The practices, training, and self-discipline it took to be able to help my team weren't exactly the high points, but that was where my character and confidence came from to be able to perform well. We have to trust the finish line exists and that our self-discipline and faith are worth it; there will be no more hurdles in heaven.

With a brain injury, I often feel like once I clear one hurdle and catch my breath, there are five more waiting on me. But I learned to let challenges excite me because I had the key to eternal hope and strength; our mindset is crucial. In Hebrews, the concept of perseverance is highlighted: "And let us run with perseverance the race marked out for us, fixing our eyes on Jesus" (12:1–2). Our strength does not come from within. I've looked all over in there, and it is nowhere to be found, not in my skill or wisdom. We must seek God and live for something far greater than ourselves, as *His* inspiration fuels us.

In doing so, I believe that God doesn't mind when we struggle. If we didn't struggle, we probably wouldn't realize that we need His help. We wouldn't ever think soberly of ourselves. We may even become self-righteous. We would live in a state of confusion because of a false confidence.

God wants us to struggle because He loves us, but there is a difference between struggling and struggling righteously. One of God's doings is to love, and we obey Him when we let Him be the fixer by trusting in His steadfast love to provide. It took perseverance to graduate college. It took perseverance to step into a new chapter in the workforce. It took perseverance to find momentum with Tyler again. It took perseverance to work and put him through more school. It took perseverance to move to another new location. It took perseverance to keep waiting ... The deeper the wound, the greater amount of nurturing is required to gently repair it. But understanding and basking in more of His love provokes a sense of healing through obedience that becomes both unquenched and fulfilling.

The book of Romans explains, "Suffering produces perseverance; perseverance, character; and character, hope" (5:3–4). The journey of life is often a struggle, but the destination is far worth the cost as we learn to let God work through our weaknesses. A professor and now dear friend, Dr. Laurel Littlefield, gave me a bracelet during my senior year of college with the word *perseverance* on it; I still look at it often to remember to keep going.

Being married while transitioning through the new normals of having a brain injury was often lonely and dreary. Moving from what had always been home and my safe place, trying to heal, trying to remember ... all of these events brought new and unique challenges. Tyler and I both got to learn a lot about ourselves: our strengths, our growing desires, our love languages, our grit, and our faithfulness to God and each other. But as the Lord led us to new and unfamiliar places, we strove to continue to walk right beside Him. "Where God guides, He provides," and that stands true in all we can remember. That is where we have always felt safe, and as our bond of marriage continued to strengthen, God's strand around us was unbreakable. Without being close to Him, we wouldn't have been able to take another step at times. We were so reliant on His Spirit to lead us in times of trial and confusion. His presence compelled us to try to be fruitful with the gifts and grace we so bountifully received, no matter the circumstance.

Through Tyler, I am continually reminded that God has blessed me so much, and I get to dance in His riches every day. He is continually stretching me to be creative with His blessings in the new, as most things are unfamiliar upon waking up from a traumatic brain injury. With most activities, if I haven't done it post-stroke, it's as if I've never heard of it before and have no confidence to do it. With some things, if I can connect a distant memory of doing a similar thing before, I get to explore that old folder of skills more confidently. Tyler shows a confident expectation in me paired with a fair amount of grace that continues to push me to be my best.

Inspired by this union, I wanted to seek to pour from the blessings it brought forth. I tried to dwell on the good things that always outweighed my struggles, but at first, I often felt scared, trapped, and lonely with the onset of so many new normals. I always sought to embody the rich principles by which I was raised, because I was confident in them. But after moving away, I missed all of my family's gatherings and second-guessed every decision I was faced with because I wasn't sure of anything anymore. I had nothing tangible from my memory, so I lacked confidence.

Many, many things continually slip from my memory so easily, but things that are heartfelt are usually remembered more easily with an emotional and spiritual connection. If His Spirit in my heart is involved, I typically remember that thing. I drew from my sweet memories of childhood and the generous outpouring of love, which I have experienced all my life from precious vessels in place by God. Everything that happens now, things that I hear of or experience, is automatically processed through what I call a "spiritual lens." I search for meaning and try to link God's presence with it. I try to be intentional with such a perspective and how I look at things. Some things may seem far-fetched, but I try to store everything up in my heart and let God saturate the meaning.

As I continued to grow, process, and heal, I tried to continually "cling to what is good" as I was able to find new strengths associated with my deficits (Romans 12:9). I strive to see in a way that Christ would, and I feel as if He has sharpened my vision in order to see the good stuff—to trash the worldly lens of gray gloom and put on that spiritual lens that gives radiance and hope. My storm was one of spiritual warfare, but the spiritual cord of three strands in our marriage has highlighted such a vision and purpose on my life that compels me to strive to move forward; I am grateful God has shared a portion of His courage with me to try to tell it.

ENDURE

Do not be anxious about anything, but in every situation, by prayer and petition, with thanksgiving, present your requests to God.
—PHILIPPIANS 4:6

Challenging seasons are really opportunities for growth, a chance to dig deep and reestablish who we are. Though for a time it felt like every single block of the tower of Malori had been completely knocked down, God wanted to rebuild a stronger one, and He was waiting for me to ask Him for His help.

After the journey to graduate college, Tyler and I were allowed to live with my parents in Lubbock for a short season until moving to Fort Worth. After an application and interview process, he had been accepted into the TCU Ranch Management Program starting in the fall of 2017. It would be a fast and furious program: nine months of an absolute academic grind. We knew it would be tough, but we were ready. Anxiety likes to sneak in when things are new; Tyler and I would both be put to the test in a new way, together.

I was offered a job through Physical Therapy Today with the billing office. I was able to learn the job in the office in Lubbock before planning to work remotely while living in Fort Worth. I was so thankful for the opportunity to have a job that would help Tyler and me through that season; it seemed to be such a reward for the discipline it took to graduate college.

The grace and help I had received from LCU to be able to graduate college seemed to cloud the deficits my brain actually had. As I was trying to adjust to the new normals of life and the unfamiliarity of a new living place that was not Lubbock, Texas, I was unmanageably overwhelmed if I ever let my mind just coast. Working eight-hour days on a computer screen was a perfect recipe for a headache, but I tried to be tough and have faith that God would bring about greater and more accommodating plans for me later on. First, I wanted to lift Tyler up by serving him.

I was fueled and inspired by the courage that Tyler showed by jumping into a completely new field of study. It is almost unheard of to enter the world of ranching like he did, without being born into that culture or having some sort of close tie. Tyler didn't have any help in this regard from people in his regular circle, but he actively sought guidance through the relationships that God had placed on our path. His determination to succeed in finding his true calling continued to grow daily, and God opened some incredible doors for us.

At TCU, he took school very seriously and studied extremely hard. He would often come home to tell me of all the things he was learning, and I was proud of the academic side of him that was emerging. I had always been the study nerd in our relationship, but I witnessed a hunger for academic excellence from Tyler that was stronger than I had ever noticed in him before.

He left early in the morning for school and typically returned home after dark. When he wasn't in class, he was still on campus in the Ranch Management building to study. If his nose wasn't in his notes, there was a rope in his hand so he could practice putting a new skill to work. He was working so hard for us, but it was a tough season to endure.

Through this time, I didn't know that I had to be patient while the mud from the storm, which was still all over me, dried up and could then be peeled off. I hadn't dealt with anything yet because my false foundation kept getting swept away through all of the changes in my life. As excited and honored as I was to try to support Tyler in this new season, my head would often start pounding as I tried to listen to all he was doing in school. I wanted to respect him by trying to learn such a new lifestyle with him and soaking in his excitement from all that was happening in his world, but it was hard to ignore a pulsing skull after using all my brainpower to work on a computer screen all day. But he encouraged me, and I encouraged him to hang in there.

I needed an outlet of something to energize me, but I was nervous to waste any energy that I needed for work so I could pay the bills for us. That felt like such a heavy responsibility, for me to support myself along with someone else, but I needed that to push me. With such a reserved mindset, I was not really good at thinking of new and cool things, but I loved to try to be fruitful with what was right in front of me, seeing dazzling diamonds in the mundane. In addition to running, I found it both essential and refreshing to write. Since I was already working on the computer, I could easily switch screens back and forth to a Word document to record my thoughts. Tyler continued staying focused in school and also encouraged my writing endeavors. After reading a little bit of the blurbs that I didn't know what to do with, he encouraged me to start a blog. I was hesitant at first but gave it a try because of his persistence. As I found momentum doing so, I was so thankful to be able to stand for something greater throughout this process. I posted my first blog on November 10, 2017, two years after my brain bleed.

I continued to strive to read God's Word because I was hungry for it and needed it, not just to satisfy routine or cover up my weaknesses. It truly gives me life, joy, and encouragement. I could tell a fire was burning inside of me for something greater, and I wanted to always remain humble and hungry for His presence. God doesn't need my actions, big or small, but I wanted to gratefully try to praise Him in whatever was happening.

I wrote about each prophetic and metaphorical instance I experienced, and this spiritual momentum fueled me. I knew I had the Holy Spirit through baptism, but I had never experienced it move like this in me. I wanted to bring the concept of seeing life through a spiritual lens to full fruition.

As God kept speaking and revealing things to me, I kept writing. Through what seemed like the longest time of silence and closed doors, I started to be more intentional in listening for His whispering. Though I felt as if I was going out on a limb in regard to my faith, the ability to share His working inside of me gave me an opportunity to add another block to the leaning tower of confidence. Seeing with a spiritual lens became my power to triumph through any circumstance.

I was so motivated to feel like I was glorifying God and contributing to the world by encouraging others, though it felt like the smallest way possible. I found that seeking to love God and others was the only way to fill my inward emptiness, and every attempt at this fueled me. I continually fought the voice of Satan telling me that I was lost in dead ends with no way out, but my competitive nature found God telling me to keep trying to dream small.

As the transition of marriage became harder in a new place, I felt fueled by a new purpose I sensed through the Lord with my writing. Writing was unknowingly helping me connect the dots of my life pre- and post-stroke. Memories of how I used to be brought Godly confidence that nullified my headaches and depression, so I found it important to remember those. Those memories helped me to find discernment and served as a filter to process thoughts and ideas. It was vital for me to remember old ways so I could build that bridge of connection to new ways.

In the movie *The Rookie*, there's a scene where Jimmy Morris, the pitcher, measured the speed of his pitch by throwing a baseball toward a speed limit sign on an old road. The dilapidated sign calculated a warm-up throw, which led him to try a pitch at full speed. After another stretch and deep breath, he wound up for an attempt at his hardest, fastest pitch. The sign read "76," which was a definite blow to Jimmy's confidence and dreams to play in the Major League. Little did he know, the bulbs were out and flickered the actual reading of "96" right as he drove away.

I find that scene to speak truth to a lot of things we do. Whenever we may feel discouraged at shortcomings, God delights to sing melodies over us as He infuses us with his strength. Our seventy-six also reads ninety-six when we allow God to intervene. He even meets us at twenty-six, sixteen, and the negatives. Only when we are living with Him can we find and grow in the true power and might that He gives, and *that* can propel us to greater things than we would ever know without Him.

But even in the search of Him and His will, we may be answered with His silence at times. That can be so confusing and frustrating. But Bart Millard with Mercy Me shared a convicting attitude when he profoundly said, "This song ['Even If'] is a declaration to God that even if He went silent and never said another word, He's still worthy to be praised and that He's our greatest hope in the midst of the trial." That is profound, solid faith. We all *have* to have that to make it. We're never just able to coast; we're either growing or falling away from God. But even in the silence, we have the privilege to trust Him, obey Him, and love Him above all else. God *is* love, and we can truly sense His divine intervention through loving relationships with others (1 John 4:8).

Tyler and I were so blessed by the genuine, loving relationships through our church home in Fort Worth. Alta Mesa Church of Christ was a body of believers who made a tremendous impact on us; the souls in that church made the presence of God feel tangible. Tyler and I felt at home immediately by being prayed over and encouraged by the precious families there. It was not uncommon to spend extra time and meals together. Alta Mesa Church of Christ is a powerhouse for the Lord, and Tyler and I learned to experience and recognize the Holy Spirit in such radical and new ways. Time with this church body was definitely a sense of spiritual glue for Tyler and me.

Through this season of grind, Tyler and I weren't exactly together most of the time, but we felt unity to *struggle together* for once. It was essential for our marriage. We both continued to grow in that time of hardship while he worked so hard in school. He chipped away at his course load one assignment, field trip, and project at a time. In the long, dreary hours he spent studying at school, I was either working remotely in a coffee shop or at home on my computer. I felt ownership through my first real job, and Tyler excitedly shared with me what he was learning in school. We continued to stay highly motivated by the responsibility of contributing to each other's goals.

Tyler's second semester consisted of a gigantic ranch management plan, among the regular class work duties, which filled up every line of a five-inch spiral notebook. He had studied in the early mornings until late evenings, while making strong relationships with his professors, so he had every reason to be confident in his work.

But the days seemed to slowly creep by as we stuck tightly to our separate routines. As my mind started to wander and become weary in such a season of blind trust, I was forced to rely on God deeper than I ever had before. I learned that my strength *had to* come from God. I knew that God had given me a miracle to live, and to live abundantly, but I didn't realize the timing needed to finish the story.

In the midst of the spiritual warfare I was encountering, I was getting impatient in the season of waiting while Tyler was in school. I often struggled with a false contentment turning into complacency. I then started to doubt myself and my ability to do anything right. I had been alone for so long, struggling in overdrive to work and pay the bills in order to keep Tyler going in school. What I was doing was "impossible" for a person with a brain injury, but I didn't know it. I sought to practice my faith with courage and vigor, though that voice of doubt was loud and almost paralyzing. In my mind, there was no other option but to keep pressing on to take hold of the hope that I hoped existed.

I was grateful to spend time at the church when I wasn't working; the relationships made there kept me afloat. Though my inward energy bank ran out quickly around people, the precious families and children at Alta Mesa continually fueled me. I was so grateful to be involved with the children's ministry and looked forward to teaching on Wednesday nights. Though I felt mentally dead for such a task, I craved this heart medicine, and my strength came from His Spirit in me.

His presence continued to remind me that I have been blessed beyond measure ... so abundantly that it was overwhelming. But as I continued pulling a weight that often felt way too heavy, I got weary; I continued to realize that it was foolish to look inward rather than upward at Him. Because He has never forsaken me, I felt like I was wasting time to *not* live for Him with all my heart. I *had* to try an outward pouring process through my writing.

While following my husband to establish a new home seemed to stretch me far out of my comfort zone, I craved a lighthearted and safe environment that radiated peace. At first, what I thought was a gift of peace and quiet slowly started to turn into a lonely sense of isolation that continually tried to make itself present in my heart and mind. In order to try to establish a new Rogers culture while juggling lots of moving parts, the book of Psalms spoke volumes to my heart. It promises, "even there Your hand will guide me, Your right hand will hold me fast" (139:10). God is *always* with us. I couldn't afford to forsake the Word because I felt Him in it; I craved that, and I searched desperately to find my new purpose and calling through Him.

But for a time, I became so desperate, searching so hard that I became desensitized to God's Word. I wasn't letting it fill me like it could have. I just read the Bible as a dry act of faith, wanting God to help me but not really letting it soak in so it could transform me. Through that dreadful season of waiting for our next step, I wasn't *fully* trusting God's Word in Isaiah that says, "In quietness and trust is your strength," because my posture said that I "would have none of it" (Isaiah 30:15). But He gently reminded me that "the Lord longs to be gracious to [us]; therefore He will rise up to show [us] compassion. For the Lord is a God of justice. Blessed are all who wait for Him!" (Isaiah 30:18).

As my inward struggles seemed to continually be brought to the light, I didn't understand how that could be God's will. I always felt alone, walking through new places and situations. Choosing to be a wife in the most absolute horrible state I had ever experienced, I continually battled feelings of being intimidated and nervous. The tasks of trying to graduate college and then put Tyler through school kept me so overstimulated that I didn't know I was really struggling. I tried to hide the anxiety by staying busy: serving, cleaning, cooking, not wanting to be caught off guard again ... unprepared and in panic. I constantly made lists of bills, groceries, and other supplies and tasks that needed to be done. I was so afraid of forgetting that I became obsessed with doing. My actions and feelings were enslaved to my mind, and I felt there was no way to turn it off or overcome this turmoil. But I kept hoping in the bigger picture during that season before Tyler graduated.

I continued to fight this unexplainable warfare with the tool set I knew best. In supplement to scripture, I craved podcasts and sermons. The powerful messages spoken through Steven Furtick continually provided a deep conviction and encouragement for me during that time. I resonated with prophetic messages, one specifically that implied that we are "chosen not despite of the cracks but because of them ... it's not about the jar; it's about the oil inside ... it's good when we feel empty, because that's when we remember the Source." We need Him desperately, and He knows that. He put that need inside of us that can't ever possibly be quenched by anything but Him. We can always trust in God's power to triumph even our greatest efforts.

While growing spiritually, I realized that the physical, tangible things in my life had always served as my base, while the spiritual was just a gloss. I had always tried to live by faith while having separate plans in the physical world too. But as the Holy Spirit was working in me, I realized the need to live convicted; I ought to let the spiritual be the base while the tangible things in life were just a dainty coat of gloss. Living by faith is a life journey, a constant and daily battle to attain and adjust to. It's like trying to catch a slippery fish, striving endlessly but never able to grasp it fully … yet we are told to keep yearning for it. We can dance in the spiritual all day long, but we are told to stay hungry and to "not quench the Spirit" (1 Thessalonians 5:19).

In a sense, I knew I had been given a miracle, so I thought I shouldn't want anything else. But in the back of my mind, I was also fueled by the parable of the lazy servant. I was hurdling what could have easily been labeled as impossible for me because I knew and feared what a shame it would be to be labeled as that lazy servant—the servant who was entrusted with one bag of gold and then hid it in the ground in fear, without even taking it to the bank to gain interest (Matthew 25). That lie of fear and timidity is easy to believe, and I have had seasons where I related to that timidity, shamefully. But God calls us to take action and sow. The reaping amount belongs to Him, in His timing, and we can always trust it.

In retrospect, I began to see how God was using this quiet time of working in the home a lot; He was sharpening me without my knowing. Thankfully, God was using such a season to prepare me to have Him as my anchor wherever Tyler and I might land. God works *all* things for good, even the seemingly unimportant details (Romans 8:28).

The book of Matthew reads, "For whoever has will be given more, and they will have an abundance. Whoever does not have, even what they have will be taken from them" (25:29). I wanted to be fruitful, with the motivation and energy that the Lord gave. I grew to realize that our earthly lives were just a mere supplement to the eternal life we get to look forward to with God and Jesus in heaven someday. He is *the* Rock (Psalm 18:2). We must seek to align our hearts and minds to be in sync with the instructions from His Word, intentionally and with spiritual discipline. The more we live and love others, the more of Him we get to experience. Sometimes we may be blinded from how He's already speaking, but we can trust Him to be ready to answer when we call.

Sometimes having to wait is the hardest thing in our faith walks. I regret to say that I became so impatient for a time that I unhooked my cable from God for a season, fed up by His silence, and started to drift off in isolation. I was so closed off from waiting and trusting that I wasn't even open to accepting anything new. I was impatient with being lonely and working so hard for something that I didn't even know how to visualize. I didn't trust God to be in that dreary and mysterious silence because I didn't feel Him anymore. I had felt Him more when I was hooked up to tubes and needles and wires; why now was this "peace" from a "healthy life" so miserable?

At first, I tried to balance my life with a fifty-fifty approach, doing my own thing while asking for His divine intervention only when I thought I needed it most. But He wants us to be all in with Him whether we think that we need Him a little or a lot. The truth is that we always need Him *a lot*. Doing His work gives us a stronger desire to relax in His holy presence as we learn to try to relate more to the life of Jesus.

The more honest I was with myself through the processing of the recent events on my life, it made me laugh about how oblivious I had been to things. I found that my passion was to be fruitful with the statutes, love, and Christianity that my family and those around me had embodied so courageously. But since I didn't have the energy or mental capacity to do so like I used to, writing came most natural. Rather than sulking in our weakness, we can choose to rejoice in His strength; our weakness plus His strength is a powerful bond that only brings growth when we have the courage to make that connection. He is so good and gracious to His children.

It makes no *earthly* sense to find joy in our struggles, but the ability to trust in Him brings about the greatest hope. Seeking to write for Him to bless others began to help me. The book of James insists that with His intervention, it *is* possible to "consider it pure joy ... whenever [we] face trials of many kinds, because [we] know that the testing of [our] faith produces perseverance" (1:2–3). I started to feel this joy through my pain because of this greater hope. Just like diamonds are created under intense pressure to develop a new and beautiful product, God does the same for us. It requires patience, endurance, trust, and hope. With Him, all things are possible; He is so good.

In His confusing but perfect timing, the time when college graduates are encouraged to grow up in this culture, God chose instead to lead me along a rocky path. *Did I not just defeat that rocky path by surviving a stroke?* Despite the sharp stones and thorns that poked and prodded at me so violently, His tender hands held me close and always brought me a strong sense of comfort. In the book of Joshua, He promises to "be with [us] wherever [we] go" (1:9). Once again, His Word always rings true.

Every new or unforeseen destination can feel like an island if we choose to see it that way, but Tyler and I worked as a team to establish a culture of peace and love to reign in our home. Seeking to be obedient has grown us a lot, and nothing seems comfortable when living with radical faith. We learned together that a deep, burning, and passionate purpose must be our driving force while we allowed our perspectives to widen.

As Tyler and I continued to seek God through our transitioning, I was honored to share in his sense of significant relief and accomplishment from his schoolwork. We both looked forward to him graduating after he finished several more big tests. His excellent efforts in the classroom and in his studies deemed more than profitable, as he graduated that May with a ranch job already lined up. We celebrated with family and his classmates and then regained focus, as he was scheduled to start work three days later. Our families graciously helped us clean, pack, and load from Fort Worth. We moved to a place outside of Roswell, New Mexico, and were honored to jump right into a new set of roots.

NEW SETTING, SAME GOAL; KEEP GOING

I keep my eyes always on the Lord. With Him at my right hand, I will not be shaken.

—PSALM 16:8

Getting to watch the sun crawl up over a mountainous skyline and fill the still world had the same effect on my soul as it did my eyeballs. The warmth of the radiant sunrays seemed to touch my heart directly, cleansing my mind gradually with every beam of light. It's so cool to know that this same sun that we get to marvel at in any part of the world is the same one giving light to every living being.

Sunrises and sunsets have always been some of my favorite things to admire, not unlike most human beings. The sun is gorgeous in the beach setting as the waves roll in to tickle its rays. It is beautiful in the flat plains of Lubbock when sitting on a blanket in a truck bed in an old cotton field. It is even pretty through the curtains of a hospital window. The sunrises in Africa, coupled with dark spots of little children running around and starting their day are beautiful too. The sun was exceptionally gorgeous in our new mountainous setting at the ranch in New Mexico as well, dotted with black spots of Angus cattle. What a gift every new morning is, as His mercies and faithfulness reign (Lamentations 3:23).

God gives us freedom to start every day anew; it is such a precious gift to be able to have the calmness that reminds us of His control. I can just feel His will saturating its way through my thick skull and giving me direction and peace every time I look to Him. I often fight it because I don't really like change. But accepting change with a willing heart is obedience, and I want God to find me faithful when His eyes are on me. Second Chronicles reads, "For the eyes of the Lord range throughout the earth to strengthen those whose hearts are fully committed to Him" (16:9). This dearness to the Lord has always been tangible to me, even as a young child.

The journey for Tyler and I to move away and start a new culture of our own was heavily influenced by our upbringing in the church. While he is the bold and courageous leader, we both seek to contribute spiritual truths in unique ways on the sliver of earth we call home. Tyler has always been a strong Christian leader; he is continually "prepared to give an answer to everyone who asks" him, wearing many different hats to serve and lead (1 Peter 3:15). His presence and leadership magnify the spiritual lens that we strive to see through together. The spiritual realm is always a place for our union to be recharged through the first cord of our marriage. God is gracious.

Tyler was eager to jump into his new job, anxious to put his hard-earned credentials to use. The five o'clock hour came early in the morning, but it wasn't as dreadful as the heat that was intentionally avoided by the crew branding calves in that New Mexico heat. I was excited and thankful to follow him into this culture, while wide-eyed and observant in such a new realm as I discovered the definition of a ranch wife. I continued trying to set up the inside of our home and settle in, after my family had helped us so graciously with organization and decor for this new move. I was in awe that Tyler was a cowboy and that we were living on a ranch, something we had always dreamed of.

On the ranch, we get to live in a still environment and be in the moment often. The conveniences we lost as compared to living in a city seemed like more of a gain with this perspective. Together, Tyler and I seek to intentionally establish Christian values in our home. If God looked down on our plot of land, we would want Him to see a fragrant aroma ascending up to heaven as we try clinging to His statues and following them closely. Getting to relate ranching to the kingdom inspires us every day.

Having both been raised in the same church for the majority of our lives, it has always been essential for Tyler and I to be plugged into a church family during our moves. In Fort Worth, the church body of Alta Mesa blessed us greatly. Their warm welcoming never stopped for the nine months we lived there. Then, in Roswell, we were led to a new and precious church family and were immediately encouraged by their friendly welcome.

The Country Club Road Church of Christ provided a tremendous outpouring of God's favor on us. This Roswell community is heavily influenced by ranching families, and we were able to connect instantaneously with all of the members there in some way. Tyler quite frequently served in the worship service in some form, and I was also able to jump in to help with the kids through vacation Bible school just a month after being there. Sensing God's presence through the body of the church has always been essential for us; He has always had an answer through what could have easily been labeled as swift and abrupt transitions. But just as Bub has always said, "Where God guides, He provides." Again and again and again.

Tyler's early mornings were always productive and full, and I was eager to ask him about all he was doing. He seemed to put all of his hard work to use without hesitance. His skin was dark, his hands were tough, and his arms were strong. A full day's work made for a tired and hungry cowboy.

I continued my job of working remotely, but I had to find a new balance of being a ranch wife and going into town to get internet service to work. I was thankful to be flexible with my hours for when

Tyler would come home for lunch; this helped us check in with each other's new schedules and workload while establishing how to create a culture under our roof that was desirable for both of us. Our new schedules were both hard and enjoyable. While we couldn't believe we were actually living our dream, we had to be intentional and work as a team to keep each other going. I tried to be well rounded and have a personality again since I had some energy left after working fewer hours. That way, I could put more energy into being the ranch wife I had always dreamed of being. But I quickly found that it was not as easy as it looked.

Without some conveniences I always had living in the city, I found myself searching to finally put a stamp on a new routine: when to get groceries, what all needed to be done in town, how long a round trip would take, and so on. I felt like it wasn't much, but I was using all I had in the tank to make new decisions and stay afloat. Tyler worked long, hard days in the heat, so it was a priority for me to prepare or perform whatever he needed for him to keep going.

Ranching together meant new roles for the both of us; I always asked him specific, repetitive questions because I wanted to learn as much as I could about what he was doing so I could find my role in how to best serve and complement him. He was very patient with my parrotlike talking and questioning, and I tried to be a sponge.

The branding season lasted about two months. It was lonely when Tyler would work on a different ranch for most of the day, so I often tried to go into town on those days. It stretched me to be both creative and responsible with the blessing of being more flexible with my job. But with such free time, I often put too much pressure on myself to fully immerse in what had happened in regard to my stroke and step back into my old life.

At first, I enjoyed living with baby standards because I was too afraid I would fail at anything else. But I had to learn how to swerve from a perspective of timidity and merge into the lane of purpose and dignity. Then I had to learn contentment in where I was, even if God never said another word. As I woke up to brand-new situations every morning for years after my brain injury, without memory of where or who I was, His mercies always struck me as new. As I continue to reflect on that season with speechless gratitude, I am reminded that I ought to strive to rely on His leading in every situation; I grew to experience a greater level of gratitude for His sweet words to calm me every time I open my Bible.

Having the abilities to take such close care of myself was a true blessing. I knew I had to take care of myself in order to take care of and love others, which was my true passion, but sometimes I felt so self-centered and lonely in doing so. It was like I was inside of a shell that had to keep growing inside. Gradually, I chose instead to talk myself into viewing this season as learning how to be a caregiver and homemaker. I would rather pour into others, especially my family, right there in arm's length, just like my family culture had engrained in my mind. I feel so full and content under a safe roof with family, and I tried to be so intentional in establishing those roots.

As I continued to require more sleep to heal, I always woke up alone, away, and already feeling behind the rest of the world. I had never woken up alone before in all my life; when I was young, my momma or someone in my family had always been there. I missed the love and encouragement from my dad and the most generous, heartfelt care from my mom while she nurtured my wounded self with all of its needs. As I longed for that same childhood need to be fulfilled, I tried to hang on and believe in a greater plan.

As the physical world often seemed too scary, with eternal options of overstimulation, I chose to keep my mind in the spiritual. I craved that sense of safety, peace, and comfort found in the spiritual realm, so I sought to establish that atmosphere wherever Tyler and I were. I remembered Papa's verse, stating that the Lord is with us wherever we go (Joshua 1:9). I could take Him with me and share Him. I could glorify Him, serve Him, and strive to see things through a spiritual lens because He is alive and active all around us.

I had heard my dad say quite often how hard it was as a parent to ever see his kids go through any sort of trouble or hurt. But, I thought, it would have to feel so cool knowing your kids looked to you for comfort. And I bet that's how God feels, so proud when we turn to Him for that fulfillment. That's one way we get to feel His everlasting love.

To keep going, I needed that supernatural help. I had tried to finish school so I could keep up with my husband's vision and not hold us back anymore. I was always trying to conserve energy to make it, so that meant more discipline that fun. Everything I did was based off of purely how this new body felt, and everything was a gut check. Trying to handle such good and exciting life events with the new normals of a wounded mind made me feel like I was stripped from comfort and familiarity and placed in a raging sea. I was called to be a lonely provider for a time with a mental wheelchair. I craved social interaction and encouragement from people, but even being around people and trying to have normal social skills was hard for me. I learned that I feared surprises because I could never find my toolbox of materials and knowledge I needed to react fast enough. I never felt confident or motivated enough to leave home because that box of life skills was missing. Being corrected in the real world seemed scary and hurtful, and my courage and confidence soon started to fade away. The real world quickly opened my eyes to such a brutal reality: I was stripped of everything I once had.

If I ever had fun, my mind constantly whispered evil things to me, "You don't deserve that joy and need to save your energy to work." I feared stating my opinion because I was often quick to be corrected or jokingly laughed at. I had no self-esteem. I feared being something and someone totally new. Fear of more attention, fear of failure, and the fear of not making the most of what God had done for me were just a few of the thoughts entangled in my mind. Even the silliest fears will turn to monsters in our mind if we just let them sit there, untouched, without using courage to be acted upon.

I realized that I had been sitting on an egg for way too long, being thankful for where I was but letting complacency turn into a deadly idleness.

Transitions in post-stroke life continued to be a little more of a struggle than I wanted to admit. At first, I was always living on edge with constant fear of a surprise or some unexpected stimulus after such drastic changes in the past couple years. Things I had dreamed of suddenly seemed to drown me because of the way I was processing new information with a victim mentality. Since everything was so new, I never encountered many triggers that called for me to remember my past. After living with my parents, then getting married, then moving cities, then states, and then diving right into the lifestyle of ranching, it was hard to find that segue that my memory needed to be myself again. I was often too overstimulated by things I could have chosen to do to help me, so I chose to separate myself and remain on that stupid island of isolation for a long time.

When I felt attacked, I wanted isolation because that meant no one could reach me to poke at me. I didn't know that when your heart is beating so fast and you can't go to sleep or think clearly about anything, it is called anxiety. I never thought that would happen to me, but I didn't know. This state of mind kept chipping away at my confidence, and it was hard for me to be so transparently different in marriage.

I was too ashamed to let the truth bubble up so it could be handled properly. I had no connections to the old Mal because I couldn't find her in any part of this newness. Nothing I did anymore had any connection to my past, except reading the Bible and running. But I didn't even read the Bible the same. I read it in order to reassure feelings that were in my mind already, feeding self-righteousness rather than being open to accepting His grace and newness that could and would sustain me. I wasn't willing to accept the correction from His Word. But the book of Isaiah reads, "I will lead the blind by ways they have not known, along unfamiliar paths I will guide them; I will turn the darkness into light before them and make the rough places smooth. These are the things I will do; I will not forsake them" (42:16). Labeling a lot of my newness as loneliness inspired me to seek God in more specific ways and to establish a loving and safe culture in our home.

At first, I didn't realize that I could grow into my new normals *with* Jesus; He *was* still there even when I felt so forsaken. Everything *can* exist in perfect harmony and union through Him. Because I have been so one-track minded since my stroke, with severe tunnel vision, I always seem to choose to dive into the task directly before me instead of first asking Jesus for His help. I couldn't feel Jesus in the ways I used to, but I couldn't comprehend jumping back into life without Him either. I longed for Him. I needed Him. Although He lives in heaven, where we all want to be, He is alive and active all around us here on earth too. We just need the right perspective to see; ranching has sharpened my vision through a spiritual lens so powerfully.

During our time in New Mexico, while Tyler was working, I heard a baby lamb near our house. I went looking for it, and my heart sank when I came across the precious straggler. Its umbilical cord was still attached, and its feeble body was so skinny and weak as it called out for help with all its might. It was guarded and hesitant at first when I came near but easily gave in as I came a little closer. I scooped it up and held it close in my arms as we walked around a little while, gradually quieting its cry. As the desire to hold and comfort it continued to build, I knew I needed to let it be with its own and near its mom. I wanted to trust the momma to take care of it and nurture it back to health.

The book of Isaiah appeared in reality before me as I tried to feel with God's heart. I tried to imagine how He sees us, His dainty little sheep, trying to make it down here.

"He tends His flock like a shepherd: He gathers the lambs in His arms and carries them close to His heart; He gently leads those that have young" (40:11).

I couldn't help but empathize with this little guy, feeling isolated and different, really discouraged. In our Christian walks, we may often feel feeble and weak, just like this wounded lamb, with snowballs of discouragement hitting us from every angle as we grow more and more disconnected from the body. As self-sufficient as we may think we are, we *need* the body. We *need* spiritual nourishment. We *need* family. We *need* love. Jesus shares His body, His flock, and His light with us so graciously.

In the early fall of 2015, my family's dog, Jeter, had three yellow Lab puppies. Homes were immediately found for two of them, but we had a harder time giving the last one away. "Hondo" slowly turned into Tyler's buddy, and we loved to take him for walks on the LCU campus as he got older. We even took him to the gym with us while Tyler was shooting. He was a little angel pup, but we had no idea the extent to which he would be used.

I had never been accused of being an animal person before Hondo. It wasn't that I didn't like animals, but I had never given them priority in the midst of my busy schedule before. However, Hondo sure touched my heart unlike any other four-legged creature. He was a loyal companion from the beginning, helping Tyler through the struggles of the horrific storm of my injury and also helping me get through a tough season of work and loneliness in Fort Worth. During the chaos of my brain bleed, Tyler enjoyed spending time at my parents' house with Hondo to escape the attention in a safe place together. They had a bond unlike any other dog and owner relationship I had ever seen. Hondo listened to Tyler more so than any other person and obeyed his commands with a sense of urgency and respect.

Hondo was a super pup, keeping up with every step of a five-mile run or faithfully lying on the floor all day while I worked on my computer in a tiny apartment. After moving to the ranch, he quickly found his role there too. He loved to chase the feed truck for miles and jumped with excitement at the click of Tyler's gun, knowing he was about to have fun on a hunt. When he got bit tragically by a rattlesnake, it absolutely tore us up to watch his condition worsen before the event took his life shortly after.

Crying from losing Hondo helped toxins escape from Tyler and me that we didn't even know were bottled inside of us still. It was like that layer of glaze that secretly secured broken feelings from the past had been popped by an unavoidably sharp needle. That garbage had to escape somehow.

It reminded me of a time at the ranch when I stepped on a big spider that got in the house, and its babies ran out everywhere. I became queasy watching them crawl away, frantically. When Hondo had to leave us, it was like all of those toxic feelings that had been tucked away through a marathon of storms crept up again in order to really be oozed out for good, just like those nasty spiders.

Hondo was like a scapegoat for our emotions. In the Jewish culture, a scapegoat was sent into the wilderness to carry away all of the sins of the people laid upon it. Oddly enough, losing sweet Hondo helped me to visualize him carrying away all of the hurt from the past seasons so we could try to put a staple on it. He helped me visualize how the scars of the past were healing, as God was opening a new chapter right before us. That little dude was sure special, and we loved him so much. It was so fun to watch how he enjoyed living on a ranch, and we will forever miss his faithful obedience and snuggles.

As sad as it was for Tyler and I to lose our buddy, it was also a victory of closure from certain monsters: loneliness, sadness, marriage confusion, and a numb soul. Things bubbled up that I had forgotten were tucked in there.

I was bubbly and thankful before, during, and a little while after November 10, 2015. Then, for a while, I felt numb to any sort of emotion, both good and bad. I was so constantly overstimulated that I didn't even know what a peaceful mind was anymore. Losing our little buddy, Hondo, the sweetest yellow Lab in the world, was honestly the first time I had felt in a long, long time. God used that pup in special ways that I had never experienced through an animal.

After such drastic lows coupled with dramatic highs, I forgot what it was like to truly feel again; I was too scared to. Being normal felt awkward. Being sad felt wrong. Being happy felt guilty. If I felt good, it was because I was just in neutral, too guarded to really care about anything. I feared some confusing stimulus might pop up out of nowhere and knock me off my rocker with uncertainty. Through such an overwhelming flood of emotions—tragedy, triumph, healing, marriage, transition to a new season and lifestyle, family deaths, family victories—losing Hondo so tragically was another new journey for Tyler and me. Hondo was a sweet sense of peace and connection for us, something for both of us to love in a lighthearted and unifying way. Getting to experience his loss together answered an unspoken prayer that God was opening our eyes to.

In the following weeks, Tyler and I learned that we had to choose to address things in order to defeat them. We can do anything we put our minds to if we ask the Lord for His help. Acknowledging that we need Jesus every second to make it instilled a "more of Him, less of me" attitude of humility that connected Tyler and me. Processing this grew a bond we were both passionate about, and we realized that we wanted a baby!

In the midst of my lingering storm to my health, I had been trying to take care of myself like my momma had always taken care of me. I was Mal on the inside, but I was having an out-of-body experience learning how to go through the stages of development again. I wanted out, but I didn't quite know how to go about that. I started to find purpose in trying to nurture my dormant self in the midst of my inner being.

As our marriage began to grow, I slowly started to connect my struggles to the possibility of a new purpose. I felt as if my inward battles were equipping me with a hunger to take care of another human being, if God chose to bless us with that. That hope gave me so much joy, and we both realized that was our unified passion.

Living on the ranch continued to magnify the spiritual lens we tried to see through. I continued trying to pour my energy and efforts into making a home because that was always a safe place of rest and escape. In addition, anytime I was around Tyler, my family, or our church body, I felt like I was able to recalibrate; I felt like

God was giving me a whole new perspective and ability to process oncoming stimuli with a tangible sense of foundation and memory. I went to town regularly, but doing so made for an hour round trip, and I was scared a headache might attack when I was away from my safe place to rest. I always craved that sweet state of peace and rest, and Tyler and I were committed to establishing home together.

"And after the fire came a gentle whisper" (1 Kings 19:12). God is in the peaceful and still, and we wanted Him under our roof. We wanted family, with Him as the head. I walked into this new spiritual momentum by quitting my job and committing to finishing my latest blog.

THE DRIVE TO
BE A LIGHT

Since we live by the Spirit, let us keep in step with the Spirit.
—GALATIANS 5:25

I found that practicing His teaching and love helps us to heal and grow; it also leads us to be fruitful to others. Gaining momentum in my faith walk continued to fuel the desire of putting His voice to action by writing. I was stirred to find a new way how, and He so graciously answered through His presence in the Word. He goes before us and is always near with His Spirit in our hearts.

The longing I had for His spiritual filling would not stop growing. After several transitions of moving, from my parents' home to different locations for Tyler's school and job, I found comfort in seeking God in new ways. This helped me grow so much, and I learned that *choosing* to see Him beside us defeats loneliness.

Choosing to seek His presence beside me, wherever I was, also continued to bring clarity to what I felt like was my purpose. I'm a little bit reluctant to say it took literal *years* before the courage bubbled up to truly put the desire of the deepest part of my heart and spirit to action, but the impossible task of writing a book continued to inch its way in from the back burner of my mind. As the blog posts turned into novels when I was bouncing around different coffee shops for work, I could tell God was on to something new in me.

I often replayed the wise words of my childhood preacher, Dale Mannon, who said, "We may not understand the command until after we've obeyed it." Sometimes we might *know* the command; that thought that won't go away, that thought we try to keep putting off because "No way ... surely not, God ... not me, not right now ..." But we may not find understanding or purpose in a task until *after* the obedience is complete.

What may seem like blind obedience takes a whole lot of courage, but the Lord longs to gloss our efforts of grit and faith with His encouragement and provision. And He never, ever fails. We will *never* understand the Lord or His ways, but if we don't open our minds and give ourselves some room to make mistakes, we will live in turmoil forever. We will never reap if we never sow.

"The servant who knows the master's will and does not get ready or does not do what the master wants will be beaten with many blows. But the one who does not know and does things deserving punishment will be beaten with few blows. From everyone who has been given much, much will be demanded; and from the one who has been entrusted with much, much more will be asked" (Luke 12:47–48).

After almost three years, the puzzle piece in my mind labeled "old ways" started to creep into the game. *Finally.* This helped me to have a backbone of information to draw from rather than being so overstimulated with new situations, most of what was humiliating through marriage. As frustrating as it was at first to process such a dramatic change and tragedy through marriage, I became motivated in a special way that was greater than myself to fight through this new lifestyle; God was so gracious to give me the gift of a husband. But through such a rough time, I couldn't even dare grasp the magnitude of the gift of Tyler.

From my perspective, marriage didn't really feel like a gift at the start. All I felt was embarrassment and shame, trying to do things I had always imagined but failing endlessly, right under a microscope it seemed. I felt as if our marriage had spiritual forces acting against it, and I tried to cling to the truth. I kept trying to be the housewife and cook I had always looked forward to being someday in a home, carrying on the culture of how I was raised so richly. But instead of focusing on Tyler's love, I was focusing on my failures. I was consumed with worldly humility, or embarrassment, rather than the spiritual humility that brings freedom.

But without Tyler, I probably would've sailed on a boat of false contentment and complacency, living for myself; I don't dare want to think about its destination. "Christ's love compels us," and so did Tyler's (2 Corinthians 5:14). His love compelled me to try things that I never thought possible. It was just as much frustrating as romantic because I felt so vulnerable to fall short right in front of him again and again. But that man is sure special, and growing *with* him helped me crawl out of the slimy pit I had slid into. I chose to trust that every ounce of our purpose must be by faith and would be tangible in the end.

My story felt like it had been bottled up for so long, unsure of how to handle it in marriage. But actually, I didn't know it was still *being written* through marriage. I could feel the change inside of me, but I wasn't sure how much of my crazy I ought to unleash in front of the man I loved. So many new normals made me a little confused, and I had no concept of a discerning filter to decipher what was going on. I was scared. I sought peace, desperately.

I had always been a Christian, and it had always been easy. I had never viewed God's way as the hard way; it had always been the way I would have chosen anyway. Walking through marriage with a brain injury really stretched me. I was confused, lost, and felt vulnerable for a long time. Everything was stripped away when I once had everything to give. I was embarrassed. But I felt so incredibly blessed and highly favored to be married to truly one of the greatest men

God created. Faith continued to compel each of us to try to attain what we felt was the best version of ourselves.

Previously, I had been trying to worship God through obedience during the silence I felt I was experiencing from Him. In doing so, He continued placing unfamiliar doors on my path that brought opportunities for me. I continued working my job remotely, using the Wi-Fi connection at home until Tyler came by for lunch. Then, I typically went into town, bouncing around to different coffee shops for a place to settle and finish my hours for my job. I felt connected to Christ through different people I got to encounter, and I received so much encouragement through those relationships and conversations. I knew God was working, as I couldn't ignore my urge to keep writing. After trying to switch windows on my computer to work for my job and on my blog simultaneously, I couldn't take it anymore. I wanted to be all in for Him and spread His message through a measly little book.

A book? How could I *write* a book without even liking to read myself? But I felt that my soul couldn't rest until I did. I had to write one big thank-you note to God for His glory and honor and hope that, by a miracle, He would help and guide me to the place I yearned for but wasn't sure of.

For a time, because I was exhausted from attention, I became selfish with the energy I did have. But "the more you pour, the more it flows," and a new sense of momentum slapped me with a realization of how tired I was of hiding my light. What a waste of a miracle if I was not courageous enough to share it and give it to God without fear of vulnerability.

Hesitance can hold people back for days, years, or a lifetime. That small voice that continually second-guesses any good thing is *not* the voice of truth. There is not a formula to perfectly solve the equation for a clear, crisp answer for what our every move should be, but as God's children, we are called to be obedient to His Spirit and His Word. I continually learned that if I did things when *I* felt like it, I wouldn't be able to get out of bed in the morning. But with

Christ, it feels good to run without chains. I realized that I had been asking and searching for so long that I had forgotten how to receive. Receiving takes intentional action, and I had to learn how to listen. Soon after this realization, I quit my job with PTT and continued adding on to the book. I was so thankful for PTT for taking a chance on me and providing me with a job that gave Tyler and me such a gracious start to our life together; I was so grateful to God for His creative, divine provisions. I wanted to receive His message fruitfully by spreading His good news, and I knew I had to get to work.

He continually motivates me to keep going with every act of obedience as His Spirit leads me. With His Spirit in our hearts, we ought to always recognize what is right and true when we hear His voice.

And when we hear His command, we've just gotta do it. We've gotta silence the nonsense of timid thoughts. We've gotta silence that stupid voice that brings hesitance and timidity. We've gotta take the risks and dive in. Idleness is *deadly*. As Christians, we all have to be ready to be leaders, and I am thankful that I married one. Both God and Tyler convict me to live with boldness every day. There are not many people going through the narrow gate, so most likely our ways will be, or should be, different from the world (Matthew 7:14). But we must stay motivated to do His will. How do we know what His will is? We must take hold of Jesus through baptism. We must be filled with and led by His Holy Spirit. It is essential to life, physically and eternally.

The book of John says, "Flesh gives birth to flesh, but the Spirit gives birth to spirit" (3:6). That is life. For most of us, this calls for a change, or maybe just a refocus; it might seem scary or fill us with timidity to think of living completely for the spiritual. But in the book of Psalms, God promises, "I will instruct you and teach you in the way you should go; I will counsel you with my loving eye on you" (Psalm 32:8). So, we can follow His ways and have confidence, trusting that He will always lead and provide.

But in the midst of my new sense of momentum, so many new stimuli had suddenly come into the picture through marriage, and I had no bank of experience to draw from. My recent past had been erased from my memory, and all I had confidence in was my childhood. All I felt was the heavy challenge that was for me; I didn't know this struggle was *actually* preparing me to live my dream better than anything else could have. All struggles lead us to our true purpose when we seek to intentionally conquer them *through the Lord*. As I had been trying to live with my spirit and stay caught up to the flood of opportunities and challenges around me, God's Word gave me comfort and stability, direction and peace.

In a devotional titled *Unbridled Freedom*, by Encounter, I was convicted with a reminder to "be pleased with what God gives and then give what pleases God." I finally realized that through my storm, God had set me on a big platform, and I'd be a coward fool to run away from that. A desire slowly grew inside of me to take hold of my story, as messy as it was, and run with it, seeking to give what pleased God and glorifying Him with it. Because of His conviction in me, I read the Bible now not just to be encouraged or to gloss my life but to seriously search for meaning and direction in life. God is *in* the Word, and He *is* the Word. I need and thirst for His presence every second.

I love how the Bible and all of its contents lead up to and point directly to Jesus. Christians ought to always strive to mirror His footsteps. I grew to admire biblical heroes like Esther, Ruth, and Mary as I studied their examples in the midst of my growth. What a blessing that would be to go back and talk with them; I am encouraged by their peace, pure hearts, gentle spirits, obedience, and examples. Thankfully, I have what seems like Bible characters in my own family, and I cling to the wisdom and examples of my parents, siblings, grandparents, cousins, and more with all my heart.

During our time in New Mexico, I heard a lesson at church one Sunday that completely changed my perspective in my relationship with the Lord. Our preacher explained a mindset I had never pondered before: our hearts can seek the Lord with a "so that" attitude or a "because" perspective.

"God, I will worship You *so that* you will bless me abundantly."

Or, "God, I love You with all my heart and want to live for You, *because* You are God. You are wonderful, mighty, loving, compassionate, powerful, and holy. You are God."

What a sweet little slap in the face. Why on earth is it so easy to act so ignorant to who God is and choose instead to idolize His powerful acts? He completely fills us because of who He is; His gracious and generous deeds are but a bonus to the reality of His existence. (OK, I'm convicted just to type these words.) We must let ourselves be convicted of where we truly are and trust God's response to our awareness and repentance. We must "be still and know" (Psalm 46:10).

I often recognized what a blessing it was to be continually surrounded by His people: church, family, Godly connections, and so on. But I also felt a lot of isolation in the midst of processing what I had lost. Through the falling of my inner spirit, self, and confidence, He brought about a sweet redemption story that fuels me to trust His Word. The words in 2 Corinthians read, "When I am weak, then I am strong" (12:10). I remained stubborn and determined to let God saturate His light on my struggles because I wanted to be strong through Him.

Psalm 16 says, "I will praise the Lord, Who counsels me; even at night my heart instructs me. I keep my eyes always on the Lord. With Him at my right hand, I will not be shaken. Therefore my heart is glad and my tongue rejoices; my body also will rest secure" (7–9). The same chapter later reads, "You make known to me the path of life; You will fill me with joy in Your presence, with eternal pleasures at Your right hand" (11). We can take this promise with us anywhere. *Anywhere.*

The sovereignty of God is a concept that ought to stop us right in our tracks. We have no need to comprehend it to believe it, and it requires no further explanation for us to be compelled to obey Him further. It ought to be completely understood that if the Creator provides another route of living or blatantly suggests another road for us to take, those under Him ought to roll with it with joy. Our plan B may actually be God's plan A, and what a joy to follow Him there.

We must readily surrender the stage to Him, always, but it took a lot of courage for me to pause the parade and ask to mourn for a second. For years, I wanted to stop that parade of my stroke journey to say, "It still hurts." The book of John records, "Jesus wept" (11:35). Though divine, Jesus experienced what it was like to be human, to feel emotion. He knew the sovereignty of God, and He knew the bigger picture. Yet He *chose* to relate and humble Himself in human form; He chose to empathize. Why? To *relate* with those He loves.

The nature of God can meet everyone's situation, everyone's love language. Choosing to tap into God's life source inside of us enables us to be well rounded and helps us to see from the higher ground He calls us to walk on. The book of John reads, "In Him was life, and that life was the light of all mankind. The light shines in the darkness, and the darkness has not overcome it" (1:4–5). God is holy, mighty, and good. He wants us to live fully and to walk in His light.

The book of John reads, "In the beginning was the Word, and the Word was with God, and the Word was God" (1:1). Just carrying our Bible around infuses His light around us because He *is* the Word. He is "a shield around [us]" (Psalm 3:3). I love to feel His presence in the Bible, getting spiritual nourishment every day, as my dad has always encouraged our family to do through his positive example and instruction. Dad never leaves home without his Bible.

Seeking God through His Word allows our minds to be strengthened by His spiritual power. We can always seek Him and find Him, which is the greatest gift in the world. But what if we truly saw God's face in the storms of life? Wouldn't we have so much confident faith instead of worry? The good news is, whether we acknowledge it or not, His presence is always with us because He loves us.

I am enlightened by the concept of the body, mind, and soul

working together to make a balanced being. When we are feeling low in one category, we can switch to another part of who we are. If our mind is entangled, we can enjoy the physical; if the physical is failing, we can get the mind right. Yet we are always full in the spiritual, with or without a pulse or consciousness, because the Holy Spirit is life giving. We can always fuel up with a quick dash or a full tank of spiritual nourishment to sustain us.

But in our physical state, we *will* have struggles. We *will* have setbacks. We *will* experience excruciating failure or complete plot twists. But with God, there is always hope. The book of Romans reads, "In all these things we are more than conquerors through Him who loved us" (8:37). God has already won, and He is so patient for us to find our place in His story.

In living this new life, when I started to gradually look as close as I could to a little more normal on the outside, there were still a lot of missing parts on the inside. The old Mal, of personality, likes, dislikes, and so on … on the inside was completely wounded, if not absent altogether. All I was able to do was try to mirror what I observed in the world of the people around me. Every time I got to be around my sweet family, I felt a little more whole, as the part of my mind that remembered who I was came on; I felt like less of a stranger in my own skin, and it was awesome every time.

I was reminded that, while searching for my new purpose, there were twenty years of living that didn't have to be flushed down the drain. Though once unattainable from memory loss, I was still that girl, just a new version. A refined version. As His Spirit, His Word, and His vessels continued to work on me, my blog broke the limit and had to be stamped with a new label. The book in your hands is proof that God is alive and active; He loves His creation deeply.

20

BEING H(h)IS BRIDE

I press on toward the goal to win the prize for which
God has called me heavenward in Christ Jesus.

—PHILIPPIANS 3:14

Due to the overstimulated factor, good, exciting, and positive things can be completely twisted into a heavy sense of anxiety or darkness if not processed properly, honoring the handicapped noggin. That is why the second I walked into the gym at LCU to take pictures after our team scavenger hunt, I was walking into my first experience with the devil. The enemy is so good at disguising himself as he constantly "prowls around like a roaring lion looking for someone to devour" (1 Peter 5:8). And he sure disguised himself really well that night when he started his attack on me.

In my case, a beautiful season of a marriage proposal, a wedding, and new lifestyle dynamics were so sneakily and ashamedly misprocessed as my life dreams began to strangle me. It's something I am very ashamed of, as the beauty and perfection of a fairy tale was distorted as evil in my mind.

This flooding factor in my brain, through what looked like the most perfect season, was so confusing. I went from just bopping up and down with my team and having fun, headed to take team pictures in my black dress, and then walked into a scene that I could have never expected.

The lights were off, music was playing, everyone was dressed up, and the gym was decorated with shimmering jewels and candles. The mood had changed from lighthearted to serious when Coach told me to step forward and walk first into the gym. My heart rate elevated a little, but I willingly followed her directions.

After going through the double doors to the gym, I was met by my brother; he led me toward a gorgeous scene. I was fixated on the familiarity and comfort that Peyton gave me as I kept greeting him and asking questions. As he continued to guide me, my eyes must have been as big as saucers as my overstimulated brain tried to soak in what was going on. But I could sense the sweetest beauty, thought, and love.

Everything seemed like a blur, connected together at ninety miles per hour, and I was too weak to understand anything. So, although such a magical scene, the weight of the event seemed to land on my shoulders, and I just wanted to crawl back home where I felt safe. I knew everything was good, as people were so giddy and smiley, but I couldn't quite latch on to that mood. I felt exposed, as my hair, dress, body, and everything about me was not really *me*.

My lack of understanding and preparation was overwhelming.

I fought myself over and over about feeling guilty about it, like it was all my fault for perceiving such a special, gorgeous, and well-planned event this way. I didn't mean to act as if I was throwing a tremendous miracle right back at God's face in rejection with a hard heart. But I later understood that those thoughts of guilt were not from God. My naïve mind was just really distorted after my stroke. That's the way it happened, and I didn't know why. I was so confused and lost while I felt that my foundation was being taken away, but I always tried to stay positive with a camera in my face and so many people around me. I had loved Tyler for a long time and knew I wanted to marry that man. But Satan's schemes were nailing me from every angle, and I had no clue what was going on in my heart or mind. This was definitely a moment of spiritual warfare that I had never experienced before.

I didn't know what to link such terrible feelings and struggles to: was it myself in my inherent introvert personality that was completely exposed, was it my brain deficits, or was it the multitude of drastic life changes and emotions all at once? I often replayed the conversation where one of my therapists casually explained a brain injury as a disease. I didn't know what that meant at the time, and I sure didn't know I had one or the severity of it. My family had always treated me like I was normal, and I believed it. But I had never been out of my comfort zone yet, as I lived under the safe bubble of what had always been home. But *disease* sounded believable now.

I had tried to be obedient to God, as I was in the phase of life that often called people to "leave your father and mother," with the honor of an incredible man wanting to marry me. In doing so, God literally provided every avenue of blessing, from the event planning, to a venue, to finances, to people, to ... you name it. God had truly opened the floodgates of heaven for us, as if He was saying, "Go, walk this padded red carpet I have laid out for you." My parents were absolute gypsies, as they seemed to master the game of Tetris with these blessings to make things work to bless Tyler and me.

But there was a spiritual battle going on. The blessings were perceived as negative because they were very overwhelming to me, and my brain was soon flooded by this good. I felt so guilty being caught in Satan's sticky web of tricks.

Satan ... was why I thought ants were running through my brain with so much going on at the proposal.

He was why I believed I shouldn't be walking down the aisle to get married.

He was why I thought of my fake hair, stupid brain, and multiple flaws as I walked down that aisle.

He was why I couldn't sleep at night, tossing and turning helplessly.

He was why I second-guessed trusting anyone.

He was why I looked inward when I was overwhelmed.
He was why I second-guessed things that were good.
He was why I struggled, desperately, through marriage.
He was why I wrestled with fear and timidity.

I honestly had never been so lost before and never had the *opportunity* to strengthen my faith muscles. I had always just been on cruise control with my faith. But through the storm, I craved the words of the Bible more than anything, being reminded that those instructions are not chains but rather insights on how to attain a rich, full life. The book of Psalms says, "As for God, His way is perfect: The Lord's word is flawless; He shields all who take refuge in Him" (18:30). God loves us a lot, and we can always live with confidence when we're being obedient to His presence through His Word.

I had tried so hard to just hang on during the journey as so many sweet souls kept popping up to help in some way. My mom is basically superwoman and did everything flawlessly … everything: planning, consoling me, driving me around everywhere, picking things out for me, and more. My mom has always poured out her heart and soul to others without end, especially to her babies. And I mean *without end.* It was all I could do just to try to keep up with saying thank you, not that she ever demanded it. But gratitude is a cornerstone quality of the Christian heritage of my family, and my mom, out of anyone, deserved every ounce of my attention and gratitude, which I felt was still not enough. All of my sweet family and precious friends helped in every possible way, and so many others offered services, time, deeds, talents, and more to allow a wedding to take place. It was absolutely the most generous outpouring of love, and I could never, ever, ever say thank you enough. God's generous provisions were another miracle and touch of His favor. *Anytime* He works on our behalf, it is a miracle.

In the midst of what seemed like such a quick, three-month parade from the proposal to the wedding, things that were lost or destroyed were quietly swept under the rug. I was never aware of my actual brain deficits until about a year after my brain bleed. The trauma of that event was never processed because a marriage was quickly celebrated. I didn't realize people's deeds were actually things I didn't know how to do for myself.

Things like open-ended decisions with multiple options were too overwhelming for me. I didn't realize this was a new weakness for me as well, so I tried to keep quiet about it. But weaknesses slapped me square in the face all at once as they became blatantly obvious to me through marriage.

After all of the attention and encouragement, I had started falling from God while trying to please people. I had great intentions but horribly wrong motives. And I got so lost. I developed a very guarded mentality and began living life like I was witnessing it, not engaging or really truly living because I was scared to. I was fearful to be fully submerged, so guarded because I didn't want to get hurt or deeply shocked about anything, good or bad. I was always wondering what I might be forgetting, so I just tiptoed around in fear with low expectations. I truly had a victim mentality rather than faithfully sowing, investing, and engaging with the Lord and His people.

I sought to find momentum in obedience to God through marriage as I grew to believe my new purpose could emerge from it. But it seemed like obstacles were waiting for me at every corner. At first, to leave my family (who I remembered most and felt safest with), to pause school (as I could only process to do one thing or the other: to be married or stay in school), to not become a physical therapist (I had chosen to follow Tyler's vision instead), and to construct a new and unplanned future (in a field I wasn't familiar with), I walked unknowingly with depression and timidity. It was confusing because it was actually the path to my dream—to live on a ranch and raise a family. But the path to get there often felt too hard. I wanted to give up multiple times.

The verse about living by faith and not by sight was made real because I couldn't *see* anything, which scared me (2 Corinthians

5:7). I was striving for independence in the real world but also trying to find a healthy sense of dependence as a wife. It was the scariest path and the greatest path. It was all faith; it was all Him.

I remember several conversations on dates with Tyler through this journey, specifically one where he asked me, "What would this Mal say to the old Mal (pre-AVM rupture)?"

I thought a second and said, "Remember all that you've believed in and tried to live out, the spiritual walk that has always been blessed and easy. Make sure you *really* live it when your course changes abruptly and all you see are dead ends, without your old skill set to navigate. Don't doubt the truth of God while relying on your own fleshly spirit. God is the same God forever, and you better still cling to Him confidently and literally."

What I was guarded from in the physical, I surely felt in the spiritual. My brokenness was vital to experience a humility that finally led to obedience and faith, and ultimately His power and divine intervention. God yearns deeply for us to look to Him, and when we do, He turns our tests into a testimony. I feel called to bring that battle to the light. God wins in every realm: spiritual, mental, physical ... He is always victorious and triumphant.

Forgive me, Lord. Thank You for loving us. Pursuing us. Molding us. Providing for us. Leading us. Oh Lord, thank You.

STEADFAST: FIXED IN DIRECTION; FIRM IN PURPOSE; UNWAVERING (COLLINS 2012)

"Do not fear, for I have redeemed you; I have summoned you by name; you are mine. When you pass through the waters, I will be with you; and when you pass through the rivers, they will not sweep over you. When you walk through the fire, you will not be burned; the flames will not set you ablaze. For I am the Lord your God, the Holy One of Israel, your Savior."

—ISAIAH 43:1–3

When a storm hits, it changes you. God intends for it to in the best way, or He wouldn't have allowed it. Romans promises that He is always working for our good (8:28), but it still may seem scary to embark on roads that you didn't see coming, without warning for preparation. But really, it's not scary once you recognize God in it and learn to accept His will.

Although storms may cause drastic pain in some ways, God enables His children to live abundantly with the new scars. "My scars for His glory," as said by Dale Mannon through one of his sermons. God provides an incredible sense of unity with Him and others when we recognize that His presence not only changes our life but empowers it. Though it takes a lifetime, we, as God's children, get to gradually and humbly learn our place in His story and be ready for whatever role He gives us. Every role is important.

Upon waking up from a brain injury, every day is new. I am constantly walking through the why and studying people's behavior and motives while trying to jump into this fast-paced world and catch up from lost time. In my early twenties, I experienced being a newborn again with the tender, loving, generous, compassionate care of my momma and dad after my stroke. As I continue to wake up, as it seems, I have mentally journeyed through every phase of growing up again. But, in a state of complete confusion and uncertainty to a new reality, I uncomfortably chose to...*live.*

Imagine being at what feels like the top of the mountain you had sought to climb for twenty years: gradually ascending so steadily through childhood, teenage years, and school years, excelling in most activities, gaining momentum to launch into the real world, lacking one last step to what I thought was my purpose and life story, and then being pushed down to not just the bottom of a mountain but even farther, the valley. Then, striving to climb up again, with every step being hindered by an ankle weight of unfamiliarity.

Surviving a stroke is not just surviving the incident; it comes with a responsibility to win a million other battles everyday to stay alive, unnoticed by most everyone. Striving to process this journey enlightened a new perspective in me of trying to see life through a spiritual lens; His presence brings so much encouragement and meaning to a situation. If God wanted to take me home to heaven, He had missed a pretty good opportunity in November of 2015. I guess He wanted to keep working on me during my short time on earth. So, I wanted to be obedient to His presence in my life, being "led by His Spirit" as my dad often says.

Thank You, Lord, for blessing us with the power of Your Holy Spirit.

I'm learning that *everyone* has a story or a burden to carry around; there's not one person who won't face adversity in life. I used to feel like that special someone who never had a big struggle and never would; I always just tried to live a Christian life the best I could, encouraging others through their shared struggles but never able to truly relate. However, there was a different story looming on the horizon.

Learning how to love myself again was a long and awkward process, but I grew to understand that coupling God's grace with a receptive heart is an empowering victory every time. It takes humility and wisdom to see riches in the simple, but God willingly helps our perspective grow to get there. John 10 says that Jesus has come that we may have life, the *fullest* life (10). God is always good.

Contentment in the quiet and simple often seems to be the richest life. In the waiting and the learning about God's character, we can't help but want to live in that fullness of life that the Bible talks about. When we are truly aware in the present moment, choosing to see the riches in it, God is very evident. Psalm 37 says, "Be still before the Lord and wait patiently for Him" (7). With a spiritual lens, the blessings seem overwhelming; it's all about perspective.

Lord, thank You for granting us unending blessings and making us so glad with the joy of Your presence (Psalm 21:6). May we remember to take hold of it, to take hold of You, Lord!

I didn't understand why Tyler loved me so much or even chose to marry me. But, as memories slowly started coming back, I wanted to choose to give myself grace, knowing that no one else would understand that fight. I had to choose to believe in God's patience to continue to finish His work in me while I tried to process and learn how to overflow to others, in His timing and ways. With my new and refined spiritual perspective, my whole world seemed to light up brighter than ever.

I didn't realize that loss of memory is kind of a big deal. At first, I thought it was silly and jokingly compared myself to Dory from *Finding Nemo*. But, in reality, I didn't realize I needed to mourn this complete loss of self. I didn't just have short-term memory loss; several years of my life were *gone*. It was like going to school without your books, taking a test without studying, or going to a job without getting dressed. I had to start everything again from scratch. But the love that our family was shown was almost unreal. The more I found out or remembered, the more inspired I became to finish the race.

Processing everything in retrospect makes it almost comical to recall my thoughts at certain times. Though I often felt so behind and hasty to complete what felt like an enormous, overwhelming puzzle of putting my life together again, I had to learn a new level of patience through healing, because those missing pieces of memory could only be resurrected in their own time. It's a weird feeling to have to do research on yourself: asking people what I was like, how things went, what happened, watching videos of myself from when I was completely unaware. Then, once on the other end of that awakening, it took courage to claim that person as me.

I often feel so silly and selfish labeling some things as challenging because I know all things are minor compared to what "should have been." I feel like I have to, and get to, roll through life using a wheelchair of faith: waiting for some memories to resurrect themselves, researching different parts of my old life, trying to label everything with meaning, and searching for God's purpose through it all. I feel so honored to have been given the miracle and sweet blessing of the willingness of others to push that wheelchair during my hospital stay and journey at home thereafter, encouraging me and loving me. Even in what felt like a valley, God, in some form, was still there.

For me, encouragement was appreciated but not believable until I actually *did* things for myself. The decision to get married kept me accountable to keep moving forward because it wasn't just myself I was living for. The journey of sensing God through relationships became more enticing than ever before. With God as the first strand of marriage, I learned that selflessness reaps greater benefits than tunnel vision, and submission becomes empowering.

During the time in Dallas for my treatment, while Papa was in the nursing home away from the rest of our family, the Christian statutes he had engrained in us all continued to infuse our minds as the Holy Spirit led the way. One of his favorite verses that encouraged him through every stage of his life-ending disease continues to provide a confident sense of God's presence for me every day: "Have I not commanded you? Be strong and courageous. Do not be afraid; do not be discouraged, for the Lord your God will be with you wherever you go" (Joshua 1:9). The Christian warriors in my family posed as such a great source of leadership, even on this new platform. As we all continued to fuel ourselves with spiritual nourishment, it was like nothing could defeat us because God was with us. Following in Papa and Nana's legacy undoubtedly kept us all alive and hopeful in what might otherwise have felt like a dreary hospital marathon. Christian family was everything, and through Tyler, I grew to believe in the blessing of establishing a new branch to that tree.

GRIT, MOTIVATION, FAITH

And now these three remain: faith, hope and
love. But the greatest of these is love.
—1 CORINTHIANS 13:13

In a culture of immediate satisfaction and gratification, it takes faith to think radically and patiently about our steadfast Creator. Why is it so hard to have patience in a greater plan while experiencing hardship following the Lord? I have to remind myself that God is big, and He is the one who performs crazy miracles. He is the one who graciously grants success. There is not a battle that He can't conquer, and all are important to Him.

Coach Gomez, the successful head coach for the Lubbock Christian University women's basketball team, winning three national championships, defined success as "doing the best you can with what you have right where you are." Doing our best is all one can do, while trusting God to do the big things.

As headstrong, stubborn, and independent as we may often want to be, God gives us opportunities to mess up big and not be ashamed. How can that be? Our weaknesses provide a beautiful platform for Him to perform. First Peter reads, "Humble yourselves, therefore, under God's mighty hand, that He may lift you up in due time" (5:6). *He* controls the outcome, and that ought to always bring confidence.

After my stroke, it took a long time to recognize that I must choose to give myself grace. Continual processing happens every day, and reality is often scary when new memories come. I felt like I was walking a tight rope with my confidence at times. Then, I learned how to fall into the pit of grace. During the times when I felt like I had lost everything, God's provisions seem even clearer in retrospect.

In the New Testament, God tells us that we reap what we sow. We must be *intentional* to sow.

"Do not be deceived: God cannot be mocked. A man reaps what he sows. Whoever sows to please their flesh, from the flesh will reap destruction; whoever sows to please the Spirit, from the Spirit will reap eternal life. Let us not become weary in doing good, for at the proper time we will reap a harvest if we do not give up" (Galatians 6:7–9). God calls us to sow in faith, generously.

It is safe to be fully engaged, with your whole heart, with the Lord. It's more dangerous not to be. We ought to always be aware of Him and the bountiful life He offers us by following His Word. We have the privilege to *always* seek God. His presence is there, but we must seek Him to find Him (Jeremiah 29:13). Seeing the world through a spiritual lens is helpful in staying in tune with Him.

Going into marriage with a brain injury was extremely challenging, something that I would never have envisioned being a reality for me. I (metaphorically) jumped off a cliff backward in full trust to try to obey the Lord in an act of submission, with little human understanding at the time. That trust was later attacked with doubt and hesitance during challenging seasons, but in retrospect, God's Word never wavered in the clarity of its promises.

Though it is inevitable for everyone to face challenges in life that constantly shape and refine us, I didn't expect to go through a big one during what everyone else seemed to call a honeymoon phase.

For me during this time, I was close to drowning in timidity, doubt, and minimal self-worth. I viewed any differences in Tyler and me as me just being lesser and wrong, still not there yet from my injury. I don't know what I was waiting on, but I was a fool for not having the courage to just take hold of the newness with confidence and passion. The new life I had been graciously allowed to live was and is my dream, and God has given me full abilities to live it to the fullest. I just didn't foresee the path it took to get there. If I had been fully conscious through most of it, I would've been too stubborn to let it happen I think. But God always works for our good.

In a lesson on humility and submission, our preacher, Dale Mannon, implied that we might not understand the command on our lives until after we have obeyed it. *What does that mean?* We must take the first step toward God while relying on Him to continually nurture that base of trust through our obedience. I find this to relate to my journey of marriage.

I knew that I loved Tyler, and my family did too; they supported us so generously. To have my parents' approval and blessing was a huge encouragement to me, especially when Satan attacked me with guilt for leaving my family.

At first, submission to Tyler was a robotic action produced by my fear of forgetting something. I was embarrassed to be caught off guard again, after being so empty-handed at a wedding proposal. I operated in survival mode, with a reptilian mindset; I had no sound logic. Everything I did at the beginning of our marriage was a mimic of what others had shown me because I didn't have a bank of experience (memory) to draw from to give me confidence. But I knew I loved Tyler. I did remember him, our inside jokes, and our chemistry. I had simply been too overwhelmed to acknowledge a lot of things regarding just us.

It was weird because although I didn't remember, I just *knew* when it came to Tyler. I just did things, whatever popped into my head, because I loved him. But doing so for so long made my heart and mind feel numb, as I was only following my to-do lists so cautiously, embarrassed to forget anything. A lot of the things I did felt Spirit led, but I could never understand the big picture. It is amazing to reflect on the power of Jesus in our marriage cord of three strands.

Thank You, thank You, thank You, Lord, for stripping and emptying me in order to fill me anew, showing so much favor to even a stubborn child like me.

The wisdom of God says, "There is no fear in love. But perfect love drives out fear, because fear has to do with punishment. The one who fears is not made perfect in love" (1 John 4:18). As I continued to grow in Tyler's love that mimicked the Father's, my fears and doubts became silent. God molded a deep desire in my heart to serve and complement Tyler the best I could, without fear of him judging or analyzing my deficits. Though I felt they were so obvious, he always reassured me there was not a trace of a flaw that he noticed.

The things I mentally struggle with are invisible to most. With a brain injury, I process information differently. No one else may understand, and they don't have to. But God is a gracious God and knows our hearts. He always knows, even if He is the only one who understands. Marriage helps me daily to realize the power of God's truth in the Bible; getting to rest in the comfort of His love is a beautiful thing and forever reassuring.

I started feeling more confident whenever I was able to start linking things with my old self to how life is now, post-stroke and post-marriage, and finding similarities. Things like plot twists, changes of plans, corrections, discipline, and so on remind me that I am human and don't have to have life figured out; *no one* knows all the answers. I remind myself that those things are normal and not just because of my brain injury. It has given me spiritual and mental momentum to try to link both lives together. Though this puzzle has been a booger, I have silently sought the Lord to remind me who I am. He is always listening and watching over His children.

Sometimes, too, it's OK to not be able to figure things out. The book of Psalms reads, "I do not concern myself with great matters or

things too wonderful for me. But I have calmed and quieted myself,
I am like a weaned child with its mother; like a weaned child I am
content" (131:1–2). Such still seasons present good opportunity to
build the base required for a steadfast nature of contentment and
trust. I think of an object being placed in a concentrated, violent
environment—like a huge, solid rock in the ocean during a time of
hard waves. As the crest of each wave tries to tackle the rock, the
wave is deflected, and it crawls down the height of the rock, which
remains immovable and steadfast.

I also think of a time in middle school when I attended a morning
devotional with the Fellowship of Christian Athletes group (FCA). A
preacher came to speak and showed us an example with a big glass
jar. In this jar, he was trying to fit five golf balls and a bag of sand.
If the sand was put in first, the golf balls wouldn't all fit. But if the
golf balls were placed in the jar first, the sand was able to disperse
through all of the extra empty space and fill the jar with the ability
to securely close the lid.

The golf balls represent living for the spiritual. If our priorities
(golf balls) are solid, steadfast, and engrained in the truth, being
lived in intentional prioritization, all of the overflow (sand) is able
to complement them fully. Such extra blessings are like a sparkling
coat from God on everything we do.

For a long while in my post-stroke recovery phase, in constant
fear of forgetting things, I kept trying to fill my jar full with sand.
I was struggling to close the lid and gain satisfaction because I was
anxiously trying to fill my jar without discernment. My golf balls
and sand filling were so off, and it was such a sad and empty way to
live. I had no backbone of who I was; it was as if I was living life as
a human doing, not a human being.

It wasn't until God led me to complete satisfaction exactly
where I was, in the new, that I was able to see Him more clearly.
It takes time for stuff to digest and process, in faith, every day.
We must be intentional to willingly take that extra step to look to
Him. Thankfully, His kindness, mercies, and compassions never

fail. They are new every morning! *Great is Your faithfulness, Lord* (Lamentations 3:23).

Humble pie doesn't ever taste good. But the nutritional value far outweighs the yummy stuff. God calls us to be humble, and He is sure creative in how He helps us to attain this state. When God strips us to a state of humility, we can still be confident if we are following His lead. His ways are beyond comprehension, and He always has good in store; we can trust in His promises and unchanging nature forever.

God's Word is so true, and every single part of it is holy. It is truly the power that sustains us. The book of Proverbs says, "Every word of God is flawless; He is a shield to those who take refuge in Him" (30:5). The Bible is a precious tool from God, something that is holy and tangible at the same time. We ought to seek to make our lives mirror the Gospel as a whole rather than trying to justify random verses to specific situations. Tyler teaches me this profoundly.

Prior to my stroke, I had always read the Bible to find encouragement and to affirm the actions I had already chosen for my life. God later transformed that encouragement from His Word into a strong desire to be obedient, putting that nourishment into practice in a more literal way. It had always been so easy and natural before; now, I often battle self-pleasing desires that stand in opposition to God's will with every step. But being a Christian calls us to die to self and to live *fully* for Him. The book of Matthew states, "For whoever wants to save their life will lose it, but whoever loses their life for me will find it" (16:25). God's grace saturates our every effort to gain spiritual momentum. There is so much freedom, hope, and promise in Christ. We don't have to understand it because we probably won't. But we can still trust that where God guides, He provides. Literally. Truly. Fully. And richly.

When Christ is in us, having the Holy Spirit in our hearts through baptism, we can always tap into His presence. With the ability to literally carry the Almighty God in our hearts, we can truly do anything. It's easier to be courageous and have peace when we aren't relying on ourselves; looking inward is selfish and foolish, but it always seems to be a first instinct in our fleshly nature. But God graciously allows that occasional slice of humble pie we may consume to digest into a little reminder that we need Him for literally everything. Plans do not exist without Him.

The book of James reads, "Instead, [we] ought to say, 'If it is the Lord's will, we will live and do this or that'" (4:15). He is in charge, always. As my dad always says, "Lord willin'!"

There is a time and season for everything: sadness, joy, grief, love, enlightenment, excitement, and so on. I've learned it is *essential* to tap into the spiritual realm and climb that ladder to be in His presence so that we may triumph over the brokenness in this world. I realized that sometimes being sad means I am really choosing to not tap into that fount of joy that He has placed in my heart, delivered directly from Him for my enjoyment and hope. We don't have to be miserable in longing for Him because He wants to satisfy us during our time on earth too, until we meet in heaven. He is our faithful and trustworthy Companion.

23

THE JOURNEY TO
OVERCOME

*So in everything, do to others what you would have them do
to you, for this sums up the Law and the Prophets.*
—MATTHEW 7:12

One of my favorite and most fitting descriptions of my dad is him helping me train in track. During meets, I always wanted him to be at the start of the last hundred meters from the finish line. His voice yelling, "Come on, Mal!" in that last stretch is a scene that always gets me going when motivation seems to slip through the cracks.

My life had always been so good and easy and abundant, making me so very naïve about the reality the devil. But while we are living in this world, we are in Satan's kingdom. The book of 1 John says, "We know that we are children of God, and that the whole world is under the control of the evil one" (5:19). I guess I must have always skipped over the part about the evil one because I hadn't met him yet. I had always just enjoyed the abundance of the Lord's rich blessings on my life. But that passage continues to read, "We know also that the Son of God has come and has given us understanding, so that we may know him who is true ... He is the true God and eternal life"

(20). My whole life, I'd skipped right over the meaning of that gift, thinking it sounded cool, but just saving that thought for later on because I was enjoying this earthly life plenty. But there comes a time in everyone's life where faith gets tested, and I grew to believe that an eternity with Jesus is the most desirable destination. With Christ, each test can be better labeled as a "refining moment" because He is sure to work it out for our good through His love and faithfulness.

For a while, I thought Christians ought to be shown special protection and mercies in life. I thought, *Why would God let anything bad happen to His people since He has full control of the whole world?* But I had never met Satan before, and he is very real. I was so confused with the despair I was experiencing upon my first encounter with the evil one.

After realizing the agony of what my family went through and the pain that my body went through regarding my stroke, my approach to life became pretty passive and absorptive as the hard truth gradually seeped in to my understanding; I sometimes felt like a witness to life rather than a character in it. It's like I had to catch up with the world by observing details, processing the why of the actions of others, while trying to gain confidence to try out a certain calling of my own. After living what I feel like was the most blessed and full life with family, friends, and an absolute abundance of everything, and then trying to find and chase new dreams, foolishly seeking to be the director and pioneer of my life before being humbly redirected, my approach to my new life became more cautious and hesitant. But seeking to live fully takes a lot of courage and growth and may mean taking risks and struggling some.

Since my brain injury, I have often tried to escape my thoughts by going walking or running, and I am so very thankful to have the outlet of physical abilities. Often when I thought I was processing things by letting my brain chatter to itself, I was really just slamming into the same glass door a million and one times, not getting anywhere. But I was trying to let myself believe and process what had just happened.

As hasty as I became to recover, I felt guilty complaining about anything because, literally, God had already conquered every battle and made everything good. *Why was accepting it the hard part?* But pairing so many options of opportunities and blessings with my new difficulties, I became overwhelmed. After fall upon fall, I was graciously humbled to be so richly content in the back seat, quietly praying for the discernment on how to handle the blessings along the way. My thick skull sure needed to be chiseled through a long time ago.

The hurt I felt through my own storm was not visible from the outside. I cowardly feared correction and wrongdoing a lot, scarred from the discipline of some. I kept trying to dilute this monster in my mind because everything truly was good from an outside perspective. But a completely new and implausible story was emerging on the inside, and it took a lot of courage and patience to let God write it. In the waiting, I had to let myself embrace the transformation of such a new self being brought forth through the rubble.

When approached by others throughout my journey, I said, "It's all good," for a long time; I was a coward who did not want to acknowledge such drastic changes in my life. I constantly searched to process and understand things before I made any action to step forward with courage. While most people measure reaction time in seconds, I have to measure mine in years. But as I yearn to measure time with God's watch, I am comforted remembering this: "Do not forget this one thing, dear friends: With the Lord a day is like a thousand years, and a thousand years are like a day" (2 Peter 3:8). He is always, always present.

Some of the unforeseen struggles from my angle seem so silly and foolish in retrospect. I used to view every day as a gut check, measuring myself by what I could remember and accomplish. Things I was supposed to get done independently would cause fear due to my lack of confidence in my memory. So, I would try to get everything done before I forgot it and/or hit a wall of a big headache, which I always feared was near. Because I was so obsessed with writing every task down in order to get it done before I forgot it, I showed zero flexibility or patience toward others and myself. I soon found myself forgetting how to just be. But there is power in the stillness and quiet; being still before the Lord is awe-inspiring, exciting, and truly sacred.

Trying to find my new self seemed to take longer than solving a Where's Waldo picture. I was so desperate and selfish trying to search so hard for the purpose in this new life that I often found myself blinded to the blessings lying directly in front of me. I had been blinded to my selfish ways, not knowing what I was missing. I couldn't seem to get motivated for anything except for defeating the monster in my mind the way *I* was led by God to. I wanted to conquer and overcome, but I was growing impatient and weary dealing with the people swarming my path. Through this spiritual search, I was convicted that if I couldn't even handle what I thought were small tasks with wisdom and discernment, then how on earth could I be trusted by God with anything bigger? In the waiting, I needed to be getting ready, working on my heart, rather than trying to understand God's plans. He is too great for me to grasp.

He graciously taught me that I am not the creator or director or leader; that is the Lord. I am simply a quiet observer now, truly finding joy and fulfillment in watching the success of others and graciously sharing in that, with a thankfulness to take part in any of it. God is so good, and reflecting on Him for a second ought to always grow a deeper love for Him. *Thank You, Lord, for shining meaning on every situation for us. Thank You, Lord, for eyes to see and a spirit to feel Your presence.*

Though walking in faith, I kept trying to find the missing puzzle piece that made me feel like myself again. I knew there was a missing link that I needed to figure out in this journey, but I didn't know what in the world it was. I didn't realize that I needed to put the pieces together of life before and life now, post stroke, to truly feel like my full self again. I didn't want to go back and process that actual change that had happened inside of me. Having to mentally remember the loss of self I had experienced didn't seem enticing at all, but it was definitely selfish of me to keep tucking away that silly monster. I didn't want to put on that cold, damp wetsuit that was saturated with the real truth, so I left it hanging up for a long while in the closet of my mind. But that wasn't fair to any of my loved ones who all still treated me with absolute generosity and love, consistent throughout my entire life. While I could function perfectly normal in the physical realm, my mind was still hung up and guarded to a lot of things.

As I became more aware of and sensitive to my errors, I felt like I had to monitor myself so closely and intentionally in order to live without embarrassment. It felt like there was a small child inside of me who needed a lot of care, and I had to slowly learn how to nurture my own needs. I had lost my person, but God was continually reminding me I didn't need to worry about the lost pieces. He was waiting for me in the new, and He felt tangible through Tyler.

Amidst this journey, I was convicted by a podcast by Steven Furtick, when he emphasized the point that the more we pour by being generous, selfless, and thinking outwardly in life, the more we're filled. Of course, motives for pouring ought to not be for selfish gain, but we can be encouraged to sow in faithfulness with confidence to reap richly in God's plan. Instead of searching so hard to be filled, we can be encouraged to pour instead; it is God who fills us in His own design. I found this to be true in marriage.

Being married meant to completely die to my plans and envisioned future that I thought I had always wanted. It was hard to do that in my fleshly, selfish state. I've always been one-track minded, but that quality became even more amplified with my brain injury. Mentally, I can't process two things at once; once my mind is set on something, I want to be committed and all in on that one thing.

That is why my dream of marriage was just as hard as it was fulfilling. Through a long process of discipline, pruning, and correction, I feel as if God was showing me what I *actually* wanted. To think my hard heart almost missed the opportunity to take His highway because of my own timidity scares me. That long, windy, confusing path was actually Him calling me out upon the waters of my dreams. Once I realized the mirroring of God's redemption on our marriage, I was more confident in God's presence and Him leading me through my hero of a husband. In my relationship with Tyler, I can't be halfway in. In my relationship with God, I can't be lukewarm either.

I was hesitant to get married because I knew I wasn't myself yet. I loved Tyler so much but just didn't have the self-worth to think I should be able to do something that amazing; I surely didn't deserve that honor of being a wife, *Tyler's* wife. Everyone was encouraging me that I could, but I knew I wasn't there yet; I didn't really know how to get there or where there was. Something was missing, a lot of things were missing, in my memory. Though things were all looking great from the outside, it was just happening so fast, and I didn't feel like there was any escape to normalcy or stabilization.

It was definitely selfish of me to not try to overcome even when I felt I was at my lowest and that nothing good would come. It wasn't fair to the hero who married me and proved he would love me in any state. Goodness, he's such a patient faith giant. I didn't feel deserving of that love, so I didn't accept it or let it fill me, like it could have from the very start. So in this most beautiful season, Satan was still trying to get me through little things, stealing my joy and peace and making me feel overwhelmed in the midst of a dream.

It wasn't until my mind started rolling in the ability to link my current self to the person I used to be before my brain bleed that I started gaining some confidence and spiritual momentum. I realized this new life may be a continual journey of trial and error, struggle and growth. Sounds like my old life was too, but isn't everyone's? Remembering previous life changes helped me to find encouragement that I am *normal*, whatever that means.

As my dad has always encouraged and practiced, I tried to fill my mind with good things: talking to myself instead of listening to myself. In 2 Corinthians, the Bible tells us to "take captive every thought to make it obedient to Christ" (10:5). So, just because we have a thought doesn't mean we have to think it. The mind is a powerful thing, and we must choose to intentionally dwell on the positive. Such spiritual nourishment was truly my fuel, and I needed it desperately to even think about accomplishing anything.

Graduating from college was definitely not easy for me, like I had envisioned it would be. Because of my parents' support, instruction, and encouragement, excelling in school had always come naturally to me and was something I took pride in. However, right as I thought I was near the finish line of what I thought could be labeled as my final academic accomplishment, I tripped so hard in the mess of unforeseen hardship. Without encouragement and my parents' generosity in paving the way for me to graduate college, I would not have finished. Also, being married to Tyler gave me a new sense of accountability because I didn't want him to have to change his plans while waiting on me to finish. The love, patience, generosity, and encouragement that was shown me by countless angels on the journey to finish school is what I take from that degree, and I feel strongly inspired by the education I was given through that road of perseverance.

I am sure thankful for that piece of paper that so many dear souls helped me to attain, and I didn't want to just sit on it. I wanted to be fruitful. Through silence and listening, God taught me patience and trust in new ways. I wanted to truly know what God's ways were and then seek to follow them with all my heart. I meditated on the book of Psalms that declared truth on my life before it was even created: "[His] eyes saw my unformed body; all the days ordained for me were written in [His] book before one of them came to be" (139:16). I was fueled to press on to know Him and fully take hold of His ways. I wanted to put a degree of love and generosity to practice; *that* is what inspired me to wake up in the mornings and live. I wanted to put *radical* faith to action and remember I was not supposed to be so cautious. God has calmly made the passions of my heart so clear to me; it just took a long time for me to be still so I could listen.

My parents', siblings', and extended family's support and involvement in every stage of my life, from birth to school to marriage to graduation and forever, reflects an embodiment of Christ and Christian living, and that is the education that reigns in my heart. I am forever inspired and driven by my family; God is love.

I am continually reminded what a tremendous blessing it was that my papa had led and established such a powerful family legacy, truly a Christian dynasty. If we are to "be fruitful and multiply," as God implied after creation in Genesis 1, then following closely to his legacy seemed very wise. Papa was a preacher, and my nana was a teacher, raising children and working in the home. As I continue to cling to this heritage as I try to walk in new ways, I am comforted to find rest and peace in their examples.

Really none of my life plans have made it to existence, and I am grateful for that. I wasn't going to go to LCU, play volleyball, or stay in Lubbock for college. But I wanted to end up back in the Lubbock area eventually and be near family. Of course, His plans truly are higher and greater than anything the human mind can understand. God is so incredibly good, holy, and mighty. In retrospect, those minor life adjustments were truly God giving me opportunities to put coins in the jar of trust and obedience that I may be allowed to cash in someday. Remembering His tender mercies on our lives all along the way were such sweet reminders of how His plans will always trump ours, and we ought to rejoice in that. God is so good.

Thank You so much, Lord, for never giving up on me. God, remind me who I am.

24

DON'T GIVE UP, LOOK UP

*The Lord is my strength and my shield; my heart
trusts in Him, and He helps me.*

—PSALM 28:7

God works through the broken and the whole. God works through the sinners and the righteous. God works through the weak and the strong. The whole Bible is full of testimonies that explain how God works even in the details of our lives to lead us to the fulfillment of His ultimate plan. There is *always* a greater plan behind everything as a Christian because God is *always* working for our good; He promises that clearly in Romans (8:28).

In the story of Ruth, God's providence is at work through every scene. Naomi, the mother-in-law of Ruth, is inspired to bring fruition through a tragedy. After losing her husband and two sons, Naomi remained motivated to follow God and restore her family, even as a bitter widow. Ruth, the Moabite daughter-in-law to Naomi, brings her healing by the boldness and loyalty she displays in following her to Israel. She tells Naomi, "Where you go I will go, and where you stay I will stay. Your people will be my people and your God my God" (Ruth 1:16). This journey to Israel led Ruth to meet a man named Boaz, who was working in the field and was full of generosity and grit. This Israelite farmer served as a family redeemer by marrying Ruth shortly after. Boaz called Ruth a woman of noble character and was inspired to step in as a husband to love both her and Naomi. His integrity paired with Ruth's boldness is such an act of faithfulness and love contributing to Naomi's redemption from hardship, mirroring the heart of the Father. Boaz was the grandfather of Jesse, who was the father of David, and, most importantly, in the family line of Jesus.

God's will permeates steadily through the book of Ruth, although He is never actually mentioned by name. God's sovereignty continually saturates light on our stories, too, as He intertwines His divine plan together with ours in unimaginable ways; His presence is even loud in silence. God can use the faithful obedience of His people to bring about redemptive stories, and the story told in Ruth is just one of many examples in the Bible. What may seem like hardship and discipline may actually be a pure expression of love from the Father. He is even present in the mundane and simple, but it can also take a tragedy to get our attention.

Convicted by His presence, Tyler and I continue to strive to be intentional in remembering Him as our first and most important cord in the powerful Christian bond of our relationship. Taking my first real step of faith, on my own doing, was awesome and scary. I didn't realize I had always walked in the shadow of the legacy set before me, and my faith felt more physical than spiritual. Trying to process and figure out the miracle I was blessed with left me feeling empty and miserable. *Why?* Because with real faith, we *can't* solve for x; we just have to trust in God. There is *no way* to comprehend the Lord, and I was trying too hard to figure everything out. My conclusion of that windy trail led me to believe that God calls us to a simple life of peace and praise. Though we can't understand Him, we can still trust Him. He always takes care of His sheep. Tyler reminds me of that promise every day with his quiet and bold way of living and working with his hands. His hands provide, protect, and love even when I can't see.

Upon realization that I had severe memory loss coupled with residual damage from a brain injury, I felt bitterly robbed. I found it miserable to walk in such a tunnel vision state of confusion, searching endlessly for an answer with all of my resources stripped from me. All resources except for my Bible. In Ecclesiastes, Solomon often states, "Everything is meaningless" (1:2). He describes wisdom, pleasures, folly, toil, oppression, advancement, and riches all as meaningless.

As humans, it's weird to think that we are more than our brain because our brain seems like the main thing about us. But it's not! Freedom and life are found by tapping into our spirit, the *Holy Spirit*, which completely trumps our "meaningless" wisdom and understanding. God, in all of His splendor, is forever on the throne. We don't have to sweat the small stuff anymore.

But trying to make it in the real world after being afflicted with a brain injury was a drastic transition for me, and I often felt worse the more I tried to figure things out. My brain didn't work the same way it used to; I couldn't even trust myself with the smallest tasks because my memory and focus seemed to burn out faster than I could complete anything. I have never found comfort in viewing things so meaningless, but Ecclesiastes provides a unique perspective that sets a Christian mind at ease in an unusual way with the power of confident surrender. This type of meaningless seems to be a result of a spirit of humility and confidence in a greater hope.

In the midst of this battle of my mind and spirit, I continued to struggle in striving to conquer. I remained very rigid because I would never let myself adjust to even the slightest change of plans. My brain had already worked so hard to create, remember, and act upon whatever list I had already created to do that day. I would often get so discouraged when my plan of action didn't take place after all of that work toward the mental preparation.

My head down, determined personality was beneficial when I

was a provider for that short season for my husband and me. I felt so very weak and discouraged trying to do this but tried to trust God by supporting my husband with everything I had. With my love language being acts of service, I tried to love God and my husband through obedience to their leadership. Tyler has always been the visionary for us, and our trust in God and each other has grown so much through this practice.

In retrospect, while Tyler was in school, I once felt guilty for what I thought was selfishness that I displayed. Because I was the provider for a time, this meant doing anything that didn't contribute to working or retaining my energy so that I could work was not permitted. I had become so accustomed to not wanting to let myself waste any energy to fill my cup or have fun because I feared I wouldn't have anything left to make it through the day to do my job and provide for us. I felt like I was walking on a tightrope to make it through a whole day, trying not to fall down into the lion's den when I crashed and hit a wall of frustration and loneliness.

Tyler had been working in school with a passion stronger than anything he had ever portrayed before academically; the way he studied, read, researched, and learned was truly incredible. I often wallowed in loneliness while he was away working, but now I reflect, gratefully, on how amazing it is to know of God's presence intervening through what had felt like darkness. Even though He was carrying us, I was so blind to His presence for a time, much like the poem "Footprints in the Sand." God had helped us through it, and I am joyfully grateful to look on that season in retrospect. God calls us to live in full surrender and promises to take care of us. The cord of three strands in marriage is truly a miracle when He is number one.

> See, I set before you today life and prosperity, death
> and destruction. For I command you today to love
> the Lord your God, to walk in obedience to Him,
> and to keep His commands, decrees, and laws;

then you will live and increase, and the Lord your
God will bless you in the land you are entering to
possess ... This day I call the heavens and the earth
as witnesses against you that I have set before you
life and death, blessings and curses. Now choose
life, so that you and your children may live and that
you may love the Lord your God, listen to His voice,
and hold fast to Him. For the Lord is your life, and
He will give you many years in the land He swore
to give to your fathers, Abraham, Isaac, and Jacob.
(Deuteronomy 30:15–16, 19–20)

Every day, I'm convicted and inspired by the blessings through
the lineage in my family. My relationship with my dad has blessed
my marriage. My dad radiates positivity with the most pure heart
and soul; he makes being a Christian literally contagious. We have
the greatest relationship, and he has always provided for, cared for,
and nurtured me as if I was the only human who mattered in the
world. But He gives everyone that feeling through his empowering
encouragement. It's amazing what you can do when someone
confidently believes in you.

My dad's love has bubbled over to give me an incredible sense
of worth as a wife. Honestly, all of the males in my life have had
a tremendous and powerful impact on how I see the Lord and
thus live my life. My grandpas, uncles, coaches, professors, and
all who I see as male father figures have all been incredible men of
faith who nurture my vision of our heavenly Father. Not everyone
experiences His goodness in those specific ways, and I can't even
describe the magnitude of that fruitful blessing. I believe in the
power of generational blessings and curses, and we must choose to
be intentional in focusing on the blessing.

I feel empowered by such a rich generational blessing of the
Father's provisions, specifically by having had the opportunity to
work for the company of which my dad is a part owner. This helped

Tyler and me to get through Tyler's additional school needed for him to be a rancher and start a life of our own. I enjoy with all my heart any opportunity to do a little ranchin' with my husband, and I know this joy stems from the base of love I have received from my dad every day of my life. Now, I want to work for my heavenly Father, seeking to do His work and being led by His Spirit.

After searching for a specific job title for what seemed like so long, I remembered that, first, I am a Christian. Being a Christian means wearing many hats, often a new one every day. In whatever it is I'm able to do with the opportunities, connections, and circumstances given, I want it to be fully for Him. Our Christian title will always weigh more than anything else, and my parents exemplify this with the life of service they willingly perform on a daily basis. I feel like I have the gracious honor of carrying their generational blessing with me every day, and I am inspired to be fruitful with that. In regard to sharpening those around us, Paul says in Colossians, "To this end I strenuously contend with all the energy Christ so powerfully works in me" (1:29). Though the path may not be easy, we can always trust that He will lead us to exactly where He has designed for us to be.

Steven Furtick once made the analogy comparing God to a teacher: a teacher is silent during an exam, much like God may seem silent during our hardest trials. But He tenderly promises in Psalms that "even there [His] hand will guide me, [His] right hand will hold me fast" (139:10). We don't have to understand what God is doing in order to trust Him. He forever owns the stage of our lives, and it takes patience to wait for the punch line to finally convict us with the reality of His sovereignty.

Sometimes the discipline that quietness requires may seem even harder than the storm, but we can endure because we have hope. We have no idea what God can do with our trials and no idea what He can create with our junk. We never will on this side of heaven. It may not be until hundreds of years later when the clarity comes, but our faith can remain confident and strong because of God's promises and steadfast nature. Striving to see with a spiritual lens enables us to sense God confidently and consistently, in everything.

In light of my spiritual walk and trying to begin a new life, I felt accountable to God to simply trust and obey. The Bible was and is my life manual. While I seek to pursue courage, timidity is often in accompaniment. But the book of Zechariah challenges us not to despise such small beginnings because God can do a lot with even the tiniest acts of obedience (4:10). Fueled by this truth, I chose to walk in faith even if that meant I had to grit my teeth for a while. While continuing to process the meaning of my struggle and chase triumph, a spiritual lens continued to bring me clarity; processing life in this way is crucial to my joy.

It is a journey of discernment to be able to find the good in everything. In light of this truth, I truly feel like God had sheltered me from what may have looked like a tragic catastrophe by giving me a gift of memory loss. After the marathon of regaining consciousness, understanding, and memory, I came to recognize that God chose to give me immensely more than what I finally remembered I had lost. Being so naïve to the severity of the tragedy that happened to me was merely an act of love from the Father. My father-in-law often describes God as kind, which is so true.

Getting to stop working gave me so much relief. What I had worked for was to put Tyler in a position to be the provider, and I was so grateful our sacrifices and hard work had paid off in a sense that I got to stay home and finally allow myself to heal on the inside. God had blessed us tremendously, and I was so thankful to finally be able to process things without as much pressure. That pressure had been building up for what seemed like far too long, but I knew it was creating who I was meant to be as I learned to trust the process of enduring.

Life is a marathon. To chase triumph is to chase the Father; to chase the Father is to chase triumph. I enjoy chasing Him through obedience. Obedience is a controllable when lots of things are not. Within our mess, God is harder to see, feel, and experience, yet He is truly the only tangible escape route. It takes patience and perseverance to seek Him, and it is a lifelong journey. But if our vertical relationship toward heavenly realms is good, all of the lateral stuff takes care of itself.

At our wedding, I was so nervous and scared to walk down the aisle, but I found purpose in seeking to be obedient to God and Tyler. In my mind, instead of experiencing any sort of romantic excitement, I was just being passed from one caregiver to the next and thought, *So Tyler is gonna take care of me now.* Mentally, I was still walking through my childhood years. With big eyes, I clung to my dad's arm, where I knew I was always safe, really hesitant to let go and start something new.

The ceremony continued smoothly, and we were so honored that our professor and dear friend, Andy Laughlin, conducted everything flawlessly.

But despite the absolute flood of blessings, encouragement, and help from my sweet momma, family, friends, and others, there was no shot of me feeling any kind of beautiful. I felt like I was dressed up for Halloween with fake hair glued to my head, and I couldn't wait to get out of my costume. I had always been confident before with the all-natural look, using minimal effort on anything extra for myself. But this time, I just tried to go with all of the fakeness while everything was happening so fast.

After the ceremony, the celebrating took place. Whenever Tyler and I were called to go out on the dance floor, the song "YMCA" was playing, and it took everything I had not to start crying. I felt like a bug being burned under a magnifying glass, more vulnerable and miserable than ever. I tried to be engaged and focused with each person asking for my attention through conversation and picture taking, wanting them to feel appreciated and important. But this drained me to no end, and there was nothing left of me before long. I was unsure of who all was there because I didn't have the chance to go talk to the people I wanted to. With big eyes, I tried to keep up but had no backbone; I was lacking the discernment and mental preparation to know how to handle the situation.

After finally getting the courage to pull myself off of what felt like the stickiest glue, people who felt like piranhas nipping at my heels to take pictures, my sister and I went to the dance floor for just one song. We enjoyed that fun and silly sister moment until I was commanded to hurry and change to leave immediately after it was over.

I felt safe getting to go with Tyler but knew I was so undeserving of his love. But every second I am with him, he makes me believe otherwise. We were thankful for all of the love shown us through such an extravagant ceremony, and I clung to the hope that all would continue to work out for the best in this leap of faith.

I am so thankful to relive this special moment through the DVD recording because I was so lost during this time; I had to learn how to reprocess this situation. I often envisioned scenes where I felt completely probed and prodded, and it hurt to remember how certain people made my heart pound in my chest like that. Of course, everyone was full of an outpouring of love, but I couldn't help the reality of my inward struggle or try to hide it any longer. I was different and had to practice giving myself grace by starting afresh with people I had labeled in my mind as either safe or dangerous, due to how they made my head feel.

Tyler's and my relationship was different and difficult to pick up after all we had been through, but God really does make beauty from ashes. My memory loss, self-doubt, and lack of confidence had hit me like a plague, but I knew that Tyler was my significant other. Trust was all we could do as we endured the hardships that rained on our stubborn love for each other. Each of our competitive natures as college athletes was used to better each other because of an unquenched sense of wanting to finish the race, together. God's favor and love sustained us faithfully through the storm.

God has since replaced Satan's grip on our marriage with gentle whispers of purity. With a beautiful ring on my finger and my hand in Tyler's, God has made marriage my safe place because God is our Rock. It took what felt like a long time, *years*, for this good thing to spring up. But now I feel the words describing the year of the Lord's favor in Isaiah 61 come to life: "The Spirit of the Sovereign Lord is on me, because the Lord has anointed me to proclaim good news to the poor … to proclaim the year of the Lord's favor … to comfort all who mourn, and provide for those who grieve in Zion- to bestow on them a crown of beauty instead of ashes, the oil of joy instead of mourning, and a garment of praise instead of a spirit of despair. They will be called oaks of righteousness, a planting of the Lord for the display of His splendor" (1–3). I had to trust that something might would grow in our marriage if we were doing things for His glory.

But for our marriage, there wasn't much of a history to draw from at first, except for the recent past following November 10, 2015. When Tyler had come to Dallas for my recovery journey, I remember being so giggly and excited when he came to visit me in therapy. I knew him and loved him; I felt safe with him when he came to visit. For someone to sacrifice his life with all of his pursued endeavors to fight for me like Tyler did, it didn't matter how much I remembered from before or understood. I wanted to follow and obey him and resurrect this new love, despite the voices of doubt in my head caused by my lack of memory. I was everything *but* worthy, but we were both committed to forever before we even realized it.

Tyler and I had become close one summer at church camp and were both raised in church, always having been Christians. But the journey of our relationship became a new testimony for both of us. Tyler's faith had been tested the hardest *through* me, yet he had chosen to fight this battle *for* me. I hadn't even started my own faith battle yet but felt like it also came through Tyler in a way. Once I came to the conclusion of how our marriage was a mirror of the story of Jesus, I found hope and purpose. Jesus felt tangible again, and my faith became less foggy.

25

Included here is a chapter from Kathy Crockett's
"Courageous Men of Faith" series

WITH GOD ALL THINGS ARE POSSIBLE

MARRAY MADDOX AND TYLER ROGERS

Marray

It was a normal day for us. Malori had a game that Tuesday night, so we were sorting through when we needed to leave. Maci was supposed to stay with a friend (since it would be a late school night) but that friend had gotten sick, so we were bringing her along for the ride. I picked her up early from school, got Sarah from work, and got on the road around 2:30. We got to Wichita Falls, TX a few hours later - about half an hour before the game.

One of the cool things I got to do was help the team warm up by shagging balls while they served balls over the net. Typically, the dads retrieve loose balls while the girls serve, but I made sure I gave Malori hers when she got up to the line to warm up. Everything seemed fine. She looked great, said she felt great. She looked relaxed but was obviously focused. This was one of her last games before the conference tournament, and as a senior that meant that this was one of her last games period. It was shaping up to be a good one.

Tyler

Since I was on the Lubbock Christian University basketball team, I had practice and couldn't make it to the volleyball games that night. I planned on hooking up my computer to the TV so I could livestream the end of it once practice got out. Everything was looking great. It was Mal's and my senior year and both of our seasons were looking good. They were about to get into their big end of year tournament, and our team was looking good for the start of season.

We got out of practice and I set up the TV. I had this big order of wings that I couldn't wait to dig into when I got a call. It was Mal's little sister Maci. I picked up.

"Hey, something is wrong with Mal," she said.

I didn't think too much of it. I figured she might have rolled an ankle or messed up her knee or something. You know, like a normal athletic injury. But Maci sounded scared – like real scared. I must have been on speaker phone or something because when I asked if I needed to come up there, it was not Maci but Mal's mom Sarah who spoke.

"Yes, you need to get up here,"

That's when I knew that this was the real deal.

Marray

The game started just fine. Malori served and went through a whole rotation before there was any indication of a problem. A ball got hit to Malori's right, and she didn't make a play for it. That was unusual. Malori was never one to ever give up on a play. She rotated out, and Coach Lawrence motioned Sarah and me over to the bench.

"Does Malori have a history of migraines or anything like that?" she asked.

I glanced at Sarah who had her brow furrowed.

"No," I answered hesitantly, "Not that I know of,"

"Alright, thank you," she said, and went back to coaching.

We returned to the stands. Our first thought at that point was that her headache was related to finals stress or something like that. The end of semester for a student athlete is hectic to say the least, so it would have been no surprise for all of that to have caused a headache. A few minutes was all it took for us to realize that it was more than just stress causing problems.

Typically, the girls stand at the end of the bench and encourage those on the court when they are rotated out of a game. Malori was not standing with her teammates but sitting down.

Coach Lawrence motioned for us again. We all came down this time; Maci too. When I got to where Malori was sitting, she turned to me.

"Dad, I can't see out of my right eye, my head is killing me."

We stood her up and walked her to the locker room. We figured we would get her off her feet and try to assess what was going on. After a few steps, Malori spoke again.

"Dad, I can't see, it's killing me."

I turned to Sarah, and she said out loud exactly what I was thinking.

"We need to get her to the emergency room."

I nodded.

"Let me go get the car and pull it around so you don't have to walk," I said.

I ran out and got our Tahoe. I pulled around to the locker room, parked it, and jumped out, not so much in a panic at this point but definitely anxious. As I was running to the locker room doors, the soccer coach (Doug Elder) from Midwestern crossed my path and asked what was happening.

"Hey, if you're going to the emergency room, don't take her to the big hospital. It'll take too long, and we can get you an escort to the smaller one. I took one of our soccer players last week and they got to see her very quickly." We didn't know at the time how vitally important it was for us to go to this small rural hospital. That's where the neurosurgeon was actually waiting for us. Thank you, LORD.

I just kind of blinked at him, speechless for a moment.

"Thank you; thank you so much," I managed, before taking off to the locker room doors.

As I began to get Malori the associate athletic director (Kyle Williams) was carrying Malori outside. She couldn't walk anymore for some reason. With his help, we managed to get her into the car. Sarah jumped in the front passenger seat, and Maci got in the back bucket seat beside Malori. A campus security guard pulled up in front of us in an old, two-door, brown Chevy pickup with a portable flashing light on top and led us out hurriedly toward Kell West Hospital.

Soon after we got in the car, Malori started throwing up and passed out. Sarah threw off her seatbelt and jumped into the back seat to support her. Malori's body was rigid, there was vomit everywhere, and Sarah was telling me we needed to go faster. All I could do was follow the security guard and hope we made it in time. We began praying in desperation as we were rushing as fast as we could to get medical care at the Emergency room. It seemed to take a long time to get there but was less than 10 minutes.

Tyler

I'm freaking out a little bit at this point. I had picked up on the urgency and panic in the phone call but knew absolutely nothing about what was going on. Naturally, my mind went to the worst possible things. I called Coach Duncan, my coach, and did my best to explain.

"Hey, something's wrong with Malori and I need to go to Wichita Falls right now. I don't know if I'll be back tomorrow for practice or what, but I have to go."

"What happened?" he asked.

"I, I don't really know, they didn't tell me. I just know I have to get down there."

"Alright," he said, "have you told your parents?"

"They're going too. I'm going to meet them there."

"Look, just meet up with them in Plainview. It's on the way, they can drive you there. You're not really in a state to be driving right now."

"Coach no disrespect but…" I started but he interrupted.

"Promise me you'll meet up with them."

"Yeah, yeah you're right. I will." I agreed.

I was frustrated, but I did as he asked.

On my way to Plainview I remember trying to pray. I knew it was something I needed to be doing, and I really wanted to, but the whole ordeal had me frantic and I couldn't focus enough to get the words out. I calmed down enough to call my cousin Aaron. He's more like a brother than a cousin. We've always been really close, and he had the sense to be worried about my well-being as well as the situation with Mal. He was able to pray too, so he did, and I drove. After all that though, I think he could tell I was still in freak out mode, so he ended up calling more than once during the drive to check on me. It's good he did, too.

During one of those calls he asked me how fast I was going. I was in Mal's little car and had flipped the cruise control on when I'd gotten out of town. I looked down to see that I had set it at 105mph. That surprised me; I didn't think you could do that, but I had, and I was flying. I was flying, but it didn't seem fast enough.

Marray

We got to the ER and Malori was completely stiff in her seat. There was a nurse waiting for us in the parking lot with a wheelchair. I know someone had called ahead for us, but when I picked up Malori to put her in the wheelchair, she couldn't stay positioned in the chair. She was too stiff. We didn't have time, so I just carried her inside to the treatment table. The nurses there began cutting off her jersey and peppering us with questions about her current health and medical history. Malori was in the best shape of her life and very healthy. She didn't drink cokes, she ate healthy foods, there was nothing I could think of that might be the cause of something like this. The ER doctors decided that a CT scan would best determine what was going on and quickly took Malori back to get checked out.

All I could do at this point was pray, and all I could think to pray was, "Please Lord, save our daughter."

In all this rush, I distinctly remember a small, older woman coming up to us and saying, "Everything is going to be okay, trust me on this." I didn't think much of it at the time, but it stands out now. She was an outlier staff member in the small waiting room, an island of unjustified calm in the middle of this mess.

The results of the CT scan came through after a few minutes. It seemed out of nowhere, a neurosurgeon (Dr. Kameth) came in to talk to Sarah and me. "The CT scan found that your daughter has a terminal bleed in her brain. If we are going to have a chance to save her life, we're going to have to attempt to perform surgery right now." We sat in silent shock as he continued, "She has no time to be sent to Dallas or even be transported to the larger hospital across town; she has approximately 15 minutes to live. We have to take her to surgery immediately to even have a chance of her survival."

We didn't even need to discuss before answering, "Do whatever you need to do to save our daughter."

He nodded. "I can't make any promises on the outcome," he said, "but we'll do what we can." All we were thinking was please save her LORD. We knew she was in HIS hands and we needed a miracle for her life to be saved.

Tyler

I reached Plainview and met up with my parents. As we were getting in the car, the weight of the situation fell on me, and I just kind of lost it. I was holding a water bottle, and I threw it as hard as I could in a fit of rage. I was frustrated and confused and angry and about 15 other things I couldn't identify in the moment. But mostly, I was helpless.

You must understand, that's not a feeling I'm used to. I was a college athlete in the best shape of my life. I weighed 210 lbs. without an ounce of body fat on me. I was about to graduate college and go live my life. If I needed something done, I would get it done. For all intents and purposes, I was a grown man. And I was <u>in love</u> with this girl. I had plans in the works to ask her parents if I could propose to her, and now, I don't even know if she's going to make it through the day. It was too much to process all at once, and I had finally reached a breaking point. For about 30 seconds or so I just exploded.

And then my parents were there. They just came over and hugged me and held me there. I felt like a kid again; I felt so small. But I was so happy that I had parents that would do that for me.

After I had calmed down a bit, we got in the car and headed to Wichita Falls. We were getting updates on surgery and word of what was going on there as well as questions from people who didn't know what was going on but figured that we did. I had to put my phone away because it was all just too much. I barely knew what was going on, and I certainly didn't have the words right then to tell them. For some reason, I still had my wings with me. They had made the trip from Lubbock to Plainview in one piece and somehow made it with me into the car. I think I had taken one bite from one wing and that was it. My mom asked where I got them and suggested I should eat but I had no appetite.

My uncle Ken Stephenson is an orthopedic surgeon so we would funnel information we got to him for an explanation that we could understand. That helped us get a grasp on more of what was going on. He doesn't tend to sugarcoat things, so most of what he said was scary to hear. It made the drive to Wichita Falls seem endless.

I passed some of the time planning how I was going to get through the hospital. I was thinking it was a big place. I mean when you think brain surgery you'd naturally think of a big hospital. So, I was going to have to find the right entrance, find out where she is, and all that. When we got there, I thought we had stopped at a school. Honestly, the place looked like a small West Texas elementary school.

All I could think was, "Really? This is the place you sent her to get brain surgery? Come on, you've got to be kidding me." I didn't know all of the circumstances up to that point yet, and even if I had, I would not likely have seen God at work in that moment.

Marray

In just a matter of minutes, an operating room staff member brought us Malori's ponytail minutes after the surgery started. To perform the craniotomy, half her head had to be shaved so that the doctors could remove part of her skull. They gave us the ponytail in a large Ziploc bag as it could be the last thing we had left from Malori. It was a sincere but sobering gesture. I found it amazing that neither of us panicked in that moment. Amazingly GOD gave us his spirit of trust in Him at that moment. We just prayed. We prayed for healing, for God to be with the doctors, and for the safety of our daughter. Specifically, I remember praying that I would get the chance to walk hand in hand out of the hospital with Malori.

We started updating with numerous calls and texts to family and friends, praying the whole time. Before I knew it, the small waiting room was full of people. Coach Lawrence and the LCU volleyball team had shown up, and most of their families had come over from the game as well. I called our son, Peyton, and explained the seriousness and urgency to drive there that night. He was playing baseball at the time at Southwestern Oklahoma State in Weatherford, Oklahoma. He left the grocery store and grabbed a few things from his apartment and rushed to begin the two-and-a-half-hour drive to Wichita Falls. Everyone we knew we asked to be praying that night, everyone. All of us in the waiting room were praying. Heads were bowed quietly, small groups whispered together, read scripture, and at times the whole room would join hands in powerful group prayer. The word had spread to Lubbock and beyond, and prayers were being offered on Malori's behalf from thousands of people around the world. We knew, we all knew, that only the power of God could give Malori a chance that night, and so we prayed as fervently and faithfully as we possibly could.

Tyler

I could see the foyer, which doubled as the waiting room, through the sliding doors. It was packed with people, all praying. That should have been a welcome sight, but it scared me. It really brought everything to life; it made it real and gave all my fears serious legitimacy. There wasn't a situation I had been in before that had merited this much prayer, and there was a heaviness to the place, an absolute weight in the air. I immediately realized something about myself in that moment – the crisis made me want to be alone. I was immensely grateful for all the people there and what they were doing, but I wanted to turn and run somewhere that I could be by myself.

Luckily, the first person I ran into was Mal's mom, Sarah. She came over and hugged me and checked on me. I was stunned. It was her daughter that was in there; by all rights she should be the one being comforted. And yet, here she was with me. I'm sure I looked like a mess: pale, shaky, scared – I know I felt like that at least. She noticed that, I think, and was strong enough for both of us in that moment.

We all sat down in a side room for a bit, but it was all too much. As I said before, I needed to be alone. So, I left and went outside by myself. I paced around the tiny, empty parking lot until I finally lost it. I broke down and started crying. All of the things that I had blown up about before hit me again, just differently. Mal was super healthy, she ran all the time, she ate well, never drank cokes. Why her? And why here, in this tiny hospital? None of it made sense, and once again, I could do nothing about it.

The helplessness was the worst. I wanted to be Mal's protector, a man that her family could trust to take care of her. And what could I do? Nothing. Literally nothing, at least by myself.

I kind of got myself composed and stood back up. I turned to walk back to the building and saw my mom disappear back inside. She had seen me walk out and followed but stayed back and let me work it out by myself. I was blessed by mothers through this, both Sarah and my mom Kelli. The strength of these women is enormous, and I thank God that they were there for me in this situation.

I got back in the building and everything just blurred together – time, faces, events. The next thing I really remember clearly was when Marray was about to start a prayer chain. I was standing in a side hallway on the verge of another breakdown. The helpless feelings had returned, and the mass of people wasn't helping. A nurse saw me and figured out what was going on. She let me go sit down in one of the rooms branching off the hallway, away from everyone.

At some point during the blur, I had ended up with Malori's bible. Looking for the comfort of familiarity, I turned to one of my favorite stories from the Old Testament. Saul's son Jonathan and his armor bearer were going up to fight the Philistines, just the two of them. Jonathan decided to use the Philistines' reactions to the pair to gauge whether they should fight or not, and basically if the Philistines asked for a fight then God was with the pair and they would win. It's a great story, but I wasn't really there for the story, more for the comfort of God's word and something else to focus on. Besides, the premise and outcome were counter to the position I was in. I had no Philistines to fight, there were no bad guys that needed vanquishing; all I could do was wait. I wasn't exactly reading, I knew the story pretty well after all, but as I was looking at it, something jumped out at me that hadn't before. After Jonathan explained his plan to the armor bearer, the unnamed man just said, "I am with you heart and soul." And that hit me. Hard. My continuous prayer changed, and it was one of the hardest prayers I've ever had to offer.

"God, I know you may not save Mal. I know that. But even if You don't, I am still going to serve You and love You. I am with You heart and soul."

"I am with You heart and soul."

I do not wish a situation like this on anyone, but at the same time to be forced to see, or rather to be allowed to see, the absolute power of relying on God is life changing. A situation like this, where there is nothing, literally nothing, one can do but desperately rely on their faith... I would not want to do it again, but I am eternally grateful for it.

Soon after my little revelation, my family came into the little room. I heard them come in but stayed bowed over the little chair that I'd been kneeling next to the whole time. I felt a massive hand come to rest on my back and immediately knew my grandad had joined my parents. His hands are carpenter's hands, tough and scarred, bruised and broken, and awash in memories. But that's Granpa D. He's a rock star, and one of the best men to ever walk this earth. His presence growing up was a major reason that I was in this room with a bible in the first place. Easily one of the toughest and yet most touching moments from my younger life was seeing him turn to the Word during hardship. I had seen him once before crying quietly at something he had read, much the same as I was doing. Now the tables were turned, and I was suffering bowed above the Word. In the midst of all my pain and confusion, he knew just what to do. He simply leaned down and said,

"I love ya, and I want you to never forget how you are feeling right now."

None of the correlation between where I was at that point and what I had seen him doing hit me until later. I was following in the footsteps of the men whose ideals I had seen played out before in my life. The exemplary Christian men in my life prepared me to face this hardship. My dad and grandad's influence were present in me and showed itself in these moments of pain. Having my grandad tell me as much in that room was both comforting and reaffirming in equal parts.

We rejoined the rest of the group to wait and pray.

Marray

After they took Malori back, we were stuck in a limbo of sorts. Updates would come via nurses every 15-30 minutes. Always, the nurse said the same thing:

"She's holding her own," she'd say, "She's doing fine, still holding her own."

Those words were so encouraging. Holding her own meant she was still alive and that's what mattered. I knew I needed to stay positive, as a husband and a dad. I needed my family to be able to find solace in me, so I did what I could to stay encouraging. I trusted God and knew He was in control, but I never wanted to accept that she wouldn't make it. We remained confident in trusting in God and His healing hand. We knew of the miracle of the timing of this life-threatening event that just happened to Malori. She was in the best possible place she could be at the time. Thank you, Lord.

Eventually, the nurse emerged with a different message.

"Dr. Kamath has finished surgery. He wants to talk to the family about what we need to do next." We all took a sigh of relief and were thankful that she made it through this life saving surgery.

Tyler

Once the surgery finished, a nurse came out and asked to see the family. I was just kind of hanging back, I was only the boyfriend after all, not exactly family. After a few steps toward the door, Sarah and Marray both looked back.

"Tyler, come on."

I was surprised, and evidently, I wasn't the only one, as someone replied,

"I'm sorry, it's only family allowed."

Sarah and Marray didn't budge. "No, he's fine. Tyler, come on."

I did as they said and went. I was humbled and more than grateful that they thought about me in that moment. Just as it had been earlier that night, both of them had no reason to be thinking about anyone other than Mal, and yet they considered me without a second thought. I remember wanting nothing more than to be part of the family in that moment.

Marray

Dr. Kamath explained that they had stopped the bleeding and reduced the pressure on Malori's brain. This was a life-saving measure. Thankfully and miraculously, Malori was still alive. Dr. Kamath did amazing work to save her life. He didn't remove the AVM (Arteriovenous Malformation) but was able to stop the bleed and pressure. Although not out of the woods, Malori was alive and now being flown to Zale Lipshy hospital in Dallas, which was part of UT Southwestern medical school, for post-surgical care as well as needing to have another surgery later to have her AVM removed. We were blessed again, as their neurosurgery center, we were told, was one of the top three in the nation. Dr. Kamath said one of us, us being Sarah or I, could ride along in the small airplane with Malori. Due to thunderstorms in the area the medical helicopter was not an option.

I asked Sarah what she'd prefer, and she said I should go. She knew she would get motion sickness on the small plane and didn't want anyone to have to take care of her instead of Malori. Selfishly, that was what I wanted to hear. I really wanted to go and be with Malori, but I knew Sarah would've wanted to just as much as I did.

As Dr. Kamath calmly explained the surgery he had performed, and what to expect next, we were anxiously wanting to see Malori. We were glad we were able to see her; most importantly, glad to see her alive. Thank you, Lord. We witnessed a miracle that night. The timing of how and when the events of the AVM rupture happened that night and the intricacies of Dr. Kamath's surgery, we couldn't help but acknowledge GOD and thank HIM for the timely events we witnessed the past five plus hours.

We were amazed. I have no doubt that our many prayers were answered, and that God caused the bleed to stop through Dr. Kamath's surgical interventions. He could have stopped and given up any number of times after the treatment didn't work, but he didn't and that made all the difference. We could only thank the Lord and Dr. Kamath for how the night had played out. We knew that Malori was not out of the woods yet, and we continued praying as they prepared her to go to Dallas.

Tyler

They took us back and explained what had happened. All I heard was that Mal had made it through this first part, and that was miraculous, but she was not out of this yet. Good news, to be sure, but there was still plenty that needed to happen before she was well and truly on the mend. They said the next step was to take Mal to Zale Lipshy, and, after some consideration, that Marray would be flying with her there.

I mentioned before the great Christian influences in my life. Marray is undoubtedly one of those men. He's an absolute rock. Through the whole ordeal, he stayed positive. The man radiated calmness, and all I could think was that is what having absolute hope in the Lord will do for you. It is a pretty special thing to be able to count your girlfriend's father as one of your heroes, and I am blessed to be able to do so. He was definitely the man to go with Mal on that flight.

We asked if we might be able to see Mal before she went. The doctor considered the idea for a moment, before agreeing to let us. "But," he told us, "just understand that she does not look like the Malori you knew before surgery."

That statement was intimidating but did not deter us. We knew what was going on, I mean, she had just had brain surgery, but didn't quite understand until we actually saw Mal.

Just hours before, Mal had the most beautiful long blonde hair. Now, almost all of her hair was gone, and what was left was brown because of the blood. The rest of her head was shaved, and a line of staples ran from her forehead all the way behind her ear. It was scary to be sure, and yet, it was also comforting. Hard to see her that way, but it was good to see her at all.

I could tell it was affecting Maci more than anyone. I mean, why wouldn't it? She was in junior high, and she loved her sister deeply. I couldn't imagine how it would have affected me had I been a middle school kid. Maci and I were close, too, since we shared a lot in common, maybe even more than Mal and she did. I remember wanting to love on her, just reassure her that everything was going to be okay, even though I didn't know that for myself.

Then they wheeled Mal out to take her to Dallas.

Marray

We took an ambulance from the Kell West hospital to the airport. On the ride over, one of the two medical staff members who was riding with us turned to me.

"I'm trying to wrap my head around all this. It's crazy. Do you realize how incredible this is?"

I just said, "Yessir, we are thankful and Dr. Kamath did an amazing job."

"Amazing is an understatement," one of the men said. "I've been in medical transportation as a medic for a long time and have never seen anything like this at a small hospital. The magnitude of this surgery and Dr. Kamath being there to perform this life-saving surgery was a miracle. And all over the hospital people were just praying and praising God. That was a miracle if I've ever seen one, it's unheard of."

We arrived at the airport around then. I thanked the staff members for taking care of Malori and for telling me their perspective of the miracle we witnessed. I thanked the Lord again. As mentioned earlier, it was a stormy night – high winds, lightning, thunder – so we couldn't take the helicopter. We boarded a little airplane instead. Malori and a nurse were in the back, and I got up front with the pilot.

The flight to Dallas was bumpy to say the least. I remember

thinking that if the plane went down in all this storm, that it'd be okay. I was eerily peaceful about everything at that point. Like any parent in a such a situation, I wished that it was me that was in the back of the plane and not Malori. I didn't want her to have to go through this. Such choices were not given to me though. As it had been through the whole ordeal, it was all in God's hands.

We landed safely at Love Field airport and transferred to another ambulance. Riding in the ambulance, I am certain that we hit every pothole between Love Field and Zale Lipshy. Everything was bouncing around in the ambulance, almost like we were experiencing turbulence on the ground, but we made it to Zale Lipshy at about 4:30 am where a neurosurgical team was waiting to take Malori under their care. Our Lubbock family doctor and friend, Joel Landry, texted me as we arrived at the hospital and said he had a family member who had prior experience with Zale Lipshy and told me they were outstanding. This news was comforting as Malori and our family begin the next phase of our journey.

Dr. Boudreaux, the neurosurgeon at the time, spoke to me following the initial CT scan they gave Malori upon her arrival. "I wanted to let you know that Dr. Kamath in Wichita Falls did exactly what we would have done here. Malori is in good hands. You're with the best team in the country – this is what we do." I immediately called Sarah to tell her this good news. Sarah, Peyton, Maci as well many other family and friends were all driving from Wichita Falls to Dallas.

All I could say was, "Thank the Lord." There was no better news that I could have heard at that point.

Dr. Boudreaux said, "These next 72 hours are crucial for Malori and her progression. We're going to track her progress and see if it trends up or down. I won't make any promises to you, but she's in the best possible situation."

Malori was placed in a medically induced coma, and all we could do was wait and continue to pray. During this time, I ran into a doctor from Lubbock in the ICU who had heard about our situation, and who spoke to me in passing.

"Hey, I heard your daughter is here and that all the stars were lined up for tonight."

I bristled a little at his description of the circumstances. I told him we give all the glory to God. It was a miracle to be sure, but it was a miracle from God, and I believe we did everything we could to point people to that through the situation. Once again, we found that faith was all we had and all we needed, and we settled in to watch God work.

Tyler

It was 2:30 am or so when Marray and Mal left in the ambulance. My cousin Aaron and his wife Amy had just arrived at the hospital. They had left Houston when I called Aaron on my way to Plainview. Both were in school to get their doctorates, and they dropped everything to come support Mal. For them to do that, I mean, it's not like high school where you can make it up, it meant so much to me. He didn't even have to tell me he was coming either, I just know he loves me that much to come. In any case, they got in right around then, and I hopped in with Aaron to drive down to Dallas.

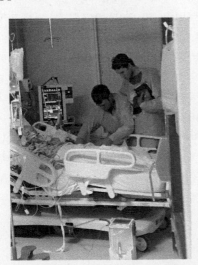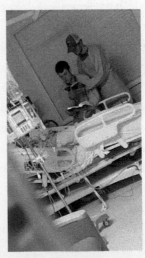

Aaron Stephenson praying and reading with Tyler

It was just us on that ride, and that was probably the best thing for me at that point. When we're together, we goof around a lot. It usually ends up getting us into trouble, and we have a lot of stories from our times together. I was in no mood to goof around at all that night. Our ride together snapped me out of my misery instead of letting me just wallow in it. He never actually said it, but he kind of just implied that I should lighten up. He talked me through everything, kept me positive, and made me laugh even though I was sad. He's basically my brother, and I will always be grateful for his presence on that night and afterwards.

We got to Dallas and stayed there overnight. Sometime the next morning, I was struck by the sudden realization that I had basketball games to play in Colorado in a couple of days. We had one of our big tournaments where we would get a chance to play many of the teams we would face in conference and in the post-season. My family was an LCU basketball family. My grandad, my dad, both my uncles, and my aunt all played ball at LCU. It was something I had spent my whole life working for and it was my final season, but in that moment, I had no desire to go.

Dr. Laughlin, a close family friend and professor at LCU, called me. He had experienced something similar, except he was not the boyfriend in the situation, but rather a husband and father. He had to support his two kids while his wife, Gina, fought cancer. For all he knew, she was dying, and he could do nothing but watch. She made it and is healthy now, but I remember watching him go through all of that and felt a certain kinship to him because of it. His call came almost immediately after I realized I had games. Good timing and the idea of coincidence are all well and good, but I believe God had a hand in his call. After making sure I was okay, Dr. Laughlin got straight to the point.

"Hey, you've got games in Colorado this week."

"Yeah whatever, I'm not worried about it." I said.

"You're going."

"What?"

"You're going. You need to be with your team in Colorado. I remember wanting so badly to stay with Gina, but I had to go to work. I had to do that with my wife. I had no choice. You are a college athlete; this is your job. You have to go. It'll be good for you."

I was not having any of it, so Dr. Laughlin got harsher.

"Look, what are you going to do for Malori? There's nothing you can do. She doesn't know you're there and doesn't care right now."

That hurt. It was everything I had agonized over that night, all things I knew were true. Dr. Laughlin laid it out in no uncertain terms. It hurt, but it was what I needed. He was right after all, and I knew it.

Coach Duncan called me too. He never once asked if I was going to Colorado, but instead asked to pray with me. It was incredible to me that my coach, an intense, serious leader, did not care about the games as much as he cared about my well-being, and not just me physically but spiritually as well. He told me my spot was secure, and not to worry about practice, but that he and the guys were thinking about and praying for me.

I was dreading going to Colorado, but I was going. I flew out from Dallas to Denver and got to the College of Mines where the tournament was being held. Dr. Laughlin was right, it was good for me. I walked into the conference room at the hotel we were staying at and was greeted by the biggest, smelliest group hug from the team. It's hard to be down when you're surrounded by a bunch of guys just being dumb and doing everything possible to keep you happy. They wanted to know what was going on too, and I was able to explain what I knew. Mal was in a medically induced coma in ICU and all we could do was wait and pray. After everything had calmed down, one of my really good buddies, Matt, just leaned over and asked,

"Are you good? I mean, with everything, how are you doing?"

"I'm good, just ready to play." I managed with a small grin.

It took everything I had not to lose it again right there, but I barely kept my composure. That would be the mood for the tournament, just trying to hold it all together, and I did for the most part. There was a point where we were taking the court for our first game where it all kind of hit again and I just turned around and started heading back to the locker room. It was all too much, the pressure to play, and play well, while Mal was still fighting for her life back in the hospital, and I needed to do well for my family and for hers and for me and I just – it was all too much. They could play this game without me. I only got a few steps back toward the locker room before someone grabbed my arm and hauled me the other way. One of my teammates, AJ, had seen me start to balk and wasn't having it.

"Look man, let's go. It's gonna be okay. Let's go."

I stopped and turned, before nodding and running out of the tunnel with him, tears streaming down my face. I know I looked like a mess and wanted nothing more than to run away in that moment, but he was right, and I got the message. It wasn't so much a 'hey I feel sorry for you,' but more a 'I know this is hard, but you've got this.' Any of my teammates would probably have done the same, but AJ was the only one who saw me and got me back on track, which meant a lot to me.

We started warmups and all of the pent-up stress and emotion from the past few days reached a breaking point and manifested as anger. Any coach will tell you that basketball is as much a contact sport as any other, and I was as physical that day as I could be without going too far. There are different types of anger, especially in sports. You see the lose your head, out of control rage monster a lot. Sometimes you see the imploding kind, where someone just gets frustrated and melts down during the contest. This wasn't either of those. It was a tense, coiled anger. It was focused, and I played alright because of it. Anyone guarding me was in for a rough day, and more than likely some bruises from heavy shoulders and elbows.

Anger like that can only be contained for so long though, and it boiled over on a referee that I thought had made a bad call. I was giving him an earful and should have been given a technical foul. Coach Duncan called a timeout and I didn't even realize because

I was still jawing at the ref. Coach got me over to the bench, just looked me in the eyes, and said,

"T – calm down. It's going to be okay. You're alright."

For what felt like the umpteenth time, I nearly started crying. I was so tired of feeling like this. I wanted nothing more than to be with Mal, but I also had a commitment to my team and my university. Basketball was helping put me through school after all, and I owed it to them and myself to do the best I could. But still, I was torn.

Coach spent the entire timeout calming me down, and I got a handle on myself. Then the timeout was over, and we were playing again.

That's how the tournament went. We played a couple games, and I headed back to the airport to return to Dallas. While I was waiting for my flight, I ran into a coach from our rival school who had recruited me before I decided to attend LCU. He was curious as to how I was doing and about the whole situation. It seemed everyone knew what had happened to Mal. It registered pretty quickly that I was going back to see her, and the fact that I was her boyfriend was the natural conclusion. Once Coach Flickner realized this, he asked if he could pray with me. I said yes, and in the middle of the busy airport, he and his assistant coach put their hands on me and just prayed. It didn't matter that I played for a rival school, or that I had chosen that school over his. He saw a need for prayer and faithfully fulfilled that need, regardless of the circumstances. I am very thankful for that occurrence and think a lot of Coach Flickner because of it.

Marray

We spent the next few days in ICU. We found that Malori's phone had an alarm on it for 10 pm every night for her to pray. It became a priority for us to do that, and we would ask everyone in the ICU waiting room to pray with us as well. Not one person ever turned us down, and we would pray for Malori and their loved ones. It was a powerful. It amazes me how God was able to use us and our circumstances to share hope and assurance in Christ with total strangers. His ability to work through crisis and make it work for Him was incredible. So many people were touched through Malori's story, and we were constantly receiving videos and news from people all around the world that were praying for her. Prayer at all times, just constant prayer, was our answer to the storm we were in. God's word through scripture was powerful for us.

Through this time, people would come up to us and thank us for using the situation to point to God. It was almost, well not exactly embarrassing – we felt unworthy of it all – but we just had to ask God for wisdom and discernment to help us use this in a way to honor Him. I thought much of the verse in 1 Peter that speaks of being able to be ready to give anyone a reason for the hope we have in Christ. We had a reason, so many reasons actually, and we prayed that God would work through us to show them. I wanted to stress that it wasn't anything we did, it was all the Lord, but it was one of the best compliments that anyone could give me to ask how we could show our faith even in the midst of a crazy time like this.

Sleep. Well, sleep was interesting to say the least. It's amazing how little you can get by on. We stayed camped out in the ICU waiting room or Malori's room. Someone brought us a blowup mattress at some point. Sarah and I would try to get a few hours of sleep at a time. Always one of us was in Malori's room, she was never alone, but I don't remember ever getting more than a couple hours of sleep at a time. I know Sarah was the same way.

After six days or so, the doctors extubated Malori so that she could speak. To be able to see Malori awake, to see her eyes open and to hear her voice was the best thing for me beyond the doctors telling us that she was still alive on that first night. She didn't know her own name at first, and she started calling us all by our middle names. God created a funny thing in His creation of the human brain. The fact that Malori could remember our middle names and connect them to all of us but couldn't remember her own name was amusing and amazing at the same time. She thought her name was Sarah. We laughed and told the doctor we were delighted and that we could teach her that her name was Malori. It was the most awesome sound to hear her speaking again and hear her sweet voice.

Coach Lawrence and her volleyball team were there at the hospital, and they had to make a decision on whether or not they would be going to play in the conference tournament (a monumental time for LCU volleyball to be eligible for the first time in school history as NCAA Division II to play in the conference tourney.) The girls didn't want to play – they wanted to stay with Malori. I got a chance to speak to them on the behalf of our family. They had just cancelled a Thursday non-conference game vs. Panhandle State in Goodwell, Oklahoma on Thursday night. We were thankful again that Malori's bleed didn't happen on that night where there was no hospital within 60 miles. Ken Stephenson and Zach Galbraith were with me during this time and were so helpful and encouraging. I told the volleyball team that our family wanted them to go play, and that Malori would want that, too. I said that we wanted them to go play in such a way that honored God and that would make Malori proud. And when they were finished, that they could come back through and stay as long as they wanted. After a lot of hugs and tears, they decided to go. Sarah, Malori, Maci and I were able to watch the match online while we were in Malori's ICU room. The girls fought really hard and lost a close match, which was tough for them. But in the end, it was a win because they were able to return and see Malori after playing their hearts out.

I will never forget what happened when they returned to the hospital. Mal was awake and was adjusting back to a semblance of normality, speaking and regaining some faculties. The team came into the room, and Sarah and I stepped back to let them see her. They all circled up around Malori's bed to say a prayer, and as it happens sometimes, they were silent for a few seconds while they determined who would be saying the prayer. It was none other than

Malori who took over and led it. It was an emotional moment. To see my daughter so full of joy and spirit-led and thankful, it was all I could have asked for in that moment. If you were there, you would have thought the team had just won the conference tournament and they were in the locker room afterwards rejoicing. It was an amazing thing, to see the Lord working through my daughter in that moment. It's something I'll never forget.

Tyler

I was worried on my flight back to Dallas that Mal might not remember me. I had gotten news before I left that they were going to take the breathing tube out so that she could come out of her coma. There were no certainties when dealing with a brain injury, and no one had any concrete idea as to what shape she would be in when she came out. I felt like I was being selfish. There were plenty of things that could be worse than her not remembering me, but I was focused on that. I hated it. I mean, it wasn't like we were married, but I loved her, more than I had even realized at that point, and I wasn't sure what I would do if she didn't remember me.

I know I prayed on that flight. I don't know what it was for, I just knew that I needed to be in prayer to God. I needed His peace and knew that prayer was the best way to get close to that. I wanted to be like Marray, to exude that calm confidence that came from a great faith in God. But I can't lie, I was scared.

I received a text when I got off the plane that said Mal was remembering her family. That gave me hope but I was still afraid that I might not hold a place in her head like her family did. When I finally arrived at the hospital, I was hesitant to even enter her room for fear of her not knowing me. I didn't know what I should say. In my hesitation, something just popped into my head. There was this joke that Mal and I had together. I would always ask her,

"Mal, do you know how much I love you?"

"Yeah." she'd reply.

"Nah, no you don't." I'd say back, teasing, knowing she'd have to answer 'no' the next time. And it was true, she didn't. I mean I didn't really understand until all this happened how much I really did love her. But that's beside the point.

I steeled myself and went into her room. Everyone gave me a few minutes with her by myself, a fact for which I was grateful since I didn't know how all of this was going to go down and how I might react. Mal was groggy. She was in and out of sleep, and I sat next to her bed not knowing if she would wake up and be able to talk. It would have been agonizing to wait any longer to get my answer, to see if she knew me, so I leaned in and softly said,

"Mal."

Her eyes opened immediately. I just kind of laughed, she recognized my voice and that gave me all the hope I needed, but I continued,

"Mal, do you know how much I love you?"

She just smiled and shook her head no. Warmth cascaded down from my head to my toes, and joy welled up in me. She remembered me, and nothing else mattered. Something else hit me in that moment too. For the first time in a long time, I realized I was tired. I hadn't been sleeping or eating at all. After seeing Mal, after talking to her, I felt like I could eat and sleep again. As Mal was nearing sleep again, I told her I loved her one more time and left the room.

I found my mom in the waiting room.

"Mom, I have to get something to eat right now. I'm starving."

I could tell that made her happy. She had watched me not take care of myself that week and could tell that my need to eat signaled a return to normalcy.

She smiled and said, "Alright, let's go."

We went down to the hospital cafeteria where it was all you can eat nacho day. All the better for me. I put the hammer down on some nachos. It was glorious and probably a little off-putting to anyone watching. I didn't care. Once I'd finished, Mom laughed.

"I've never seen you eat like that."

I grinned sheepishly.

"Well, it's the first time I've been hungry in a week and a half."
I had lost a lot of weight since the night Mal went into the ER.
A lot. I think I gained every bit of it back in nachos that day.

Marray

Our journey was far from over. Malori was going to need a second
surgery to remove the AVM, as the first surgery was lifesaving, but
she needed to recover as much as possible and be stronger before
that could happen. She went through daily rehab processes during
this time, too. Occupational therapy, speech therapy, and physical
therapy sessions became the daily norm for a while. Later we would
take her to sessions in a nearby facility. A few things really stick out
to me from that time before the second surgery.

In the ICU, Malori was limited in using her right hand. She
had always been right hand dominant. Dr. Kafka (one of her
neurosurgeons) told me to move my chair from the left side of the
bed to her right side and make her use her right hand. It was a tough
love kind of deal, and might seem mean, but we did as they told us. I
always made her get things with her right hand. It was frustrating for
her at first. She had to think far more to make her right-side move.
Simple things like grabbing a cup to drink or using a fork or spoon
to eat were extremely difficult. It seemed a little harsh to make her
concentrate and take extra time for her to relearn how to use her
right hand, but I knew it was the right thing to do. Gradually she
fully regained strength in her right hand and to this day she has
no physical deficits in her movement or strength in her right side.
Malori was always a hard worker and as usual, an over-achiever. She
also still had her soft, gentle spirit.

Once Malori was cleared from ICU and was moved to a regular
room, Sarah, Maci, Peyton and I were able to use the Ronald
McDonald house. We were grateful to be able to sleep and shower, two
things that we had gotten far too little of while she was in the ICU.

While we were there, our Peyton told us, "Once Malori made it through that first night, I wasn't afraid anymore. I knew God had it all in His control and that she was going to be okay. I had nothing to prove that other than faith, but I knew. I know she'll be okay."

Hearing her brother say something so profoundly spiritual was greatly encouraging, and it only strengthened our family's hope and resolve.

Malori had a little bit of hair left after the surgery, but it was a mess after all that had happened. One night a couple of nurses, aides and I did what we could to clean it up. They brought all kinds of shampoos and things from their homes to clean her hair up. We worked on it for a couple hours in the 4 am – 6 am range. It was a good time for Malori, and we all had a lot of fun trying different concoctions in the hope that they would work. I know she appreciated that we could help her with that, if only a little.

Another neat thing that happened involved Malori's favorite song at the time. It's called "The Well" by Casting Crowns. I found it on my phone one day as Sarah and I were sitting in her room and played it for her. She started singing it word for word. Hearing her sing this song, a song about God giving you what you need if you'd only ask, was wonderful, and fitting too. Sarah and I were crying joyfully as we heard her sweet voice and heart felt words.

About a month after the original surgery, the doctors were prepared to remove the AVM. We were a bit anxious about the surgery – with any kind of surgery there are risks but especially with brain surgery – there were no guarantees. Malori wasn't fazed. Out of everyone, she was probably the least worried. In the time before the surgery, her brother found a song called "Brain Wash" and played it in her room. She found it hilarious. It kept everything light in what was a fairly tense situation. Malori was amazing, just so at peace with the whole thing. We learned a lot about faith through her example, and I constantly thanked God for her faith.

Once again, there were many people including family and friends with us in the lobby praying when they took her back into surgery. We prayed for a successful surgery and continued thanking God for His healing hand beginning November 10th in Wichita Falls. I don't recall many of the small details – how long it was supposed to take, updates, that sort of thing – but I do remember the surgery being over remarkably quickly. It went as good, if not better, than we had hoped, God be praised. Dr. Welch, the neurosurgeon for this operation, showed us the before and after CT scans. It was remarkable. The AVM in the before scan looked like a conglomerated bird's nest with veins spider webbing out. It was just a malicious sort of thing. It was completely gone in the after scan. Dr. Welch and his team managed to remove the entire AVM; Dr. Welch showed us the scan and told us all there was no chance that she would ever experience the brain bleed from it again. The AVM was completely gone. Thank you, Lord.

Tyler

After Mal woke up it began a time of constant back and forth for me. I was in Lubbock for school and basketball during the week, and in Dallas with Malori on the weekends when I could make it. Having to make myself go put an orange ball in a steel hoop felt pointless, but as it was with the tournament, it was something I needed to do.

The fact that I was a college athlete raised some complications. People had recognized a need for me to go see Mal and were trying to donate money, plane tickets, and even private flights to get me there. I had to turn it all down in the beginning because it would put me in violation of NCAA rules. Our liaison to the NCAA, Scott Larson, called me to discuss all this outpouring of support and to talk about what we could do within the regulations the NCAA imposed. We had to get approval to use the funds that were pouring in, and there was precedent, but it typically only applied to immediate family and I was just a boyfriend. I didn't expect to be approved to use the funds, but to my surprise, the NCAA acquiesced. It was such a blessing and just another thing I can point to during this time as a credit to God.

I will forever be thankful for my coaches. Coach Duncan and Coach Imes cared for me so much. They did everything they could to accommodate my need to be with Mal. My spot on the team was never in jeopardy, which was crazy to me. These guys' jobs were in the hands of a bunch of 18-22-year-old kids, and their performance on a court. That means that if one guy isn't putting in the same work as the rest, then his spot should be up for grabs. It's a competitive world, and both of my coaches were extremely competitive people. And yet, for me, they threw this out the window. Coach Duncan would let me leave games early if we were up just so I could make a flight to see Mal. They took care of me and genuinely cared about how I was doing. They moved practices to accommodate me. The respect I have for them is immense, and I would not want to play for anyone else.

I wasn't the only one going back and forth either. Maci was going through all of this, too. Junior high is hard enough as it is, and she had to deal with all of the pressures that come with it while doing makeup work, playing basketball, and travelling back and forth to Dallas on the weekends. She was an absolute trooper. We had always gotten along since we were both competitors. She'd claw your eyes out, and I say that with all the pride and respect I can muster. But even more than I respect her for that, I respect her for how she handled the entire situation. She's an incredible little girl and an incredible sister to Mal.

The time came for the second surgery to take place, and everyone was hopeful. There was a good chance of a positive outcome. Mal was young and healthy, all things considered. She didn't quite understand everything that was going on, and the days leading up to that second surgery were weirdly fun. Her brother kept singing this song called "Brain Wash" and Mal would just laugh. She still had some short-term memory loss, so things would happen and she wouldn't remember them. For example, I remember feeding her a chicken nugget and her saying it tasted really good. A little later I asked what it was she was eating, and she didn't know, but she said it was good. I don't know why exactly but just being around her and her family at the time was so cool to me.

The day came, and all of my fears from that first night came rushing back. I was scared again. I was in Dallas when they started the procedure, but had a flight scheduled just after she had to go into surgery. I wasn't happy. The only thing I wanted to do was be there for the surgery, but I had to do my job. I got off the plane in Lubbock and headed right into practice. Typically, we'd start practice with about 30 minutes of warming up. Once the buzzer went off after those 30 minutes, then it was all in, full go. When the clock went off, the guys and I were just kind of left looking around. The coaches didn't start practice like usual. The guys kept shooting, and I followed suit. Coach Duncan called me over a few minutes later.

"Tyler," he said, "Your dad just called. They've finished surgery and Malori is okay."

"Okay," I said.

It took about five seconds for that to actually sink in. When it did, I hit a jog into the closest tunnel in the gym. I just laid face-down and cried. I was trying to be quiet, but I was sobbing loudly, like the big can't catch your breath kind. I heard someone come up behind me and turned to see who it was. It was Matt. He didn't say anything. He just laid down by me. It was the weirdest thing. All of my emotions, my fear, my sadness, my joy, all of it came out in that three-minute span. Once I got it out of my system, I sat up and took a deep breath. My face was a mess, all dirt and tears. Matt looked at me.

"You good?" he asked.

I nodded.

"Alright then, let's go."

We walked out and the rest of the guys had already started a drill. We jumped in line and started up again like nothing happened.

Marray

After the surgery, they kept Malori at the hospital for a few days. She moved out of ICU a few hours after surgery and was discharged from the hospital after a few days. She was going to get to come home for the first time since that night in November. We were told to continue therapy in Lubbock and come back in three months, and we did exactly as asked.

During those months, Sarah and I were guarded with Malori. She's always been very independent, and it was a challenge to discern how much we should let her do and how much we should try to help her. As always, we made it through with prayer.

Speaking of prayers, amongst the many answered through the whole ordeal, God found it appropriate to answer one of mine specifically. On the day Malori was discharged, January 6th, I got to walk hand in hand with my daughter out of the hospital.

We made sure to stop by Wichita Falls and Kell West to see the staff and Dr. Kamath before we headed back to Lubbock. We figured it was appropriate, like the story of Jesus and the ten lepers. God had worked through them to save our daughter, and it was the least we could do to thank them. It was a special day. They knew we were coming and set up a big lunch. They had big pictures of Malori's head (from volleyball), like the ones you would see at ball games, all over the place.

Dr. Kamath and Malori's meeting was something special to witness. He just took her face in his hands, acknowledging the miracle had happened. They walked hand in hand around the hospital. He showed her everything, and never once let go of her hand.

Malori meeting Dr. Kamath

Tyler

I got to go on the trip with the Maddox's back to Lubbock. We stopped at the hospital in Wichita Falls on the way back. They had a big meal, and everyone was so happy, a stark contrast to the mood when we had been there last. Everyone was so taken with Mal and her family. So many questions were asked of them. The way they reacted that night had not been human. It was spiritual and it was a mark of their deep faith. Even in this case, they deferred all praise to God. It was all God, not them. That's one of the things I love about them.

We got to Lubbock and went straight to the Maddox's home church, Greenlawn, which happens to bump right up against LCU's campus. It's a big church but the auditorium was packed. We walked down the aisle to the front, where Coach Lawrence and the volleyball team were waiting. My team was there too, but they were scattered around the auditorium. Mal sat with her team all of whom were thrilled to see her. I sat kind of off to the side in the front. Everyone started singing and praising God. Marray got up and spoke to the assembly. I'm not sure exactly what he said because I was crying again. I was overwhelmed by the outpouring of support by all these believers. It was so good, just pure. It was heaven. It was a deep journey over a short period of time, and I thank the Lord that it ended the way it did.

That was the last time I really cried over what happened to Mal.

Marray

Romans 8:28 says, "in all things God works for the good of those who love Him, who have been called according to his purpose" (NIV). That was not one of the scriptures I was thinking of that night. I was more cognizant of things like having the faith of a mustard seed, or the prayer of a righteous man availing much, but in hindsight, it seems very appropriate. People talk about storms of life, usually in reference to a bad situation, but in this case, it was for the good. Dr. Kamath, the neurosurgeon, was not supposed to be there that night. It was late, and he would have usually been gone for the day. He told us after the surgery that he was actually supposed to fly out to see his mother in India, but something had kept him from leaving. We also learned later that the timing involved in treating an AVM is touchy to say the least. The difference between life and death is a few minutes. If this had happened anywhere else, Malori would not have had any sort of chance. It was God, it had always been God.

On April 6th, three months later, we saw Dr. Welsh and he did a CT scan. When the results came back, he looked at Malori.

"Malori, you are being discharged and released. I want to see you in ten years. You go live your life."

Words cannot express the amount of gratitude I feel toward those involved in these events. Malori's situation taught me the virtue of constant thankfulness, and as always, the power of prayer.

I am so thankful for her, and the people who surround her. My amazing wife Sarah, son, Peyton, and youngest daughter, Maci were incredible faith giants and prayer warriors. Both Peyton and Maci had to juggle sports and school while traveling back and forth to be with our family and see Malori. We all grew closer to each other as well as closer to God. We understand the spiritual journey as we were being led through a storm. There are so many people to thank: Sarah's sister, Rachel and husband, Scott and family; Sarah's brother, Stephen and wife, Jenelle and family; Nana and Papa, as well as other family members and friends like Zach Galbraith; Ken and Jana Stephenson; John, Terry, and Kathy Delaney; Phil Bryant; the Roger Talanyi family; Jimmy, Shelly, and Jalen Moore; the Jerry and Carla Shelton family; Dale and Lauri Mannon, and many others (I failed to mention) praying and supporting us through this time we'll never forget. Our family from Big Spring; LCU family including President Perrin, Brian Starr and others; Greenlawn Church; Lubbock and surrounding community; Coach Lawrence and LCU volleyball team; Coach Duncan and LCU men's basketball; all LCU sports teams; Peyton's baseball coach, Zach Saunders and SWOSU baseball; and all Malori's medical staff, we can't thank everyone enough. I also want to thank my business partners, Bill Lewis and Rick Stepp from Physical Therapy Today for their constant support, time off, and prayers as well as all our PTT employees and the many Lubbock medical doctors and offices that reached out to us through this time. For every person's prayer that went up on Malori's behalf on November 10th and following, we thank you. Tyler, Tye, Kelli, Nici and the rest of Tyler's family were amazing as well. Wow, through these events, Tyler juggled basketball, school, and flying back and forth out of concern for Mal. We knew from his love and devotion to her through all this that he was the one we wanted out daughter to marry someday. So, when he asked, of course we gave him our blessing.

God can use any situation for good. Never underestimate what He can do. He helped us through the most difficult storm of our life, and that is something we will never forget. Above all, we want to use this story to honor God and point others to Christ. Rejoice greatly, give thanks in all circumstances for this is God's will for you in Christ Jesus and don't quench the spirit. 1 Thessalonians 5:16-19 Hopefully, it will help others through their storms, too. I continue to wear, as a reminder, a bracelet on my right wrist that says With God all things are possible. Matthew 19:26. I thank the Lord every day for His healing hand. I'll never forget what God has done for Malori and our family.

Tyler

You can guess how my story ends. Malori and I got married the following summer. The circumstances leading up to the wedding were directly influenced by that night in Wichita Falls, and taught me an important lesson: never underestimate the memory of the woman you love.

After Mal started feeling better in the time between surgeries, she started getting a little stir crazy being stuck in the hospital. We asked the doctors if we might be able to take her to the mall for a change in scenery. They agreed, and our little excursion was on. We loaded up in the car and headed out to the mall.

Mal was noticeably anxious, and for good reason. This was before the second surgery, so she was still missing part of her skull. Her peripheral vision was nonexistent at the time as well. I remember holding her hand and feeling like she was going to rub a rash on it with all of her nervous energy. I wanted to cheer her up somehow. On an earlier trip to Lubbock I had purchased a ring. A few days before the mall trip, I showed Marray and Sarah the ring and asked if I could marry Malori. To my great joy, they agreed wholeheartedly. I didn't have it with me, but I figured I could tell Mal and it would cheer her up. There was no way she'd remember it. I mean, she couldn't remember putting a chicken nugget in her mouth long enough to finish chewing it up.

We were sitting in the back of the car together, so I leaned over and whispered,

"Hey Mal, I know you're feeling kind of scared and timid and anxious. Can I tell you something that will make you feel better?"

"Yes," she whispered back.

"I bought you a ring," I whispered, smiling.

"You did?"

"Yeah, I did."

She cheered up immediately, and I thought that was that...

Well, it turned out that she never forgot.

Fast forward to March. We were back in Lubbock several months after the surgery. I got a text from Sarah.

"Um, did you know that Malori knows you have a ring?"

I called her immediately.

"Hi, Sarah. Yeah, it's me. I just wanted to ask what that last text you sent me meant."

"Malori told me that you told her that you bought her a ring," she told me.

"I mean, yeah," I said, "but that was in Dallas like a month and a half ago."

"Well she remembers." She said.

We both started laughing. I was a little bummed because it wouldn't be a surprise anymore, but I was excited too. She remembered, and that meant that she must want to marry me too.

A few weeks after that, Malori and I were coming back from Plainview in my truck.

Offhand, she said, "I thought we were going to get married this summer, but I guess we'll have to wait until next summer."

I was taken off guard. We had talked about having a short engagement before getting married, but that was before the AVM and we weren't engaged yet. She was mad too, for the first time in a while.

Biting my lip to keep from laughing, I looked out the window and said, "Well, I just wanted to make sure you were okay."

That was not the answer she was looking for.

For her sake, I had been waiting. I prayed for wisdom and discernment so that I would know when to ask. When I was sure, I told our parents about the incident.

"She's pretty fired up about it." I said. "She really wants me to ask so that we don't have to wait until next summer. It's something I've been praying about a lot."

I turned to Marray.

"What do you think about this next weekend? To ask her, I mean."

Marray was a little shocked, but being the man he is, he regained his composure quickly.

"Woah, next weekend huh … You know what? Yeah. I think that would be good."

It was late March, after basketball season was over. I figured that I had a small army of guys, my teammates, who could help me do a bunch of special stuff if I needed them to. I got permission to use the Rip Griffin center, our gym, and we got to work. We blacked out all the windows with tarps and made sure the lights were turned off, so the place was pitch black. We made an aisle out of candles down to midcourt. I worked with Coach Lawrence and the volleyball team to get Mal there. They took her on a scavenger hunt that was to end at the Rip for a team picture, that way she'd be dressed up. When she got there, I was waiting in the circle of candles at midcourt. She came down and I read some scripture to her and danced to a song.

Matt, my buddy who'd laid down in the tunnel with me, he was my DJ. He had shown up wearing a bolo tie – just the weirdest looking bolo tie – as a part of him dressing up. I remember that he'd come in to help that day wearing it and asked if I liked it.

I said, "No. I mean – sure. You know what? I don't care, wear it." Goofball.

Anyway, as the DJ, it was his job to play the song after I read the third verse. Those were my specific instructions. He got the timing exactly right, and when the song finished, I got down on one knee.

"Mal, will you marry me?"

She said yes!

All of our family and friends who had been hidden in the darkness jumped out and we had cake and punch to celebrate.

We got married in July of that year, three months later. It was originally going to be a small wedding. God and our moms had other plans. When all was said and done, there were 600 people there. It was a beautiful day, and we got to thank so many people who had been a part of our journey to get there. Dr. Kamath came, and so many other people came. And Malori, the amazing girl who had nearly died just six months before, Malori became my wife. What an amazing God we serve.

GIVE HIM THE
STAGE ALREADY

"Not everyone who says to me, 'Lord, Lord,' will enter the Kingdom of
Heaven, but only the one who does the will of my Father who is in heaven."
—MATTHEW 7:21

Jon Gordon once said, "Everyone wants to be great, but you can't be great without sacrifice. When you lose yourself in the service of a greater cause, you find the greatness within you." As Christians, we are safe when we follow God's lead to our greater purpose and really *live*; He seems to put a safety net around our sacrifice.

I like to keep my old planner flipped to November 10, 2015, to remind myself that my plans don't have to work out because His are greater, always. It makes me chuckle to think that bulleted task list of homework and various responsibilities was once so important to me on that day. It is both humbling and freeing to know that God doesn't need us to accomplish His greater plans. The world actually does spin without the completion of our to-do lists. He has everything under perfect control. But hardships and trials are blatant reminders that *we* need *Him*.

God's wisdom is infinitely greater than anything humans can

possibly produce, plan for, or be worthy to receive. Paul puts it perfectly in 1 Corinthians when he says, "For the foolishness of God is wiser than human wisdom, and the weakness of God is stronger than human strength" (1:25). I need this affirmation in times when I try to be obedient to God, through the Bible and nudges from the Holy Spirit, but my human spirit leaves me hard-hearted, unsure, and selfish. He is always right, and we can trust Him with everything.

Upon coming out of an intense storm, spiritually and physically, the journey seemed endless to find my path again. It is still a daily choice to intentionally walk the path of God's choosing … temptations are so believable. I often wondered how to be fruitful or shine my light when I felt like I didn't have anything left. The truth was that the waves of the storm didn't actually take everything away; they had just clouded my vision of all of my blessings.

I knew I was richly blessed beyond measure, but I couldn't feel those blessings for a while. My new baggage of weaknesses was completely swept under the rug because of miraculous celebrations. While I praise God for that, certain things needed to be addressed, mourned, and sifted through in order for me to sincerely be myself again. The blessings were perceived as hardship for a time without the knowledge of how to juggle them. No one seemed to recognize this, and I was so confused by the treatment of those who loved me. In light of such innocent yet preventable hurt, I knew I had to take a stand for others who had a voice needing to be heard, specifically in the population I now identified with: brain injury survivors.

During my stormy season, I was ashamed to bring anything up because I never seemed to go without. I never allowed myself to admit any problems, so I just kept trying to change my perspective. I constantly assumed I was in the wrong because of my memory loss. This tested my faith and endurance while hardening my heart. But I sought to embody the attitude of Job who, in the midst of His storm, never blamed God: "The Lord gave and the Lord has taken away; may the name of the Lord be praised" (Job 1:21). May we all strive to reflect this attitude of never blaming God for our afflictions (22).

Getting to process in retrospect has been helpful and reassuring to affirm that the God of powerful disaster is the same God that creates, renews, and restores. Rather than dwell on past weaknesses, I want to reflect on stormy seasons with a renewed perspective of gratitude and confidence, never wanting to forget what He has done and can do.

Even though God's stage is often magnified at rock bottom once we humbly realize our need for Him, it is there that it may be easiest to overlook Him. I find it encouraging reminiscing on journal entries during my times of struggle because witnessing how God answers prayer, tangibly, inspires me to move forward. His "light shines in the darkness, and the darkness has not overcome it" (John 1:5). Though I had to be broken in order to fully taste His healing rain, I'm so thankful that God showed me a deeper level of His grace than I had ever realized by reading His Word or sitting in a Bible class. In terrible hurt, He still works. He saturates meaning and purpose on us through His Spirit; He waits for us with immense patience and a mighty love, every single day.

I feel blessed to taste the holy proof of His patience by hearing about the stories of those who waited in a hospital lobby, praying fervently, during a brain surgery the night of November 10, 2015. *They* are the true heroes. Prayer is the most powerful thing in the world, and it's because it's 110 percent God at work while we simply remain still and trust Him.

I bet the four hours my family and dear friends endured by praying for me during that surgery felt a lot longer than the turmoil I have endured with a brain injury, though measured in years. Their faith was tested from every angle as they willingly walked that broken road for me, while proving to be true. The Bible warns that trials come as opportunities to show the genuineness of our faith, and that is exactly what my family and friends, my heroes, did. Much like fire tests and purifies gold, our faith may also be tested and refined by drastic measures. It's a guarantee, actually. However, the end result of solid faith is praise, glory, and honor when Jesus

Christ comes and reveals Himself (1 Peter 1:7). That promise gives us both warning and hope. As Christians, we must inspire one another with testimonies that continually fuel and empower our walks.

I continued to recognize that I went from a college athlete in the best shape of my life to having my brain exposed to air on an operating table within minutes. Dr. Kamath, who I now am honored to call a dear friend, was an angel to me that night. He persevered more than the protocol called for; he performed measures to stop the bleed again and again and again. After hearing the stories of the firsthand witnesses in the operating room, I am speechless and awestruck to know the timing, perseverance, and endurance of His vessels being successful in a lifesaving event.

Why did God decide to save me?

What was He waiting on for the miracle to happen?

What was everyone in the waiting room doing in that moment when the bleeding stopped?

Was God wanting that one person to believe?

Or for just one person to look to Him for the first time?

Was He using me? Me? For a miracle?

I don't know, but I am in awe that God looked down from heaven to spare a sinner like me. It seems like it would take longer than four hours to drive anything through this thick skull because I know I'm about as stubborn as they come. But He saved me.

On the night of November 10, 2015, my mom knew exactly how to react to care for me within seconds of seeing my condition. She knew it was serious and even assumed it was an aneurysm. She led the way of orchestrating a speedy route to the hospital. Dad followed her orders quickly and was met by Doug Elder, the MSU soccer coach, who I believe served as an angel for us. He was in the hallway outside the gym and had advised my dad to go to the small, rural hospital so we could be seen in a swift manner. His recommendations were based on previous experiences with his players, and we are grateful for his presence and truly life-giving advice.

My wide-eyed, brave sister sat beside her stiff, unconscious sister in the back seat of the Tahoe while following a police escort to the hospital. Mom later climbed back there with us to scoop the vomit out of my mouth so I wouldn't choke. My brother was contacted, and he uprooted his plans to immediately respond to the call to be with family. Nana went to the nursing home to tell Papa before getting in her car to speed to be with family. Tyler stopped his delicious meal of wings after basketball practice to come to the scene, followed by his family. My aunt and uncle also met and rode together, ditching their previous plans for the evening. People flooded to be with and bring comfort to my family, offering prayers the whole way. The Lubbock Christian and Midwestern State volleyball teams faithfully waited in the lobby through the night, wrestling in prayer. The Kell West Hospital staff worked tirelessly through the night as heavenly instruments of a miracle.

Mom had the supernatural instincts to know how to act with urgency and accuracy. She is an angel who never takes a day off. Dad later chose to fly through treacherous weather on a small, sketchy plane to be with his daughter to the best hospital for treatment following my first surgery.

Peyton and his whole baseball team later shaved their heads in my honor; he proved to finish that season and school year with intense perseverance. Maci was passed around from family to family while also choosing to sacrifice her activities and be with her own whenever she could during her basketball season.

My extended family was always involved and prayerful, offering the most generous services in every form. Hudson, my nine-year-old cousin at the time, passed out Bibles at his school and encouraged people to seek God in prayer for my healing. Countless souls took off work to be with my family and me, catering to any need we had: food, money, deeds, encouragement, social media updates, and so on. Tyler and several players on his team also shaved their heads to walk alongside me during this battle as well.

I feel certain that these miscellaneous, sweet humans were

heavenly tools, rock solid and unwavering in their faith. *They* are who shined their lights on the dark valley I was in to pave the way for me. *They* are what made therapy motivating and exciting. *They* are who I feel blessed by and accountable to in finishing this journey.

The book of Proverbs says, "Trust in the Lord with all your heart and lean not on your own understanding" (3:5). I knew my trust had to be greater than my understanding because I couldn't rely on myself for anything. I chose to follow His voice and vessels to keep me on the right path.

I feel like I had a convicting advantage through the storm by having such incredible examples to follow. But even when following God wholeheartedly, obstacles can often clutter our path. Daggers still try to pop my confidence.

"Oh, you still have headaches?"

"Don't you remember when I told you?"

I try my best to ignore such ignorant comments so that they do not belittle my confidence. Such people created a danger list in my mind of people I couldn't fully trust, but I also realized that I couldn't expect people to understand.

As I strive to keep moving forward through the fog and frustration, I must carry the responsibility of handling new weaknesses while trusting God to faithfully help me through them. Though I have continual headaches and fatigue amidst the new struggles and obstacles of trying to rewire every neuron connection in the brain of a twenty-four-year-old girl, I must choose to rejoice in the Lord as I recognize Him at every corner. In responding to various hardships, the book of Habakkuk reads: "Yet I will rejoice in the Lord, I will be joyful in God my Savior" (3:18). We can't look to Him without receiving a response that strengthens, inspires, and motivates us.

Though I lost everything, silently, because of my memory, it was not evident to everyone. It was so confusing to me learning who I could trust because, without a memory, I couldn't even trust myself. My family at home always encouraged me and provided a sense of normalcy when I was around them, and I was so grateful. But being so vulnerable while entering into marriage was humiliating to me.

I opened my mouth way too much in trying to process things with Tyler. I knew I loved him and that love would continue to grow, but without any tangible foundation of memories in the beginning, it was hard for me when I was alone the majority of the day. We sought to find the right balance of work and rest, bouncing from apartments, cities, and then ranches. I had no discernment factor to filter through my feelings, and everything was still new without a memory. Without God, I would have had no foundation. Even in the good seasons, I need Him as my firm foundation to cling to.

It was interesting to keep waking up in the same body that went through such a massacre, and it's amazing to me what God has done. I keep trying to understand it, but I can't figure it out. What is more awe-inspiring, though, is *who God is*. Continuing to study His nature and divine qualities through His Word just keeps me curious and hungry for more of Him.

Why would He spare me when He hasn't others who were more worthy?

Why did my family have to go through that and I did not feel anything, physically? (And they didn't have to; they chose to. Wow.)

How can I share this inner peace and confidence that He has shown me through such a terrible storm?

I am thankful to try to embody the qualities of God that I have been shown through Him and His vessels. I have been blown away by the courage, faith, and encouragement that was and is continually modeled in my family and community.

Though I have been far from perfect, or even good, I rejoice in the fact that God's Spirit dwells inside of me. That is the only reason I have been able to hold on, conscious or not. It truly is "God Who works in [us] to will and to act in order to fulfill His good purpose" (Philippians 2:13). He forgives us when we fight it.

Thank You, Lord.

I don't get it. God trumps and shines through every crack and weakness when we have a willing perspective to trust and rely on the direction from His Word. All I know is just to say, "Thank You, thank You, thank You, Lord," forever and ever and ever and ever and ever. He gave me life, and He is life for all of us.

It is one thing that my body experienced a miracle in physical form, while not really even being present mentally; it is another to process and walk through this new life as a changed person. But I'm reminded that the miracle involving my brain bleed was not my first showing of grace. Being born into a home that fosters Jesus and love might be my favorite blessing.

I feel as if I was placed into a huge, comfortable pit of grace from day one of my life. Not many are aware that that is all of our reality as Christians, and we ought always to feel immensely blessed and favored by Him. Such an attitude of humility grants us the permission to bring struggles to the light. In sharing, we find great joy, confidence, motivation, and purpose to finally surrender and let God work to bless others. In doing so, we learn that grace is free, but it is not cheap to own. It comes with a calling inspired by the price that was already paid. It takes intentional faith to remember this price and be fueled by it; it nudges our purpose to action.

When I kept thinking I had to figure things out to move forward, I remained frozen for so long. I learned that without pouring out and sowing, nothing would ever come about. We must sow in faith, hope, and trust, then let God do the work.

I wanted to grow something by striving to give back the love I was shown all of my life, specifically reminiscing on the childlike needs that were satisfied by dear loved ones as a wounded adult. I desperately searched for meaning in everything, the meaning that *God* wanted me to recognize through it all. Tyler and I wanted to mimic this love of Jesus in our quest to raise kids and establish a new branch in our family tree. I feel so highly favored that one of my deepest desires is still to be with my incredible and loving family yet grow in the courage it takes to establish a new branch. This battle of searching has fueled me to pursue one of my deepest desires that I felt was blocked for some time: to emerge from the battle of becoming a broken bride, His broken bride, and be fruitful with a family for Tyler and I to call our own.

I truly feel the blessing and favor of the Lord on our marriage when I reflect on the culture of my family through the generations: strong marriages, fruitful families, fun trips and vacations, and deep support for one another in various ways. I am so thankful for that backbone of faith from my upbringing through such a rich Christian heritage, and I am confident that God's grace has kept Tyler and me afloat through that.

Although I wasn't conscious to remember or know what all Tyler did and went through for me in light of my aneurysm, I knew it was unlike any faith or love story that ever existed to my knowledge. At first, every motive in my mind to love him was purely because of my faith in God, and it is so evident of the Holy Spirit's work in our cord of three strands (Ecclesiastes 4:12). Of course, that ought to always be the case, but during our early stages, the tangible memories of Tyler and our dating history did not exist for me. Everything was by faith, and faith gave birth to courage.

I continued to learn things that Tyler had been through on my behalf. After flying into Lubbock the morning of my second surgery on January 6, Tyler had two basketball games that week. I remember my family had the game on in the ICU room, although I wasn't sure all of the details. At this point, I remembered Tyler as part of my family; he was there when I woke up along with my immediate family. There was no history of dating in my brain yet, but deep inside, I knew that I loved him and that he was mine. Three years later, I read that he had led his team to two wins that week. He had scored nineteen points against Newman on January 7. It was such an honor to read of this victory for my man, knowing the strength and heart with which he has always played. I was in awe but not the least bit surprised.

It was an unspoken purpose for both of us to fight for the symbolism of our marriage. It was as if we were supposed to use our competitive athlete drives to better each other in a selfless, fulfilling way. In an unconscious state, I was told that I even remembered to pucker up for two more kisses after Tyler had given me just one during my first round in the ICU; he always kisses me three times, meaning "I love you."

But upon being married, we did not exactly have a riding off in the sunset moment. I was completely caught off guard by new weaknesses I had that presented themselves loudly in marriage. Things that I tried to sweep under the rug, the unknowing effects of my stroke, were so obviously exposed in the most embarrassing ways, especially in the kitchen. Sometimes my mental absence protected me from embarrassment but would eventually slap me in the face even harder when light bulbs started to come on. The scale of humility and confidence was a tough one to balance. During my quiet time, I trusted there had to be purpose in my pain, but I was unsure of how to let it emerge through marriage. So, I really lost myself for a while as I tried to escape from the person who occupied my skin.

I operated everything in fear. I was defeated before the day even started. I was lonely. I was without direction. I was so confused. I was impatient. I was so empty but so desperate to be filled. I grabbed for things that were meaningless and temporary. I didn't have the whole picture mentality to sow things that could not be immediately reaped. I didn't have the memory for long-term sowing. I didn't pour at all because I feared there wouldn't be anything left in the tank left to survive on. I was so self-centered and anxious, worried and nervous. I have to be intentional to quiet those voices every day.

Marriage was tough for me as I tried countless times to make that my deliverance from the storm. With a husband as steady and faithful as Tyler, it seemed like he should be my anchor. That was foolish of me to be so ignorant and closed off to anything else, but my lack of memory made me second-guess my every thought, and I wanted something or someone I could tangibly trust to lead me. Marrying Tyler through that time seemed to sweep me from that terrible destruction of a physical storm; however, my naïve mind continued to be cornered in confusion when I didn't know where to stand. It seemed like obedience just kept leading me into countless dead ends, but I remained determined to find my way in Him. I knew God was right and that I could trust His Word to be true, even when I felt impatient. I tried to use being stubborn to my advantage, as I was determined to let faith be my sword against the cobwebs of my mind. This journey with God was a new one.

Through so many drastic transitions, I wasn't even sure how to act as a Christian. It was so easy for me to love people, which fueled me every day to do so in my comfort zone. But following God seemed to remove me from the natural ways in which I had always served Him, which was the base of who I was. What then?

I struggled so much with thoughts like, *What do I do when God does something for me like this? When I have experienced Him like this? Like I don't get it, and I literally have no clue what to do. Being obedient has stripped me from all of my people, the doors I have always seen Him through, and now I'm in a remote place by myself a lot.* I realized that the harder it was to have faith, the more real it became when I chose to put it to practice. I am still learning to listen, to be content, and to seek to sow. Without the familiar ways of affirmation and direction from people in arm's reach, I often became confused and discouraged. But spiritual nourishment was the only thing that could truly fill. And it still is.

God, in His infinite mercy, must have thought, *OK, daughter. Since you're so stinkin' stubborn, I'm gonna switch the roles of your brain and heart. Since you've been doing your own thing for so long, all your life, I'm gonna highlight your heart, where my Spirit is, and humbly quiet your stubborn noggin.* God is crazy at working for our good. He means it when He says it in Romans (8:28). He has been leading me to the best life through the power of His Spirit by transforming my whole heart with new desires and purpose. God wants all of us—spiritually, mentally, and physically. Everything is possible with Him.

To get started, I felt like I had to grow up again, on my own, and it was so scary. I didn't have a voice of reason on how to process what all on earth was going on around me. I didn't know how to keep up with the world, be social, and maintain relationships … I just wasn't getting it. I wanted nourishment spiritually, physically, and emotionally.

I labeled myself as homebound, with minimal energy and untrusting reactions to stimuli, but I sought desperately to find purpose. Staying busy and trying to be fruitful in the home seemed somewhat lonely and meaningless at times, monotonous and unworthy of the calling God gives His people. But that's all I felt I was able to do.

But in trying to move forward, to do something, to do something with this tremendous gift of life and love of family and experience at LCU through such a horrific tragedy, I just didn't know. I didn't feel that I could possibly find a calling that would praise God and thank others enough. I couldn't find the answer in anything I accomplished or anything I could see. Nothing felt tangible like it used to. I can't say there wasn't a season where I didn't hear God or question His presence throughout my uncertainty. It was tempting to not have the courage to own my life anymore, so I had to be intentional not to dissolve in the false humility that zapped my worth. I learned to view making mistakes and adjustments on my own while experiencing the world again as a necessary part of my healing. In this journey, I wanted to be a leader in the waiting.

A servant leader.

It took a lot of self-discipline and motivation to attempt to do things that were once so easy, even the small tasks that are mindless for most. Those were things that had made up my personality and character for twenty years, but I had to go find them all again to remake those connections and create a new me. I honestly wasn't really interested in taking the time and effort to go through a lot of old files. A lot of them were exciting to open, but with a lot of them, it was sobering to realize that those things had been taken away. I started to grow in the trust that God's new provisions would outweigh old joys. My dad always reminded me that every new season in life was greater than the past one.

I became encouraged to gradually remember the base and roots of where it was I came from. Peace, contentment, and thankfulness flood my heart with any reflection of God's goodness through my family. I realized I shouldn't be afraid to jump into the old Mal's skin with a new life perspective, because I got to take Jesus with me, always. I felt united in spirit with my Christian family, and I was thankful that sense of family was growing everywhere that Tyler and I went.

I've thought things like, *I need to be baptized again, I need to get married again … I need to do all of these things and thank all of these people again and again and again. I just can't quench this season …* Thankfully, nothing depends or relies on our understanding. I believe blind obedience is just as adequate as sound understanding, and maybe even greater. We will never understand God, even the smallest detail about Him. When I think about how I wanted to give back, live up to, and fulfill the calling from this unbelievable blessing on my life, I am frozen. I am confused. But I am in awe. There's no way in the world that I can ever live up to this gift of life from God, with the powerful miracle He has given me. But as my dad has often said in regard to what our family went through, "There's no way to ever pay God back, but we can do our best to try." That's what I knew I had to do. And get to do. All of us. Walking in circles is not purposeful; we've gotta do something. I like to dream small and let God do the big things.

As I continued to listen and write through this process, I quickly grew to realize that I'm not good with words unless I'm typing. I can't even think or process fast enough for normal conversation pace a lot of times. With a fragile memory, I frequently type things in my phone to go back and say to people the next time I see them. Therefore, writing a book seemed like one of the only outlets to express myself and finally satisfy my purpose. I could gather all of the scattered notes of thoughts I had jotted down through different seasons and ask God to make it into whatever He wanted. I am finally learning to enjoy the ride rather than trying to control it. I've never liked surprises, even good ones, but His surprises are always fulfilling.

For a time, I just did the same thing, the same routine, the same schedule, because getting off schedule made me fear that I would forget something. I made routine an idol and was very disturbed if it was interrupted. But a hunger continued to grow inside of me to defeat the negativity.

Starting as such a broken wife, I became motivated to cultivate the stomping grounds in our home with positivity. A new love emerged that taught me that I would love to be a stay-at-home mom, just like my mom, and be able to love, serve, and care for others like she does. I missed the natural cup-filling sense of being in her wonderful home. She uses the gift of being available for her family and also for others, being fruitful in everything. That is my dream—to be like my momma.

My mom has always decorated her home with verses. Since God is the Word, His presence continually fills the hearts and minds of everyone under her roof through signs of scripture everywhere around her living space. Those staples continue to be imprinted in my thoughts and keep me accountable to God and my family. I am so thankful for my gracious and generous upbringing of family.

"My son, keep your father's command and do not forsake your mother's teaching. Bind them always on your heart; fasten them around your neck. When you walk, they will guide you; when you sleep, they will watch over you; when you awake, they will speak to you. For this command is a lamp, this teaching is a light, and correction and instruction are the way to life" (Proverbs 6:20–23). When temptation filled my mind to often think, *Man, I'm still not out of the storm. I feel lost and just haven't figured it out yet. I don't know how to move forward*, the thought of accountability to family kept me going.

I wanted to live as a fragrant offering to the Lord, step up when I am called, fill in where help is needed, help and encourage those in my path and on my heart, love everyone, live fully, thank everybody, and go to heaven. That is my momma's heart, and I wanted it to be mine too. In God's perfect timing, He stripped me of myself and filled me with greater things. I had to turn the gears from being an empty receiver to being a continually filled giver because of Jesus.

I had to get my mind right in order to clarify and justify my new purpose. I needed to put a label on my why. One reason I knew that I wanted to get healthy and take care of myself was so that I could seek for a way to use my restored abilities to give back to people for what they did for me. I wanted to honor God, my family, and community and be the best wife to Tyler after he had walked through fire for me. I was fueled not just by what these people did but also by who they are and what they live for.

I guess my desire of wanting to be a wife, mom, and homemaker came to light in a really unexpected way, with efforts to mimic the love I was shown through such brokenness. I wanted to be Tyler's wife not because of what he did for me, and always does, but because of who he is. He deserves the best, and I knew I had to get there. There is no one in this world like that man. I don't get it. Every day, I don't get it. He is something else: a gift from God given to me to understand Him more. Our marriage inspires me to view everyone this way, how God would. There is power in God's presence, and with a spiritual lens, we can sense that more evidentially. The spiritual fuels, motivates, and empowers me.

It took a lot more faith once I remembered myself; I was more than my body that had just taken a beating. There was a girl with a voice inside that body too. The more I became aware, the more scary things seemed. I was in this broken body and still trying to find the missing pieces of my puzzle after important decisions had been made for my life.

My brain doesn't seem to work naturally with a big-picture mindset; I live very much in the moment because that is all I am able to focus on. Since I couldn't think about more than half of a thing at a time, it was so hard for me to think big picture. I could only focus on whatever the tiny task was right in front of me; even the simplest tasks took 110 percent focus to remember what I was doing and bring it to completion. There is no such thing as a mindless task for me. Something as simple as tying my shoe or as complex as giving a speech takes the same amount of focus as I feel the neural pathways being sketched into being. I felt frozen until I could finally regain independence and do things for myself. I knew that being the doer would give me confidence again as new connections started to rewire in my brain.

Thinking ahead is not a natural way of thinking for me because that implies thinking of something beyond what is right in front of me. I would often just sink inward with sadness and loneliness, waiting for a Deliverer for so long because I didn't have a confident sense of direction for my life anymore.

My new life requires a lot of rest, and I would often fight the need to lie down because I was so lonely. I loved people but didn't have the energy to love them in ways I used to. When I had the peace of mind to lie down, God often spoke to me during these times of rest, and I was always excited to listen or see what memories He might bring to light. I felt more connected to God and people as I tried to be fruitful by thinking outward, as He inspired me in these quiet moments.

I didn't feel like I was really living until I realized it wasn't my purpose I needed to find. I wanted to figure out the new role God had for me in how to best bless others. I count it a huge blessing that I have the physical abilities to do a lot of things. The reason I can walk and talk is because of His restoration, and I owe it all back to Him.

I am spiritually convicted by the testimony of our marriage; the symbolism of being Tyler's broken bride is plainly analogous to being Christ's broken bride. All of us are broken, unworthy, saved, and redeemed. While it is true that we don't deserve God's goodness and grace, it is just as true that we get to accept His blessings anyway.

God gave me a special gift in a very special man. My husband can do anything; he carries the heavy load of my weaknesses and makes them seem invisible. And defeated. The man I got to marry keeps my life filled with beautiful and mysterious purpose as we try to pursue the Lord together in new ways. We are so grateful for the bountiful blessings on our lives and seek to be fruitful and obedient in our ways. I need Tyler as a leader, and God has formed such a sweet bond of trust in our relationship. The passion that that 6'5" goober has to lead and provide is pretty special, and we continued trusting God and following His lead on our union.

GIVE, MORE

*"For everyone who asks receives; the one who seeks finds; and
to the one who knocks, the door will be opened."*
—MATTHEW 7:8

*Wow, I just experienced God moving in my heart again. I sure must keep
Him busy up there with the service project that I am. In a Bible study
group I am involved in, we just learned about the property of blood in
a life being. "For the life of a creature is in the blood, and I have given
it to you to make atonement for yourselves on the altar; it is the blood
that makes atonement for one's life" (Leviticus 17:11). There is power in
the blood; there is life in the blood!*

I know that through such a horrific event as my brain aneurysm,
God allowed "triumph through the tragedy," as my dad so positively
put it. As toxic as that blood was to my brain and physical body, I
truly feel it was cleansing to my spirit. The Spirit of the Almighty
God, living inside of all of us Christians, has been working so
patiently in me in trying to endure the search journey of His purpose
being revealed. I want to view my aneurysm with this same triumph
of answered prayers that my family chooses to rejoice in every day;
God has already won.

The biggest tragedy in the history of the world was when Jesus was sacrificed on the cross, but God brought triumph and victory through that tragedy. It is through Jesus's blood that was shed that we can live cleansed, forgiven, empowered, and inspired. There is power in the blood; there is cleansing in the blood. There is new life in the blood! And that stands true forever. I want to view my aneurysm, that killed so much of my flesh and brought so much anxiety, turmoil, and terror to my family, as cleansing and renewing to the life that He sustained because it was in God's will and He used it for good. I can't help but to share this victory in Jesus's name!

In Exodus 14, God told the Israelites through Moses to stand firm and to never be afraid. The Lord promised they would see the deliverance He would bring for them (13). Moses delivered the encouragement, "The Lord will fight for you; you need only to be still" (14). The God we serve today is the same God who led the Israelites along the road to their rescue from the Egyptians. In His faithfulness, God sent a pillar of cloud to guide their journey by day and a pillar of fire by night, giving them light and direction with His presence. The Lord was with the Israelites and sustained them both day and night (Exodus 13:21–22). Just like He sustained the Israelites, He continues to sustain us as well.

With a calling saturated in faith, it is a mission to wake up every day with Jesus shining through our pores as we follow His pillar of light in its various forms. We can't run in front of God when He is working. He needs our attention and obedience but not our will. It is hard to be still but easier if we remember that He is *forever* on the throne; He is always available and ready for us to look His direction. He is ready for us to climb the ladder into His heavenly presence.

I felt like I used that ladder when my brain was turned off, but when it started to turn on, I seemed to forget it and relied more on my own ways, excited to put my working brain to use. But I kept falling and searching to finally find my way. I had to consciously rely on Him, too, in every way. Now I know that I *must* reach for that ladder that brings life and perspective because it leads us to eternity with Him.

I am thankful that my parents and family have always had a tight culture rooted in the Lord for generations. Growing up, friends were always welcome in our home, as both of my parents were equally involved in providing support and encouragement in any and all ways they could. I didn't ever realize what a rarity that was and how that had always been an unspoken source of fuel for me. My faith seemed tangible because of the plethora of blessings, right in arm's reach. This base of family love and support kept my cup full every day, and it spilled over to every category of my life. To seek God was an easy and natural act that mimicked the examples around me, and I tried to live boldly in ways that I knew were right.

As a student athlete, I always worked hard, with optimistic expectations for great things. It seemed automatic to rely on God for things like big games, and I was always eager to ask for His strength and direction when I had the opportunity to perform on the court or in the classroom. It was exciting to relate Bible verses to whatever activity I was doing and have full trust in the God I was familiar with to show up and deliver me, time after time. I loved to be a leader, with confidence and humility. Everything I did was enjoyable and exciting to me, and I always stayed motivated to grow. One of my favorite verses in Colossians reads, "Whatever you do, work at it with all your heart, as working for the Lord, not for human masters, since you know that you will receive an inheritance from the Lord as a reward. It is the Lord Christ you are serving" (3:23–24). It has always been natural for me to do just that.

My drive and work ethic were second to none, as I plummeted over every molehill without even noticing it. I had always been a dauntless leader in all of the countless activities I was involved in, seeking to love and encourage the ones I was trying to serve. This snowball of momentum got bigger and bigger every day for twenty years of my life, and I was finally ready to graduate college and start life on my own.

But what if that snowball disintegrated into millions of particles of dust and I had to start over as a wounded warrior? What would be my true source of foundation then?

In the Bible, there are several examples of people starting from scratch and putting radical faith to action. God often leads His people along wild goose chases just to test their obedience, and *He* proves faithful every time. His nature never changes; this same God is alive today.

Noah put radical faith to action by obeying God's command to build an ark and save his family, although mocked and ridiculed by many through his efforts (Hebrews 11:7). Abraham obeyed God and moved to a foreign place, even without understanding; he had hope in bigger plans for a home whose "architect and builder is God" (10). His wife, Sarah, gave birth to their son long after childbearing age, and she recognized God's promise to them as faithful (11). God blessed them with descendants "as numerous as the stars in the sky and as countless as the sand on the seashore" (12). By courageous faith, Abraham also answered God's test to sacrifice his only son, Isaac, even after waiting so long to have a child (17). He reasoned that God could even raise the dead, and God crowned his obedience with favor (19).

Moses took a humble stance to endure being mistreated alongside the people of God when in Egypt (25). Moses had "regarded disgrace for the sake of Christ as of greater value than the treasures of Egypt, because he was looking ahead to his reward" (26). Miracles happen when God sits on His throne: He parts the waters of the sea, tears down walls, shuts the mouths of lions, raises the dead, and turns weaknesses to strengths (33, 34). He is a God who shows tender, generous favor to His people.

Even through the twists and turns of our own journeys, we can fix our gaze on God at any point and know that His sovereignty is constant. Hebrews chapter 12 encourages us to fix our eyes on Jesus's example: He is the perfect pioneer of faith, attaining a righteous reward after the horrendous act of being nailed to a cross (2). Even through excruciating pain and desperation, Jesus sought God in His crucifixion. As Christians, we must grow in our trust in God *through* the storm, seeking to pour from the abundant ways He fills us *after* the storm, just like Jesus did for us.

Along with reading about heroes of faith in the Bible, I get to see and talk to faith heroes in my family every day. I consider my dad one of the most legendary faith giants ever created. He consistently pours from a cup that never runs dry and blesses others with his every breath and ounce of energy. Alongside him, my mom lives so faithfully with both of her arms extended to reach out, serve, and love, *deeply*. Their examples and heritage truly sustain and inspire me every day. My brother is so hardworking, skilled, and determined in everything he sets out to do, and it seems to be in his blood to be a provider someday. My sister makes sunlight seem dim when put in comparison to her own heart and personality. "The Maddox five" is surely a special thing to be a part of forever because God radiates through that Christian heritage, powerfully.

I am in awe of how my family, established through Papa and Nana and other ancestors before them, has remained faithful through trials to prove triumphant. When I was in the hospital through the physical journey of my stroke, everyone in my family stuck closer than ever and *chose* to grow in faith. They even brought in others, relying on Jesus together and giving Him an even bigger platform to perform. My parents led the way, followed by my brother and sister, grandparents, aunts, uncles, cousins, and dear friends. Hearing about each of their journeys has inspired me to persevere through my own and desperately try to "finish the race and complete the task the Lord Jesus has given me-the task of testifying to the good news of God's grace" (Acts 20:24). Though each and every Christian has a story or struggle, God continually proves to conquer for His children and turn every battle into a testimony through His name. Even without a tangible Christian dynasty to hug, talk to, or learn from, we are all a part of one by faith when we learn to recognize *Him* in any situation.

God so willingly even turns the bad to good when we allow Him to intervene. We don't have to be sad or depressed or anxious forever. That is *not* His will for us to live in permanently, and we should never believe the lie that that is His will for us. I used to think it was, and I just had to tough this life out until getting to heaven. But God didn't create us to suffer here. He is perfectly fine with us going through trials, because they sharpen and refine us, giving us opportunities to trust Him more. We can always trust His faithfulness to be waiting for us, even when we feel like giving up. His ways are higher, and He gives us instructions on how to walk this high road in the Bible.

I used to think reading the Bible and following God was a separate category than having fun, but the joy that comes from following His Word is truly the greatest. He forms that in us by changing our perspective and giving us nourishment when we draw water from *His* spring of life. The greatest gift and command we can obey is to love Him back, and Deuteronomy (6:1–9) commands us how to do so.

> These are the commands, decrees and laws the Lord your God directed me to teach you to observe in the land that you are crossing the Jordan to possess, so that you, your children and their children after them may fear the Lord your God as long as you live by keeping all his decrees and commands that I give you, and so that you may enjoy long life. Hear, Israel, and be careful to obey so that it may go well with you and that you may increase greatly in a land flowing with milk and honey, just as the Lord, the God of your ancestors, promised you. Hear, O Israel: The Lord our God, the Lord is one. Love the Lord your God with all your heart and with all your soul and with all your strength. These commandments that I give you today are to be on your hearts. Impress them on your children. Talk about them when you sit at home and when you walk along the road, when you lie down and when you get up. Tie them as symbols on your hands and

bind them on your foreheads. Write them on the
doorframes of your houses and on your gates.

God's commands are a treasure; they are *life giving*.

Because of my deep Christian roots through the examples set
before me, it has always seemed easy and natural to trust His Word.
It is black and white fact that we are born and will have some sort
of hardship, but we ought to have hope and trust in the Lord to
bring what may seem like unexpected good. In light of this fact,
I have always been fueled and motivated by that hope and help
through a Christian home. My upbringing has radiated the truth in
Psalm 46: "God is our refuge and strength, an ever-present help in
trouble. Therefore we will not fear, though the earth give way and
the mountains fall into the heart of the sea, though its waters roar
and foam and the mountains quake with their surging. There is a
river whose streams make glad the city of God, the holy place where
the Most High dwells. God is within her, she will not fall; God will
help her at break of day" (1–5). He has always been active and alive
through my Spirit-filled loved ones, and I am grateful to reflect on
their faithfulness.

As a bride, I was chosen in my brokenness: all of my memory
was gone, my life tool set had been snatched away, and I endured
new physical pains every day. I had to choose to find purpose in
faith, which is not tangible, but we can see its existence with the
right perspective. The purpose I once thought I had was not the
case anymore, but I am grateful for my husband, family, and people
who have believed in me the whole time. God gives us an inner
motivation through His Spirit, a drive that can never be stopped
when used for His glory. The fact that this drive was the greatest for
me when all of the stuff of life was snatched away is proof to me that
God is real. Sure, it's easiest to fall off the path during the hard times,
during the times when it's frustrating because there are no doors left
to knock on. But in the darkest valley, He is waiting.

Despite the flood of blessings from God, I often felt trapped and lost in that exciting wedding season because discernment was so hard for me, and any decision was stressful. I was in a season of life where it seemed like there were forks in the road everywhere. All I felt was severe brain fog, and I needed God's clarity to help me with every step.

The position for which I had worked so hard for twenty years started to disappear, one thing at a time, and I always felt the need to play catch up to that old life. When reflecting on Jesus's lesson to Martha and Mary, my inherent personality is essentially like Martha in the Bible, who wanted to get things done rather than to sit, be still, and listen. I sought to choose to be like Mary when it is so natural for me to be a Martha.

"Martha, Martha," the Lord answered, "you are worried and upset about many things, but few things are needed-or indeed only one. Mary has chosen what is better, and it will not be taken away from her" (Luke 10:41–42). Although I was confused and unsure about so many things after a brain injury, I wanted to be like Mary. I wanted to choose what was better. I wanted to strive every day to have Mary's patience and clarity in decisions, choosing humility over honor and finding peace in rest. But it is *hard*. Of course, Jesus's ways are always right, but they never seem easy to follow.

As I tried to keep things simple, I found that everything that was once so tangible for me started to gradually disappear. However, it didn't make sense to cling to a firm foundation that I couldn't see either. But 2 Corinthians implies that our faith is more reliable than our sight (5:7). A lifestyle of faith does not come without struggle, but His Word equips us with all we need. My dad always reminds our family that we have to feed ourselves every day with that spiritual nourishment and positivity.

As I was in the midst of such a spiritual battle and testimony, I often blamed other things for my struggles when the root was there from the start: my AVM. That event caused heartache and pain for my family, and I hate that more than anything. But even as they waded through the waves of that fierce storm, they praised God. Not only so, but they encouraged others to do so as well. They met other people in the midst of their storms, to offer encouragement, while they were chin deep in the waters of their own.

Tyler often tells me of the time when my dad was going around the hospital praying with others while his own daughter was in a room hooked up to tubes and machines. That doesn't seem to make sense. *Who has even heard of faith like that?* But that is my dad. When someone is equipped with the spiritual armor of God, that person is unstoppable. God's ways are simply beyond human comprehension, and we get to *expect* radical things from Him.

The book of Zechariah reads, "This is the word of the Lord to Zerubbabel: 'Not by might nor by power, but by my Spirit,' says the Lord Almighty" (4:6). To let His Spirit lead your life is truly exciting and freeing. His ways are perfect, and His Word is flawless. We can always be confident when we follow His Word. And the good news in His Word applies to everyone.

In the book of Psalms, the verse "Take delight in the Lord, and He will give you the desires of your heart" doesn't mean He gives us exactly what we want (Psalm 37:4). Instead, He gives us the actual desire; He makes our desires *change* in order to orchestrate His will, and it's so cool. When falling off that cliff backward in a trust fall to follow His path, we may find ourselves growing with new desires as He starts changing and molding our hearts. It is His perfect plan to make our lives align with His will because that *is* what's best for us; He will go to extravagant measures to pursue us. Praise the Lord for His kindness, patience, and absolutely perfect love.

To have the freedom to enter God's presence with Him is a privilege, and what He wants in return is our love and obedience. I think to love God takes intentional action. It takes a pure heart. It takes a committed Spirit, all in and unwavering. It takes a selfless soul that quickly learns how fullness is actually found in God and others. Even though His plans are quite often different from ours, they are better. His ways are higher, always.

What a shame it would be to settle. What a shame to not believe and press on. Without encouragement, wisdom, and guidance from others, we wouldn't know we could. But God's presence is alive and active all around us, and it's convicting to notice; it can't help but change you and guide you to His will. Every one of us has a different story, a different journey, but an identical destination. Putting spiritual meaning to everything is the key to finding our purpose on earth while waiting for our eternity in heaven.

But while we're on earth, we can still praise God and intentionally seek Him in every moment. He says, "You will seek me and find me when you seek me with all your heart" (Jeremiah 29:13). His presence and His blessings are everywhere when we strive to see through a spiritual lens.

When Tyler asked me to marry him in such a special way, I felt like I had to turn my back on my family because, in my mind, I was faced with two choices: to continue what I was working toward and graduate from LCU and then apply to PT school *or* to get married to Tyler in three months. In my broken mind, I couldn't do both things because a brain injury causes severe tunnel vision. Therefore, I was faced with choosing one route or the other. I didn't want to look like I just fell in love and rode off into the sunset, forgetting everything else. I have always been very driven and determined to stay focused and get my work done, and it was scary to make that decision and stop all I once knew was right. But I could only be all in to one or the other, and I didn't want to let myself forget Tyler.

While God performed a miracle to save my life, I am often reminded it wasn't mine anyway. It's His, and it has been from the start, whether I choose to acknowledge it or not. It's fun to be led by His Spirit. We can do anything with God. *Anything.* Faith is the key ingredient to this fullness of life, and it is truly the answer to all of our struggles. When He answers us, we must also listen to how we ought to demonstrate our new and refined faith. This inspired faith can't be quiet or hidden; it must be a *fruitful* faith. It must be a faith with action, because "faith by itself, if it is not accompanied by action, is dead" (James 2:17).

28

TRIUMPH IN TRAGEDY: THE REAL MONSTER

For though we live in the world, we do not wage war as the world does.
—**2 CORINTHIANS 10:3**

I just experienced God moving in my heart again. We are living in my ideal dream situation, literally. Lately, though, I've been having some mind games and getting really anxious. I've been letting things I've always dreamed of *cause me stress and anxiety. I've had a victim mentality instead of practicing that preemptive planning quality, being ready and able to tackle whatever stimulus comes my way. My dream was turning into a nightmare because of the flooding of things into my brain, and I felt attacked with new stimuli. Even good stuff.*

Getting away for a second, changing routine, doing something fun, and returning to the same activities and environment has completely allowed me to regroup and get a change of heart. Currently, I'm in the exact same external situation, but my mind is sharpened and more in tune with Him. I love what I'm doing again, and it's exactly the stimuli that caused anxiety and flooding in my brain before.

I guess there's not one thing I can do to finally pay God or people back enough or feel as if I have conquered my brain injury. I am forever unquenched. May I live every day writing the lyrics to my fight song.

The AVM that had been in my brain from birth gave my life quite the twist. Although I understand that I am in the tiny percentage of being a high-functioning stroke survivor, the residual deficits from this injury have a tendency to make things very frustrating for me.

It wasn't until four years after my injury that the past memories of my life, besides childhood, started to make themselves present in my brain again. I had chosen not to rely on those memories because God was doing a new thing in me. After losing what felt like every connection in my brain, a reconstruction process had to take place. I felt so encouraged with anything that popped back into my memory bank and gave me reassurance that I *might* be considered normal. I wanted to love myself again as more than just the bald girl who everyone knew had a stroke, but I had to start giving myself grace so I could treat others the same.

I wanted to conquer my lack of memory by staying fueled with things that inspired me. Looking at pictures of the waiting room in Wichita Falls the night of my surgery trumps a nonexistent memory. People on their knees in prayer for me at the LCU fountain trumps a nonexistent memory. Family trumps a lack of memory, and I could never honor them enough for putting their faith in action for me during horrific darkness. Tyler's love and faithfulness trump a lack of memory, then and always.

Faithful love is a gift that is beautiful to receive, and I feel so favored to have been given that in multiple areas of my life. God has shown me so much grace and kindness, and I want to be a faithful steward of His mercies that are so tender. The book of James reads, "[Our life is] a mist that appears for a little while and then vanishes" (4:14). We must make every day count. I know I must intentionally reflect on these things to fuel my faith so that I will trust and obey him even when I don't understand or remember.

Losing it all to God is not a loss at all, even though it can seem scary. Thankfully, His grace washes us clean from the doubt and hesitance that might otherwise seem overwhelming. He longs to draw us nearer to Him. Though God's blessings are incomprehensible, that mysterious faith drives us to live *unquenched* every day.

I see that incomprehensible quality in Tyler every day as he works *so* hard and *so* faithfully to provide and lead; he touches my heart and inspires me daily. The gift of his faithful love, battle-tested and true, pushes me to be better. While I might not remember or ever understand how or why God has completely saturated our story with His grace, I wanted to choose to "be still, and know" that He is always good (Psalm 46:10). We both realized that we must strive to let God be God as we found our lesser role in His greater plan.

But in the midst of my journey, I felt so completely overstimulated all the time that I never had the peace of mind to just be calm and relax. Even though there wasn't much going on for me anymore, I was constantly racking my brain to test what I might be forgetting. It was traumatic to not have a memory while starting to look better from the outside; everyone started to assume I was fine and asked things of me that I thought were scary. I was exhausted from the questions and treatment due to others' ignorance of the severity of my injury, but Tyler always had my back when we were together. He was very protective of my energy and guarded me from the piranhas, as we jokingly called people who sucked my energy. Eventually, I learned to not be so naïve in trusting everyone.

Without my family at arm's length anymore, I had to choose courage every day. I was either lonely or around people who didn't understand my new struggles, but I tried to keep running even without proper understanding of what had happened myself. Though in the midst of trying to keep my head above water every single day, I was grateful for the man of strength who chose to marry me. I tried to couple my steady endurance with his monster strength as we began to run the marathon of life together. It is only through God that we can claim trust and hope.

Tyler saw me go through one of the darkest times, and we have fought through a lot to get where we are. Ultimately, God's blessings have trumped everything, and we can't help but want to give it back to Him. As we desired to start a family of our own someday, we wanted to walk with the Lord and in His light. We both chose to give it our all, to God and each other. There is no such thing as lukewarm to our heavenly Father; we have to be fully committed.

Learning how to accept myself with a brain injury has been the hardest thing I've ever had to do, especially in front of Tyler. I used to try to just shrug it off because I was too ashamed to acknowledge such weaknesses in marriage. At times, I felt like literally everything had been taken away from me. I seemed to have strayed off the path a little bit whenever I started to do things on my own, isolating myself and putting a guard up. But through the quietness, I decided to defeat loneliness by fueling it with purpose. I accepted the fact that I must walk myself through feelings in order to not have such a knee-jerk reaction to everything. I had to be intentional no *respond* to things rather than allowing my natural urge to *react* to things without a processing filter. This is something that I fight daily.

I grew to not have a preference or personality anymore because I lived in fear, feeling lonely and discouraged and paranoid of what I was forgetting. I found that whenever I was with a group of people, it seemed that everything consisted of some sort of project toward me, and as helpful and kind as it was, I just associated the help with humiliation. It seemed like I had lost every connection in my brain, the blueprints of who I was, I thought. I wanted to do stuff, and I wanted to prove to people I could be independent again. I reminded myself I had what mattered most: Jesus, a man who loved me so faithfully as a wife, and family. Practicing intentional thankfulness of my blessings gave me confidence.

At first, my thankfulness was sneakily superficial; I was thankful because I knew all of the changes that had happened were good compared to dying. I had lost a lot, but it took me a while to realize what all I had lost while also trying to jump back into life at full speed. The losses that weren't noticeable to others were the hardest for me to accept. But I didn't lose everything.

My family has blessed my whole life, my marriage, and future family by their spirituality, examples, and material blessings. They fuel me, spiritually and physically. With my dad's positive voice of encouragement in my head, I strive to claim and conquer what many may label as *immovable mountains* every day. My dad has the purest heart and has trained himself to see the good in everything. *Everything.* I hope to be like him more every day, bubbling with positivity and thankfulness. His voice of encouragement continued to whisper in my heart amid all of the dark thoughts I was having.

Growing up, his voice of direction constantly told me that I ought to view new things as stepping-stones and that no one had everything figured out. He told me to just keep trusting in the Lord through difficult situations and that He would give us everything we could ever imagine. It is such a blessing to have had the childhood I did, so full of light and love and rich tradition. Growing up is hard, but I try to live by the principles that have been instilled in me all my life by my parents and family. That Christian bond keeps me connected to the Vine that fuels me.

In all my confusion of being married through a brain injury and struggling to find new normals, my roots engrained in Jesus and family continued to graciously sustain me. This enabled me to press on and move forward, and I am so thankful to stand in the victory of having this rich heritage. That is what gets me out of bed in the mornings: a strong call to continue this fruitfulness, coupled with the fear of being a dud that would stop this legacy and be a waste of a miracle. God's blessings are so tender, and His grace is so real; He will always wait for us. I am motivated and inspired by my family heritage.

Mealtime triggered my childhood memories of family togetherness. While I was at home and couldn't drive, I tried to cook so that a mealtime would help me know what time of day it was; otherwise, I had no bearings for time or awareness after my brain surgeries. I wanted to continue this staple of family for Tyler and me someday because these memories of togetherness at the table with laughter and joy fueled me and got me through the days when I was deep in brain fog.

God, is my mind flashbacking to my wonderful childhood, reminding me of my most blessed and wonderful Christian heritage, so faithfully sustained through the souls before me, in order to start a legacy and ultimately be a fruitful vessel for you? I would love to stay home and raise kids like my momma. I can barely even leave our dog in his kennel while I go into town, so I can't imagine leaving kids at home someday. I want to always be there for them. I love You, God. Please help me and show me and guide me.

After creating the whole world, God spoke the command to "be fruitful and increase in number" (Genesis 1:28). Through faith, we are all born into this calling through Jesus's heritage. I feel honored and blessed to have that tangible calling and heritage through my own family as well, maintained through the faith of my ancestors. I feel called to carry out this legacy as a *fruitful* vine; I don't want to end it and fail God or my family in this way. After being stricken with a condition where I couldn't talk or communicate, I wanted to be sure to leave a legacy of faith that would be fruitful even if I wasn't there to be able to carry it out. I wanted to get everything God taught me put to paper so that I would never have to fear not being able to communicate again. This would give me the peace of mind that whatever happened to me, His will would be done, and my purpose would be complete.

FINISH

Who is He, this King of glory? The Lord
Almighty—He is the King of glory.
—**PSALM 24:10)**

2019—Three years from God removing that monster in my brain

This year, I want to change submissiveness that's morphed quietly into complacency and loss of self into passion, vision, and confidence. I have poured my cup to below empty trying to keep up, repay, and understand ... but that has been a chasing of the wind. God is good and deserves our praise—the firstfruits.

Processing a brain injury is a double-edged sword ... maybe even triple or quadruple. As the physical starts looking (hopefully a little) better, the mental is quietly understanding (and remembering ...) at its own speed and is empowered by the spiritual. I didn't know how to handle things for the news and interviews except to praise God. I didn't know how to process through what I felt like was the microscope of marriage that seemed to just zoom in on every struggle (through my eyes). I hate the focus being on self, so that's one reason this calling of writing a book has been growing underneath the rug for so long.

*But God did His part and is patient to let me try to find mine ...
though He doesn't need me for a second because He's already won.*

So, here's to dreaming big, embracing and tackling the new, remembering the old, and striving to let love drown out fears.

We all need God. Everyone. Growing up, my dad told my siblings and me to "always marry a Christian." That's so powerful, but I never knew the reality of that power and truth in a relationship ...

In our marriage, I had always recognized Tyler's pronounced qualities of strength and leadership, physically and spiritually, but my chronic stubbornness had always given me the green light in having the last word. Now, after a brain injury, it is more natural for me to be a submissive listener, completely opposite of my old self.

"OK stop. I'm getting overstimulated and about to get a headache," usually comes out of my mouth at least once a day, especially when listening to Tyler's explanations of his dreams and vision for us. God blessed my simple mind with a visionary partner, and gracious, he is so patient. I feel that we are still two college athletes trying to better each other before ourselves. I would not have the motivation to strive for greatness if I didn't feel the unspoken pressure of accountability to Tyler.

Living with a brain injury is something that takes an immense amount of self-motivation and discipline every day. That pride pill is sure a hard one to swallow; it seems that I find it stuck in my throat all the time. Although I don't remember the pain of *the* headache when my brain was bleeding, I know it must have tickled in comparison to the life changes it has brought me. It's easy to get caught in a circle of thought processes of new struggles that can go around and around endlessly if not stopped intentionally.

In light of this circling of thoughts that is sometimes unstoppable, waiting on God has been one of the hardest things I have ever had the privilege of doing. The responsibilities associated with this privilege can be trying: enduring and trusting while getting nailed in the face with other struggles. Waiting on anything is hard; patience is *so hard*! But waiting on God minimizes dreaded trials because of the light of a greater hope. We must always live with eager anticipation of a God who sees us trying because He says, "The Lord is good to those whose hope is in Him, to the one who seeks Him; it is good to wait quietly for the salvation of the Lord" (Lamentations 3:25–26). Sometimes, living with hope can feel like a spiritual discipline, and other times it is more natural. Katherine Wolf, a heroic AVM survivor, lives boldly in the truth that "hope heals." She said, "Everything is the power of the mind. You can, in fact, survive anything by redefining everything. Everything can be thought about different, and God calls us to ponder, recognize, wake up to what He is doing in the lives we are currently living and how we can live well within that-how we can suffer strong." It was and is a journey to be a Christian, and I crave encouragement from witnesses who share an unquenched momentum inside their souls. God is God. God is good. And because He is sovereign, it's all good. We really get to live with hope.

As I consciously acknowledged my need for God, I felt that He was silent when I needed Him most. After not hearing from Him for over a year, I grew discouraged by lack of direction in my new state of trying to be independent. My New Year's resolution in 2017 was to be intentional, but I often had a hard time silencing my desire for an unhealthy control. For a time, I was just searching wildly, staying busy as a bee but getting nowhere. I grew to believe that it's important to be intentional but not in control. Those are separate things. It's important to find the balance of being intentional and flexible. We are human *beings*, not human *doings*.

My drive to be intentional was fueled by my fear of forgetting; I tried so hard to accomplish a task before it would slip my mind. I thought the people who told me to "be still" and "slow down" were annoying because they didn't understand the hole I still had to climb out of. But when we just trust and obey, it's weird how God provides. God's presence is literally everywhere. He tells us to be strong and courageous because He will be with us wherever we go (Joshua 1:9). We really get to trust that.

Faith is real. Our lives must be a constant search of how we fit into His plan, not how His plan can complement ours. There's a difference. The foundation of God is unshakable. In Matthew, we read how the foundation of our houses, *our lives,* must be built on the Rock (7:24–27). Storms will come, but we have a welcome package with a key to a shelter than can *never* be destroyed. The insurance policy for that option is pretty expensive, but Christians qualify for the greatest benefits without having to pay anything out of pocket. *Jesus paid it all.* We must put our stock in that.

Although it has never been in my DNA to want to stray from a rigid structure or from the original plan, I have found joy in the search for purpose in such a new maze because I know He is with me. All those sayings, all those verses, in the Bible ... they're true. You can trust them. Just trust me; more importantly, trust Him. I began trying to let my example be my thank-you note and my purpose, sacrifice, and mission. I started to work intentionally to plant seeds and scatter them generously. I became able to nap without a racing heart because there I found purpose in example; there is faith in *God's* doing. I thought that I could let my purpose emerge through my example and let His praise through tragedy be a living psalm.

My example may not be through leading teammates anymore, and that's OK. I can still lead in my own family, and more importantly, under my own roof. God has given me a platform that He can do whatever He wants with and a calm boldness to share everything about my once introverted self. If it brings Him glory, why not try it? His ways haven't failed in thousands of years. His ways haven't failed ever.

I searched desperately for how to grip to this foundation when trying to make big life decisions after a tragedy that nearly shattered my identity, knowledge, and confidence. God graciously gave me a perspective that brought me contentment as a peacemaker, enabler, and encourager, and that seems like a miracle for this stubborn spirit of mine. Stubbornness can often be a good thing when it acts as an unexplainable force that allows us to remain confident and hopeful through what could easily seem like absolute terror.

My old life felt comparable to a paper sailboat dropped down a gully of water that I could only watch float by into an unknown distance. I didn't know how to operate with a broken control center—my brain—but this weakness sharpened me as I sought God's working in it. Through certain seasons, an optimistic Christian perspective is painfully hard. But God's Son, Jesus, holds the key that unlocks the treasures God has in store for those who love Him. Jesus is "the way and the truth and the life" (John 14:6). He offers us all a free ride. I found that He had given me a new control center through His Spirit in me. I often battled this surrender to God, but once I *fully* believed in who and what I was surrendering to and living for, my confidence grew. I still ask God every day to help me in this.

I have to intentionally trust God to work on my behalf through weaknesses that I never dreamed of. As the logical left side of my brain was dormant during such a crucial time in my life for decision-making, the abstract, creative right side of my brain became the new Malori as I navigated through adulting. But when old memories became more apparent of who I once was, I demanded some sort of logic to the craziness, even though there wasn't exactly an x to solve for. I tried to be patient through the confusing silence of my left brain, but I felt like a kid waiting to open presents on Christmas morning as I tried to persevere through the waiting.

I was ready to make money. I was ready to feel independent. I was ready to feel purposeful, confident, and smart. I gave myself to others so that I might help them be what *I* wanted to be. At times, I felt momentum, and at times, I felt discouraged. Although it was hard to find contentment and purpose, I had the privilege of trusting that someday, through my pain, God was going to bring a deeper knowledge to the light that might be able to help some if I would just endure.

I fight the thought of just wanting to go to sleep several times an hour, making it difficult to stay motivated to finish any task, specifically long-term ones. I fight the voice of hesitance when pursuing any task that is constantly whispering, "You really think you should do this? You really think you *can*?" I fight the thought, *You are an unexplainable miracle and really should be dead*, based off facts without God's intervention.

But the whispers of God always seem to be louder than Satan's screams.

"But you are a chosen people, a royal priesthood, a holy nation, God's special possession, that you may declare the praises of Him who called you out of darkness into His wonderful light" (1 Peter 2:9). He is calling *us*. Just because we haven't answered yet doesn't mean He isn't calling. We must learn to recognize and adjust our lives accordingly in order to follow His master plan.

Rather than being bitter about the sudden and drastic changes that my life took, I often try to emphasize and practice the art of contentment in my life. I became stubborn to recognize blessings after such a whirlwind of life-changing events had clouded them greatly. Although so many things happened so fast that were completely out of my control, it is amazing how God's direction was, is, and will forever be right. The book of Isaiah reads, "The grass withers and the flowers fall, but the word of our God endures forever" (40:8). No storm can destroy God's Word.

Sometimes it's hard to be still and mentally allow myself to wake up when my body is ready to go. It is also hard to physically be still when my brain is getting bored and ready to do something, but it hurts to move or do anything that requires energy. To minimize headaches, I crave simplicity and peace. Multiple options bring clouded thoughts that easily bog me down, so it is essential for me to attain clarity in order to act on anything.

One area of trouble for me was the art of giving myself grace in the education category of life. Struggling through what seemed like kindergarten-level material was frustrating. I will never forget being told I was on a mental third-grade level. I will also never forget people's "encouragement," such as being handed a book of elementary-level worksheets that "should be helpful." I would never want someone to feel like they weren't smart or capable; that was one of the biggest disgraces to me after being salutatorian of a large 4-AAAA high school. Such acts fuel me to want to make sure others are confident, supported, and motivated to do anything they set their mind to.

It was often humiliating for me to be so helped, so a switch flipped inside of me to just enjoy learning in the process of what it was like to be in the shoes of someone needing it. After deciding to have the courage to feel it all, I knew I needed to be a voice for the voiceless.

I love people so much, but I became a gigantic grudge holder toward people who would frustrate or hurt me without knowing it. Because several thought they were helping me, I didn't have the heart to bring anything up about me needing space or boundaries. I knew they must deserve my everything since they had probably done an act worth repaying while I was unconscious. But thinking this way wasn't fair to me, and I had to learn to be content with doing the best I could.

Although I often retreated to hide my frustration from others by seeking to find the Lord in quiet time, I had to figure out a way to love people from this safe distance. It wasn't fair to myself to try to keep up with something I desired to do but physically could not do. In regard to handling people, God revealed this verse to me in light of that battle:

> "We love because He first loved us. Whoever claims to love God yet hates a brother or sister is a liar. For whoever does not love their brother and sister, whom they have seen, cannot love God, whom they have not seen. And He has given us this command: Anyone who loves God must also love their brother and sister" (1 John 4:19–21). I wanted to find out

how I could do that best without giving myself away completely.

It seemed unbelievable to me what my body went through, and it was hard for me to merge the pre-stroke life with the present. I believed it, I saw pictures ... but I couldn't remember or grasp that girl actually being me. It felt weird to admit that, but I knew I would continue feeling like an outsider until that truth was fully handled. The book of Luke reads, "For there is nothing hidden that will not be disclosed, and nothing concealed that will not be known or brought out into the open" (8:17). I had to give my wounds permission to fester. I wanted to choose to love, but I had to bring everything to the light, in hopes of helping others and myself.

Though it takes humility, we ought to always bring our struggles to the light and ask for His grace to penetrate that barrier that sin often puts on our hearts. The book of Lamentations says, "For no one is cast off by the Lord forever. Though He brings grief, He will show compassion, so great is His unfailing love. For He does not willingly bring affliction or grief to anyone" (3:31–33). It is freeing to be transparent and humble; God works through weaknesses powerfully.

I didn't remember my twenty-first birthday, even without the use of alcohol. But when I wrote, memories of certain things gradually lit up my mind like a Christmas tree; it was fun to rebuild my mind like that. Tyler kept telling me to write a book, and I usually thought, *Ew, no.* Though I secretly wanted to, I wasn't going to if someone was going to tell me to. Plus, I didn't even like to read myself because, with memory loss and a minimal attention span, it seemed pointless at times. I have to read even small paragraphs several times before anything starts to stick or make sense.

When new information is presented, I have to hurry and write it in my notes so I don't forget it. Then I can refer to it later and relearn it several times. I often do things in haste because of my fear of forgetting to do a said thing. For example, I fold clothes in such a sloppy way because I know that a neat stack of clothes is not a completely essential thing to a full life, and I want to remember the next thing I wanted to do after the clothes were folded. There are so many tiny hurdles to jump over, and I have to be intentional to maintain a calm, hopeful, and confident headspace to do anything.

But God has intervened His presence into my life's disaster by having a sense of urgency in readiness for His coming. God has translated such weaknesses into a mindset of "I want to hurry and do that thing before Jesus comes again." All of this endurance of recognizing new struggles continued to give way to a momentum that couldn't be stopped to write this book; I wanted to write a testament to have an example of God's intervention in a tangible form for others so that it might continue to be fruitful in His name.

God brought me obvious miracles through physical healing, and He has also shown me abundant miracles through spiritual healing. But what God has done as the cornerstone of our marriage, as *truly* the first cord in that cord of three strands, is also a miracle, and I can't help but share it. I didn't want to die until I had. It's crazy what God can do when He's the Captain of our lives. When zooming out and choosing to view the blessings on my life rather than the storm, I can't help but ooze with thankfulness. There's always a bigger picture. Once this perspective became more natural for me to see, contentment and purpose found their places silently. There was still that stubborn, persevering voice that wanted to be the best version of myself possible, and I couldn't help but want to do more.

I knew I had a special purpose just by being a small part of God's creation, and I felt Him nudging me to finish the unique journey He had empowered me to navigate. The message from Paul in Colossians proclaims a profound truth that gives such a sense of spiritual unity to His flock; it confirms a purpose we *all* have as God's children.

> Now I rejoice in what I am suffering for you, and
> I fill up in my flesh what is still lacking in regard
> to Christ's afflictions, for the sake of His body,

which is the church. I have become its servant by the commission God gave me to present to you the word of God in its fullness—the mystery that has been kept hidden for ages and generations, but is now disclosed to the Lord's people. To them God has chosen to make known among the Gentiles the glorious riches of this mystery, which is Christ in you, the hope of glory. He is the one we proclaim, admonishing and teaching everyone with all wisdom, so that we may present everyone fully mature in Christ. To this end I strenuously contend with all the energy Christ so powerfully works in me. (Colossians 1:24–29)

'Tis so sweet to trust in Jesus.

Anyone can do anything with God and someone who believes in or encourages them. I am thankful to experience His presence through the heritage of a Christian family, as that message continues to toss around my mind endlessly. What a *gift* that is, such a rich treasure. The blessings that have come from my family are abundant, and I believe that I am living in a generational blessing from God because of the precious family before me. They have established a rich culture of the fruitfulness that God desires, and woe is me if I were to let that taste of heaven fade away.

I wanted to acknowledge my extended family in hopes of someday honoring them for their heroic deeds for my immediately family and me, though I can't even come close to doing what they truly deserve. I also desired to make money for my family without having to be away from them or take any attention away from my role as a wife or mom. With this book, I sought to funnel those desires into one focused source. I would "swing for the moon, and if I missed, I would still land among the stars," just like my dad always told me. I trusted God to bring that about in His timing, silently, if I sought to honor Him with the life He had spared.

Anytime God works, even in the smallest details, it is a miracle. God, the Creator, has made everything good, and we must pray for the eyes to perceive things in His way. He is always working for our good, and He never fails. Though I always had, I grew to admire my mom's example more than ever before during this time as I tried to mimic her ways. While the deeds she performs are always angelic, what seems to have meant the most to me is her faithful willingness to just *be there,* wherever *there* was. "There" often meant in the stands, in the car, at home, on the other end of the phone, at the dinner table, on a shopping spree, and more. Her often unplanned schedule is a gift because she thrives when she is spontaneous; she always proves to be equipped as "her arms are strong for her tasks" (Proverbs 31:17). The way that she has always made herself available, even without being planned, continues to give me confidence even when we're apart. *Mom* is a big title and seems to be a heavenly anointing.

My childhood preacher, Dale Mannon, had a powerful and wise lesson on a "cruciform-shaping environment," emphasizing the power in a Christian home. He proclaimed that a cruciform home is truly a taste of heaven. In my broken, twenty-year-old mind, through my stroke recovery, what sustained me was this very truth. All I had left of myself were memories shaped around this blessing of a cruciform environment, such as meals together at the dinner table, family support at school and sporting events, camping trips, vacations, traditions of celebration for baptisms, birthdays, and holidays. *That* is family. Tyler and I shared an unspoken, mutually burning desire to establish this together.

With a Christ-centered family, there is discipline, there is hardship, there is sacrifice, there is service, and there is safety. There is resilience because there is hope. There is tradition, there is remembrance of loved ones, and there is a kingdom culture; with family, there is victory and always something to celebrate. Jesus is the King and forever the head of the household. Following His ways allows us to truly experience a taste of heaven.

In the shadows of Tyler's leadership and love in our marriage, this staple of family sustained me. However, the strength of Tyler's and my marital bond seemed diluted through all of the commotion of good things, and he recognized that we needed to grow for a time *away* from the commotion. *With God as the captain, He will surely take us safely to our desired destination*, I thought, even though I still had uncertainty with so many moving parts.

For me, getting married stretched my faith because it meant saying goodbye to all the things I had worked for my whole life, even after what felt like losing almost everything from a traumatic brain injury. That took a lot of faith for my stubborn go-getter personality. The reason for this decision being such an ultimatum was my memory. I knew I was capable of doing anything I wanted, but I was fearful of my forgetfulness when my attention had to be dispersed to different things. For example, I had the confidence to be a physical therapist, but if I was fully engaged in my career, I wouldn't have the neurons left for Tyler and feared I might forget him. The opposite was also true; if I was married, I wouldn't have the neurons left for my career.

I chose Tyler.

Tyler and I choose to make our happily ever after using the hand we've been dealt. God has graciously painted our story with the generous gloss of a heavenly perspective. We both had a quiet confidence in God's greater plan, although it seemed like it took forever to start reaping tangible benefits as we tried to cling to our faith through each of our separate times of desperation.

While working remotely and bouncing around different coffee shops to support Tyler through school, I was able to overhear several interesting conversations. I didn't do this intentionally, but there were a few times when I was interested enough to think that squirrel was worth chasing, at least for a second.

One conversation seemed to be a counseling session with a middle-aged lady and a younger, college-aged girl. From the older woman's mentoring perspective, I heard her say, "Everyone makes decisions based off fear." That is something I have thought about several times daily, wondering about its truth.

Although we are told to "fear the Lord" several times in the Bible (Deuteronomy 10:12), this fear, I believe, is not the "scared to death and can't think straight" type of fear. It is a healthy fear, out of respect and reverence to the Lord our Maker. This fear once silenced me to a seeking season of submission, wanting to perfect my next steps toward His plan.

But living with such drastic life changes after my injury taunted me that the natural way of life from there on would be for me to live in fear. Because all of my new deficits were swept under the rug and hidden by the excitement of new life changes, such transition for me had to be researched and brought to light intentionally, because I didn't have the counseling or warning about the new life I was jumping into with everything that had happened so quickly. Deficits such as brain fog, confusion, memory loss, and verbal and logical functioning troubles involving speaking, writing, listening, and reading were insane to figure out on my own. But after walking the route of fear, intimidation, uncertainty, and doubt, my positivity was driven through a deep stubbornness. I wanted to conquer for myself, not because someone commanded me to. Since I belonged to a population that was unfamiliar to most, I figured I could slowly try to dive in and see how I might help others navigate a wounded life too.

The Bible *never* says we ought to live in fear but gives bold instruction and reassurance on ways to *not fear* (Isaiah 41:10). As God has heard my silent prayers and thoughts, I believe that He has answered my heart, graciously. Later, the lessons taught to me through that intense patience and endurance blossomed with a confident assurance that *nothing* was meaningless. It takes an immense amount of faith, patience, and discernment to seek answers from the Lord. But all we have to do is ask (James 1:5–6)! I believe in the power of asking Him to see with a spiritual lens so that we may try to better understand His will through a heavenly perspective.

So, a *healthy* fear of God is what drives me. I fear His divine nature being released against me if I am not obedient, and I trust Him to help me conquer the impossible because He strengthens me. He motivates me.

When given the gracious honor of a miracle, I am often reminded of the heavy responsibility that it comes with. Although sometimes it feels like I am trying to run a marathon with a weighted vest, I am stubbornly motivated. In regard to this miracle God gave me, I often think, *Lord, how can I receive this?* I still wonder that every day, but when I look to God, He removes my baggage. He releases my feet from the snare (Psalms 25:15) and lets me run again.

God funneled my terror into a motivation that kept gaining momentum. Through my struggle, I became stubborn to defeat the brain deficits of my left brain by either capitalizing on them or using my right brain instead.

The left brain is responsible for things like detail, academics, and logic. Those traits seemed to define a big part of me for twenty-one years, but when those things about me faltered, I knew I had to tap into a bigger Source. I am still stubborn about improving those things I was once good at. I was determined to graduate college, and that gave me confidence to conquer the academic and detail-oriented tasks that seemed impossible without a strong left brain. I am proud when I remember details by finding a way to connect bits of data and make them stick. When I am left brain fatigued, I try to utilize right brain strengths, and the spiritual realm is always my safe spot.

Short-term memory loss was defeated in my left brain by living in the spiritual realm of my right brain. I often remember things with my heart. I am a spiritual mentor to many, thrive in relationships, love being social, and participate in outdoor activities when I remember to use those right-side strengths. I am blessed through Tyler's profession when I get to join him and do a little ranchin' in the great outdoors. After having paralysis on my right side, I love to perform deeds with my right hand and simultaneously slap Satan in the face. Why? Because God strengthens me and has helped me overcome.

Memory loss was freeing when I stopped putting pressure on myself and remembered I was able to receive new mercies every morning. Every day was new; that's how it is to live with Christ. With such a perspective, it was more natural for me to enjoy the process; I had to stop myself from letting the destination be the goal. I learned that my circumstances may not change, but *I* can change. I never envisioned walking this road to get to my happily ever after, but I was determined to prove that my left brain weaknesses plus right brain strengths equals God at work. I had to crawl some, even turned over to roll some. But goodness, I got there. When we live in a constant state of prayer, our bodies start to respond to our minds, and we really believe the faith we once just *thought* we believed. Our Spirits take over—the Holy Spirit, that is.

"Therefore we do not lose heart. Though outwardly we are wasting away, yet inwardly we are being renewed day by day. For our light and momentary troubles are achieving for us an eternal glory that far outweighs them all. So we fix our eyes not on what is seen, but on what is unseen, since what is seen is temporary, but what is unseen is eternal" (2 Corinthians 4:16–18). The unseen is more powerful than the tangible.

This makes me think about people who are in the hospital ... they're in there. Their spirits are alive in those feeble and sick bodies, unexplainable in medical terms. I was told of a divine intervention moment that proved the spiritual power to trump over the physical by a sweet new friend, Kenee Carter Dover, who had gone to the hospital with my family while I was in ICU. She was a graduate from LCU who had also played volleyball and was still connected to that LCU circle. She told me that she had read Psalm 23 at my bedside, and although I don't remember this moment, she explained that my body had responded with a spark of an obvious recognition to the words, as my eyes opened.

When our bodies are wasting away, our spirits remain alive

because of Jesus, and as Christians, we must fuel one another with that encouragement. The innocence, confidence, peace of mind, and purity of heart we receive from God as Christians is greater and stronger than any high or pleasure from an earthly substance. We will win every battle, every time, if we feed our spirits and keep them strong.

In the book of Philippians, Paul states, "I have learned to be content whatever the circumstances" (3:11). While trying to finally recover from my stroke, I am reminded every day that I am *forever* a work in progress; I will never experience the finished product this side of heaven. But that is not because of my brain injury. No matter how high or how low we may feel in light of our goals, we can't grasp the finished product that God has waiting for us.

This is both frustrating and exciting and requires an extravagant hope. Stubbornness says, "I want it now," but the voice of wisdom says, "Persevere! It will be worth it."

In times of crisis and disaster, it's essential to return to the base of a sound mind. There is unity in Christ, and we are all bound as His children with an eternal purpose that brings forth the most immense profit: unity, hope, love, light, forgiveness, and joy. In light of this freedom, Paul also speaks of the honorable responsibility tied to it:

> Though I am free and belong to no one, I have made myself a slave to everyone, to win as many as possible. To the Jews I became like a Jew, to win the Jews. To those under the law I became like one under the law (though I myself am not under the law), so as to win those under the law. To those not having the law I became like one not having the law (though I am not free from God's law but am under Christ's law), so as to win those not having the law. To the weak I became weak, to win the weak. I have become all things to all people so that by all possible means I might save some. I do all this for the sake

of the gospel, that I may share in its blessings. (1
Corinthians 9:19–23)

In the search, it's important to do what you know, not what you
feel, and to talk to yourself instead of listening to yourself. After
being close to dying, I wanted to be able to do so with the peace of
knowing I had done everything I could to advance the Gospel.

Though I never felt like I could do anything noble, I wanted
to establish a cruciform home with Tyler that may produce ones
who may. As God gave me the privilege of bringing a child into the
world to raise and love, my sense of accountability as a Christian
soared. I now had the opportunity to rely on God even more with
the upbringing of a child.

When the title *mom* was granted to me, I felt my burdens lifted
as I saw my little guy smile, breathe, and laugh; I wanted to grow
into the greatest version I could be for my family.

McCrae Dee and Roan Rivers, you made us a family. You
connected the dots. You tied the loose ends. You empowered me
with a sense of accountability to paint your world with the brush of
Jesus. You made us a *family,* and it's my honor to hold and care for
you with my right arm that was once immovable. And as written
in the book of Joshua, "As for me and my household, we will serve
the Lord" (24:15).

I have learned that God is on the throne, joyfully working all
things for the good of His children. There is not a single second He
takes off. I have learned that heartache is inevitable and that failure
is beneficial but only when viewed through a lens of faith.

Joy is still intentional but seems more natural when we seek to
radiate the love story told in the Bible. *That* love story is available to
all, because of Jesus. God is the one working. How can we *not* trust
that? Through a tested and unpretty (on my part) journey of faith,
we made it to our happily ever after on a ship named *God's grace.*
Welcome aboard.

Malori, Roan, Tyler, & McCrae at the ranch

McCrae & Roan at the Maddox Family Ranch

at the RA Brown Ranch
Photo courtesy of Kayla Jennings

at the Maddox Family Ranch

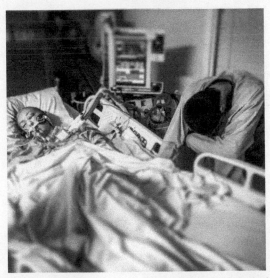

What faithful love looks like: Tyler at Malori's bedside

BIBLIOGRAPHY

Atabong, Sixtus. 2018. *My Father's Gift: How One Man's Purpose Became a Journey of Hope and Healing.* Koehler Books.

AVM Embolization. Cedars-Sinai, 2019. https://www.cedars-sinai. edu/Patients/Programs-and-Services/Imaging-Center/For-Patients/Exams-by-Procedure/Interventional-Neuroradiology/ AVM-Embolization.aspx.

The Bible. New International Version. Zondervan, 2011.

Collins English Dictionary. 2012. "Dictionary.com." https://www. dictionary.com/browse/steadfast

Crockett, Kathy. 2016. *Courageous Women of Faith Part 2.* Amazon Publishing.

Crockett, Kathy. 2020. *Couragous Men of Faith.* Amazon Publishing.

Hillsong United. 2013. *Oceans (Where Feet May Fail).* Hillsong Church T/A Hillsong Music Australia.

"Steel." *The Gale Encyclopedia of Science.* Encyclopedia.com. October 28, 2019. https://www.encyclopedia.com/earth-and-environment/ minerals-mining-and-metallurgy/metallurgy-and-mining-terms-and-concepts/steel.

Young, Sarah. *Jesus Calling: Enjoying Peace in His Presence.* Thomas Nelson, 2004.